D0085562

Tattered Banners

Tattered Banners

Labor, Conflict,
and Corporatism in
Postcommunist Russia

Walter D. Connor

WestviewPress

A Division of HarperCollinsPublishers

Published in 1996 in the United States of America by Westview Press, Inc., 5500 Central Avenue, Boulder, Colorado 80301-2877, and in the United Kingdom by Westview Press, 12 Hid's Copse Road, Cumnor Hill, Oxford OX2 9JJ

Library of Congress Cataloging-in-Publication Data
Connor, Walter D.
    Tattered banners : labor, conflict, and corporatism in postcommunist Russia / Walter D. Connor
        p.   cm.
    Includes bibliographical references and index.
    ISBN 0-8133-2911-6—ISBN 0-8133-2912-4 (pbk.)
    1. Industrial relations—Russia (Federation)   2. Industry and state—Russia (Federation)   3. Russia (Federation)—Economic policy—1991–   4. Russia (Federation)—Politics and government—1991–   I. Title.
HD8530.2.C66   1996
331'.0947—dc20   96-7425
                                                                                                                CIP

This book was designed and typeset by Letra Libre, 1705 Fourteenth Street, Suite 391, Boulder, Colorado 80302.

To the DiToros

Dominic
Marilyn
Jennifer
Joseph

Brigid, Patrick, and Columbkille bless your house

Contents_____

Preface

THIS IS A WORK ABOUT A TRANSITIONAL PERIOD, researched during transitional times and written necessarily in a transitional style. There are massive discontinuities between the politics, economics, and social life of the old USSR and the states into which the Soviet Union split at the end of 1991. But there are continuities as well between the old Moscow-centered megastate and what is now variously labeled the CIS (Commonwealth of Independent States), the FSU (Former Soviet Union), the newly independent states, or, simply, Eurasia. Economic priorities pursued for generations, habits of thought and behavior produced by the old system, and webs of connections formed individually and collectively in the Soviet period constitute a heavy legacy. All the former Soviet republics are in transition; not all are on the same trajectory. Russia's transition is in sheer scale different from the rest.

If Russia today is a mix of old and new, so is the approach taken here. Those of us formed in the old business of Soviet studies, whether in academia or government and in whatever original disciplinary affiliation, have been subjected—and have subjected ourselves—to a good deal of criticism in recent times. The object of our study, launched by the late 1980s on a path of reforms hitherto unthinkable, collapsed—an outcome unforeseen by analysts in large part but similarly unapprehended by the reformers who were the agents of Soviet disintegration. No doubt much of the criticism is deserved. Yet throwing away the accumulated perspectives of some decades would be an overreaction. Sovietology understood a great deal about the old USSR, whose shadow still casts itself over the present. Prediction is a tough business; predicting the "great" (and therefore discontinuous) events is all the tougher. The best of social science, applied in particular national contexts, would be unlikely to significantly better Sovietology's score in this regard.

Still, any work written at this time that engages the post-Soviet present and future must concern itself with concepts, images, and organizing ideas. This is true both for works that aspire to be theoretical and for those, like the present one, that set out different aims.

Thus, the first chapter deals with conceptualizations—of what the old USSR as a political system was and of what the Yeltsin government's attempt to craft a new Russia, politically and economically, amounts to. It deals with the totalitarian model and what it may tell us, looking backward, about the sources of the USSR's decomposition. It engages aspects of discussion and speculation about democratic transitions—for some years now a growth industry in political science. Democratic transition studies are driven by the encouraging emergence of new democratic polities in the earlier exceptional political orders of noncommunist Europe (Spain, Portugal, Greece) and of authoritarian Latin America and have recently been confronted with new raw material in the emergence of the former USSR and Eastern Europe from communism. It deals as well with corporatism as a mode of controlling and coordinating diverse political and economic interests; it was a variety of corporatism that Russia chose in late 1991 to regulate its own anticipated problems in government-employer-labor relations.

This book, however, is not primarily intended or written as a conceptual work. I am impressed with Russia's particularity. Particularity is not uniqueness; in a trivial sense at least, every country is unique. But Russia's particularity is oversized, large-scale, multifold, embracing elements of Soviet and pre-Soviet heritage: the Byzantine-Orthodox cultural-religious provenance; the early (by European standards) centralization of the state via the Tatar domination and its heritage in Muscovy; the early emergence of autocracy and with it a massive barrier to the development of any real class system; the Eurasian expansion; and the critical role of the state in driving economic development under late tsarism and, massively expanded, under an explicitly antimarket Soviet regime. Finally, the transition from communism involved not only a regime change that operated differently from those in the external empire, but the dissolution of the Soviet Union itself and the even older political-territorial links joining the East Slav lands. Thus, the emergent Russia was smaller than it had been for over 300 years.

Attitudes: Russia in the Mind

Fascination with the particularity of a country does not mean attraction to, or moral approval of, the object—whether the political system or the underlying culture and society. There was nothing attractive in the USSR's monstrous political system, and rare were practitioners of Sovietology in the English-speaking world who could have been called pro-Soviet. (The system's propagandists thus responded in kind over the years to our "bourgeois falsifications.") But analysts were somewhat divided, if not explicitly, on another point: the nature of what lay under the state—the society, the culture—and how to react to it. This was a matter of emotion as well as of intellect. Some liked what they saw as the real

Russia, sympathized with it, and felt engaged on its behalf while rejecting the political system that stood above it.

Others reacted somewhat differently. Although not unsympathetic, not disinclined to see the people as victims, they tended to stress the duration and depth of regime (tsarist absolutism, Soviet totalitarianism) impacts on society. On the whole, Soviet society did not look like a Western, or central, European society under a mode of rule culturally and historically alien to it. The experience since 1917 had been crucial. The project of building a "new Soviet man" might have failed, but the system had formed the Soviet people in a mix of fear, dependency, parochialism, and ignorance.

Many such observers consequently wondered how a people formed and disciplined in this system, even with the dodges by which they worked that system and survived in it, would manage under any new dispensation. Until Gorbachev at midterm, it was hard to imagine that a new dispensation might be in the offing. Even then, the building of a civil society seemed more a matter of top-down construction than of the freeing of suppressed political and economic impulses and forces.

Stephen Cohen, in his provocative *Rethinking the Soviet Experience* (1985), noted—in implied criticism of those with the latter sort of reaction—that he was "struck by how few Sovietologists gain any real intellectual pleasure or excitement from visiting the Soviet Union; for too many of them, the trip seems to be a distasteful professional duty."[1] My own reaction was always more of this second sort. The USSR, around me, depressed me. If excitement and things to do, reconnaissance to be carried out, made landing in Moscow something of a positive experience, I nevertheless felt a sense of release upon leaving. To assume that there is something wrong with such a reaction, it seems to me, is to demand that those with one set of idiosyncracies replace it with someone else's set.

The post-Soviet Russia of today, then, both fascinates and troubles me. I still experience a sense of relief in leaving, if not of the same intensity as in the old times. I am hopeful and share those hopes with people who now can speak freely. But arrivals in and departures from Warsaw still impart to me a different feel from their Moscow equivalents. Much of this turns on my feeling that in Poland, I am in a lost, now recovered, part of the West and on a conviction that in Russia, given its roots, I am not. Russia's path ahead to what so many reformers called the civilized world, then, is likely to be more arduous, its "reunion" with traditions of limited government, rule of law, democracy, and the market all the harder to achieve precisely because there those traditions are weak to nonexistent—however marginal the soil on which they have struggled in central Europe.[2]

Particularity and Generalization

A quarter-century ago, presenting a challenging and ambitious logic for comparative sociology and political science, Adam Przeworski and Henry Teune pointed to the problem of "systems versus variables" (more or less, of national particularities as opposed to what is contained in analytic frames) and argued that "the crux of the problem lies in the status of proper names of social systems within general theory." For them, the goal was "to substitute names of variables for the names of social systems, such as Ghana, the United States, Africa, or Asia." Countries ("particular social systems") did, admittedly, matter in influencing "the nature of observed relationships"; knowing about them did "yield a gain in prediction." Still, were "some additional assumptions" to be accepted, "proper names can be replaced by variables. ... Nomothetic statements can be made."[3]

These words, I admit, leave me rather cold today, just as they did when I first read them. This does not mean that I think them untrue or wholly ill-advised. Generalizing, "nomothetic" statements are made all the time. Some are more accurate (or less readily disconfirmed) than others. Some attempt to cover many systems, others fewer. Such statements assert regularities, relationships of variables across systems with proper names; they drive a good deal of social science and for many, they are what it is all about. I doubt that I would have pursued the career I have had it not been for certain proper names—USSR, Poland, Hungary, and so on. It is of no particular interest to the reader how this came about, how a perspective involving sociology and political science has been for me—however well or poorly employed—a mode of approach to societies that already compelled my interest rather than a commitment to doing social science that then happened to find material for analysis in the proper names of the countries of the old Soviet bloc. Were I a historian, there would be nothing to explain here; history is full of proper names, and perhaps this book is contemporary history as much as anything else.

People in the Sovietological enterprise, of course, enjoyed over the years the advantage that the USSR, the Soviet bloc, the East-West cold war were all important beyond the worlds of academia and social science. We had sizable audiences; unlike some other specialists on exotic areas, we had, on the whole, close relationships with the governmental world, to what I think was clear mutual benefit. People with compulsions to explain smaller countries—Luxembourg, Equatorial Guinea, Nepal—would hardly have found audiences of such size or built so large a field of studies around them. Still, as an analytic matter, all countries of whatever size can figure equally as proper names, as systems, in cross-national, comparative research, and as labels in the leftmost columns of matrices otherwise displaying quantitative indicators and coefficients of one sort or another (though in fact most communist regimes deprived us of much of such quantitative data). These can tell us that across a range of countries studied, say, political democracy (measured in a certain manner) had this or that effect on the equality or inequality of income or wealth (operationalized in a certain fashion). There is nothing wrong with this, but it is not what I am about here.

If there is nothing wrong with broad theorizing, there is also nothing wrong with addressing Russia per se. Whatever happens, each time it happens, happens somewhere. The somewhere in this book is Russia. If in geopolitical stature not so tall, in security calculations not so central, and in its information supply not so secretive as the old USSR, Russia and its problems are still important, still major preoccupations of the West.

What follows, then, is full of proper names; they are part of the picture I try to draw of a critical period in the Russian transition. Some, no doubt, are more interesting in themselves than others, and drawing that distinction will have more to do with the tastes of the reader than with those of the author. Without being explicitly comparative in intent, this book does draw on the thoughts of comparativists, avowedly more interested in structures, in variables, than in specific countries. Such a description especially applies to comparativists with interests in the dynamics of transitions to political democracy from something less, to the market from something different, and in the sources and workings of corporatism as a mode of political organization. There are lessons I try to draw from the data, framed by and expressed partly in terms of these perspectives; there are no doubt other lessons readers, or other analysts, might draw from the same facts, the same data. The point is that we need the data; we need to pay attention to the details.

It is possible to carry preoccupation with the details too far, of course. Philippe Schmitter, who has made major contributions to the study of both democratic transitions and corporatism—ones on which I have relied heavily here—recently counseled former Sovietologists against such tendencies.

> The one thing that *cannot* be done is to take refuge in *empirie*—in the diligent collection of facts without any guidance from theories and models. Given the sheer volume of data, not to mention their frequently contradictory referents, without some sense of priorities and categories for classification no analyst is likely to be able to make much sense of what is going on—much less within a time frame that might be of some use to the actors themselves. Former Sovietologists converted to the new tasks of explaining transition and consolidation would be better advised to spend more effort on conceptualization—even an alternative conceptualization—than on diligent fact gathering.[4]

Most of this is unexceptionable; all narrative, all analysis, is selective. It is surely better that criteria of selection be explicit than not, that conceptualizations operate consciously rather than unconsciously. But selecting elements in the new, large volume of data is a process of selecting out as well as selecting in. Without a good deal of *empirie* in approach to the whole disorderly mess of Russia today, it seems to me, it will be difficult to tell what one may be excluding, and why, and whether such advances or compromises one's understanding. To Schmitter's quite reasonable cautions, we might then add the homelier observation of Yogi Berra: "You can observe a lot by just watching."

What This Book Offers

This book is the product of a lot of watching. The final pages contain some speculation on the future, but much of what follows is an attempt to chronicle and explain certain developments in Russia's labor politics from the postcoup autumn of 1991 to the October crisis of 1993, when presidential-parliamentary conflicts, simmering and increasingly envenomed, turned violent and turned a page in Russia's short postcommunist history.

Schmitter rightly noted that it is difficult to apprehend what was going on. This is true not only for analysts but for the actors themselves, and I have tried in the pages that follow to convey some of this confusion and indeterminacy. I could scarcely avoid doing so; it is part of the story.

Chapter 1 deals with definitions, conceptualizations, and perspectives on totalitarianism, political and economic transitions, and corporatist versus pluralist means of regulating interest conflict. It establishes a perspective on what Russia is trying to move away from and on the nature of its attempt to get to a new set of political and economic realities. Chapter 2 covers the first full year—1992—of the independent Russian Federation in regard to the design and functioning of Russia's corporatist mechanism for regulating labor relations, the players, the politics, and the problems of a trilateralism premature but with no evident alternatives.

In Chapter 3 the focus turns to the organization, politics, and rivalries of trade unions, old and new, both within and without the corporatist mechanisms of regulation. Radically different pedigrees and political stances made for bitter conflicts between those organizations that are typically assumed to stand together for hired labor in consultative-corporatist designs. In Chapter 4 I return, for the year 1993, to the organizational dynamics of corporatism; actors and positions changed in the employer-labor-government trilateral, and the government was subject to increasing economic and political pressures.

In Chapter 5 I look back, from the perspective of 1994–1995, at the transitional experience and events of 1991–1993. Although this perspective spans a short period, it is a period marked by slow-starting but fast-accelerating changes in the structure and form of property relations, and thus potentially management-labor relations, that are still going on. On the basis of lessons drawn, I make some points about tentative future lines of development.

Walter D. Connor

Notes

1. See Stephen F. Cohen, *Rethinking the Soviet Experience: Politics and History Since 1917* (New York: Oxford University Press, 1985), p. 12.

2. I am aware that these remarks—and the ones earlier on Russia's particularity—might be criticized on the ground that they express a privileging of the West (here central Europe denotes the ex-communist lands of Poland, Hungary, the Czech Republic, Slovakia, and, by extension, Slovenia but not the Balkans and the East Slav states themselves). But I confess myself out of sympathy with, and unconvinced by, those who argue that the West has constructed an other (a process variously called orientalism, or balkanism) without, as some scholars and critics would seem to assert, an adequate basis in fact. For a strong and interesting presentation of these critics' view, focusing precisely on the central-Europe-versus-the-Balkans distinction, see Maria Todorova, "The Balkans: From Discovery to Invention," *Slavic Review* 53, 2 (Summer 1994), pp. 453–482.

3. Adam Przeworski and Henry Teune, *The Logic of Comparative Social Inquiry* (New York: Wiley-Interscience, 1970), pp. 8, 10.

4. Philippe C. Schmitter with Terry Lynn Karl, "Comment: The Conceptual Travels of Transitologists and Consolidologists: How Far to the East Should They Attempt to Go?" *Slavic Review* 53, 1 (Spring 1994), pp. 184–185.

Acknowledgments

WHEREAS THE AUTHOR BEARS the responsibility for the faults of a work (and this one no doubt contains its share of such), nobody writes a book without help. Acknowledgments are due, then, to people and organizations whose contributions to the research and writing were valuable indeed. The National Council for Soviet and East European Research (NCSEER) allowed me to draw water from the same well twice: After awarding me a grant in 1987–1988 for an earlier project, it was good enough to do the same in the 1992–1993 academic year for the one whose results fill these pages. Vlad Toumanoff and Robert Randolph of the council continue their good works for the field—to them my sincere thanks.

Boston University sabbatical support further increased my supply of the valuable commodity of time. A sabbatical is doubly welcome when it comes immediately after a five-year term as departmental chair, which in my case bracketed the decline and collapse of the USSR and the birth of postcommunist Russia.

Harvard University's Russian Research Center once again provided resources and support, organizational and moral, for this as for many of my earlier scholarly enterprises. My thanks to two center directors, Adam Ulam and his successor, Tim Colton, for their interest and support and to Marshall Goldman, the center's long-term associate director.

Travels to the new Russia were facilitated by funding from NCSEER, from Harvard University, and from the International Research and Exchanges Board (IREX).

In the new Russia one has colleagues in a sense that was difficult to impossible in the old USSR. My thanks to a goodly number whose information, ideas, and reactions have contributed much; to Boris Grushin, Olga Kirichenko, Pavel Kudiukin, Eduard Klopov, Alla Nazimova, and, most especially, Leonid Gordon and Vladimir Gimpelson. In Moscow, where so much that was once unthinkable is now commonplace, even the AFL-CIO now has an office. I am grateful to Tom Bradley and his colleagues there for sharing their impressions and insights (with an author who votes Republican!) and to Dr. Christine Sadowski of the AFL-CIO's Free Trade Union Institute in Washington, D.C.

Works in progress typically produce in their authors certain compulsions to talk about them. Some of my thinking on interpretive matters benefited greatly from exchanges with four Boston University students in a small seminar on Soviet and post-Soviet politics in spring 1994, indebting me to Kivanc Akkaya, Susan Cavan, Lisa Ameden Claussen, and Julie Roginsky. Gordon Hahn, another of my students, who advanced to the Ph.D. while I was finishing this book, was also a source of several insights. Among my more seasoned colleagues, Elizabeth Teague of Radio Liberty, Linda Cook and David Powell at the Russian Research Center, and Jay Siegel of the Kennedy School of Government at Harvard deserve special thanks for willingly lent ears and for ideas and comments that I have freely used.

Eileen, Christine, and Elizabeth Connor continue, through it all, to cope with a husband and father who surely is, at times, "a bit too much"—but not, it seems, for them. They, however, have already gotten dedications. This book, then, is dedicated to the closest and dearest friends, a family launched in the same year as my own. Our connection dates back to when two future "male heads of household" (as the Bureau of the Census might put it) met as high school freshmen in 1955, when Eisenhower was in the White House and Khrushchev was in the Kremlin. A Celtic blessing on the DiToros, despite the Slavic subjects of this book, makes perfect sense.

W.D.C.

Acronyms

ATC	air traffic controllers
AUCCTU	All-Union Central Council of Trade Unions
CBI	Confederation of British Industries
CIS	Commonwealth of Independent States
CPD	Congress of People's Deputies
CPSU	Communist Party of the Soviet Union
EBRD	European Bank for Reconstruction and Development
Edinenie	All-Russian Trade Union
FNPR	Federation of Independent Trade Unions of Russia (Federat-siia Nezavisimykh Profsoiuzov Rossii)
FPAD	Federation of Air Traffic Controllers' Unions (Federatsiia Profsoiuzov Aviadispetcherov)
FPALS	Interstate Federation of Unions of Civil Aviation Flight Personnel
FRG	Federal Republic of Germany
FSU	Former Soviet Union
FTR	Federation of Commodity Producers of Russia (Federatsiia Tovaroproizvoditelei Rossii)
GDR	German Democratic Republic
IMEMO	Institute for World Economics and International Relations
IMF	International Monetary Fund
IREX	International Research and Exchanges Board
KFP	Kuzbass Federation of Trade Unions
KPRF	Communist Party of the Russian Federation
KPSR	Russian Confederation of Free Trade Unions
KRO	Congress of Russian Communities (Kongress Russkikh Obshchin)
KRP	Congress of Russian Trade Unions
KSPR	Confederation of Free Trade Unions of Russia
KT	Confederation of Labor (Konfederatsiia Truda)
KTR	Confederation of Labor of Russia (Konfederatsiia Truda Rossii)
LDP	Liberal Democratic Party
MAKKIP	Association for Free Trade Unions of Small, International,

	Lease, Joint-Stock, Collective, Cooperative, and Other Enterprises (or) Association of Free Trade Unions of Small, International, Leasing, Joint-Stock, Individual, and Other Enterprises and Organizations
MFP	Moscow Federation of Trade Unions
NCSEER	National Council for Soviet and East European Research
NDR	"Russia is Our Home" (Nash Dom-Rossiia)
NEP	New Economic Policy
NPG	Independent Union of Miners (Nezavisimyi Profsoiuz Gorniakov)
NPS	USSR Scientific-Industrial Union
NPRUP	Independent Trade Union of Coal Industry Workers (Nezavisimyi Profsoiuz Rabotnikov Ugolnoi Promyshlennosti)
OECD	Organization for Economic Development
OFTR	United Front of Workers of Russia
PGMR	Union of Mining and Metallurgy Workers
PRC	People's Republic of China
PRIAS	Trade Union of Aviation Service Workers
PT	Party of Labor
RASP	Russian Assembly of Social Partnership (Rossiiskaia Assambleia Sotsialnogo Partnerstva)
RF	Russian Federation
ROPP	Russian United Industrial Party (Rossiiskaia Obedinennaia Promyshlennaia Partiia)
RSFSR	Russian Soviet Federated Socialist Republic
RSPP	Russian Union of Industrialists and Entrepreneurs (Rossiiski Soiuz Promyshlennikov i Predprinimatelei)
RTK	Russian Trilateral Commission for the Regulation of Social and Labor Relations
SMOT	Free Interprofessional Association of Workers (Svobodnoe Mezhprofessionalnoe Obedinenie Trudiashchikhsiia)
SP	Socialist Party
STK	Union of Labor Collectives (Soiuz Trudovykh Kollektivov)
TU	trade union
TUC	Trades Union Congress
VKP	General Confederation of Trade Unions (Vseobshchaia Konfederatsiia Profsoiuzov)
VKT	All-Russian Confederation of Labor (Vserossiiskaia Konfederatsiia Truda)

1

Slippery Surfaces: Conceptualizing Russia's Political Transition

THE SOVIET SYSTEM FELL ONLY YESTERDAY. People formed in it— leaders and led, old and new elites, the masses; those eager for a different future, those nostalgic for a remembered past—make up the vast majority of the human material of the postcommunist Russia that began to emerge in 1991. Their habits, aspirations, and fears will mark post-Soviet politics in important ways for the foreseeable future.

Politically, aeons separate the Russian Federation, whose capital saw gunfire and bloodshed on its streets on October 3–4, 1993, from the RSFSR (the Russian Soviet Federated Republic), which constituted the major portion of the USSR on which Mikhail Gorbachev attempted to work his political and economic reforms from 1985 to 1991. Rulers and rank and file, the advantaged and the weak, operate now in a context bereft of the rules, certainties, rewards, and penalties that shaped the Soviet system. The past is little guide to the present and future performance of this largely anomic polity.

All of the previous observations have been asserted as self-evident by many analysts since 1991. Each emphasizes a different general dimension of postcommunist Russia today: the recency of the collapse of the Soviet system on the one hand and the newness of the post-Soviet political game, the lack of clear rules, on the other.

Any investigation into this disorderly political realm, whatever its specific focus—here, labor politics—needs to specify two things to do justice to the complementary perspectives of the preceding observations. What was the Soviet system that fell? What is the nature of the new politics since the end of December 1991? If we cannot yet speak, really, of a Russian Federation political system, what is politics in the federation about? What are the natures of the players, the institutions, the procedures? What happened, what is happening, what is likely to happen, and why? This is a tall order. Consensus about the old USSR is elusive—less so, perhaps, on what it was, more so on why it fell when it did. As to the current Russian political scene, consensus is hardly to be expected. Things are changing too rapidly. Patterns we will with some years' hindsight recognize as emergent in 1993–1995 are still too conditional and too close to those trying to apprehend the large picture.

This chapter, then, cannot be conclusive. It offers an exploration of some currents of thought and conceptual approaches to aid in locating the recent past and present contextually.

Totalitarianism, Authoritarianism, and Transition

Is this the period of Russia's "democratic transition"? During the past quarter-century we have seen Latin American states and Spain, Portugal, and Greece move from various forms of authoritarian politics to something more or less closely approximating political democracy in its common Western understanding. Is Russia's passage, at least in the broad aspect, comparable to theirs?

This is a leading question. An affirmative answer would reflect an optimistic view of Russia's trajectory in the mid-1990s, a view that is not necessarily unwarranted. But answering yes would also indicate the acceptance of "democratic transition theory" as a major key to understanding what is going on, the nature of the central issues, and so on. If such acceptance is a bit premature—and so it seems to me—it would be mistaken to reject, at the outset, a body of theorizing and discussion large and diverse enough to encompass many differences in perspective and emphasis.[1] But there *had* been, earlier, a "rush to affirmation" in this regard, one wittily characterized (or, a bit, caricatured) by Ken Jowitt in the context of the 1989 collapse of Soviet-imposed systems in the former East European colonies and its early-1990s aftermath:

> Confronted with a turbulent environment, there is a quite understandable, predictable, and observable tendency by intellectuals to restore certainty idiomatically. That certainly is the case with Eastern Europe. One of its most pronounced expressions is the fetishlike repetition of the phrase "transition to democracy," as if saying it often enough, and inviting enough Latin American scholars from the United States to enough conferences in Eastern Europe (and the Soviet Union), will magically guarantee a new democratic capitalist telos in place of the ethnic, economic, and territorial maelstrom that is the reality today.[2]

To be fair, democratic transition theory did have a place in Eastern Europe. Poland in 1989, plausibly, afforded the scenario of splits in the political elite, allowing society (more politicized and organized in Poland than elsewhere in the region) to enter a new political process: In spring

1989 negotiations culminated in semifree elections that were a product of a kind of "pacting" between communist regime and opposition; all scenarios were part of the stuff of the transition literature. Hungary, in a somewhat different sense, had a peaceful transition with elements of pacting. Czechoslovakia, the German Democratic Republic (GDR), Bulgaria, and, later, Albania were examples of regime collapse of a rapidity that rendered pacting impossible (had there been organized oppositions of sufficient strength to pact with); but at least in the early aftermath, democratic transition theory could by implication raise questions about the difficulties of stabilizing new, avowedly democratic, governments in the absence of some of these negotiation and pacting elements.

Another reason for the rush to transition theorizing was, surely, vocational: the old "area studies versus the discipline" business. Whether rooted in the distinctness of Soviet-type systems from democratic and other nondemocratic polities or in, for students of the USSR especially, the national-historical specificity of tsarist and Soviet Russian polities, much of what this field did seemed to have little to do with the disciplines of political science and sociology.

Calls to break down the walls, to integrate Soviet–East European studies into the disciplines, to draw on their theoretical and conceptual apparatuses, were nothing new. Universities were organized on a disciplinary-departmental basis; in such structures were preferment, advancement, and tenure conferred or denied. Few have a taste for isolation; being mainstream is attractive. Surely it is unsurprising that the collapse of Soviet-type systems led to an intensified search outside a rather empirical-historical field for theoretical models. Nor is it surprising that such models were found in democratic transition theories, which had the merits of being current and to a degree optimistic at a time when students of the old communism wished the best to those who were emerging from under it.*

_____

* Although this is not the place and I am not the person to render any judgment in this regard, it does seem in a sense striking that in the vast majority of discussions of the area studies–discipline sort, the discipline was regarded as a given: Its processes, states, and directions were not subject to discussion even though within the disciplines paradigms succeeded one another, debates raged over all manner of issues, and theories ranging from the insightful to the faddish (or foolish) came into vogue and then were abandoned. A good deal of the not inconsiderable borrowing from the discipline in Soviet studies in the 1970s in the areas of interest group politics and bureaucratic-organizational models seems in retrospect to have done little to really enlighten us on the trajectories of Soviet politics, and nothing to sensitize Sovietology to the "coming of the end."

Further, practitioners of Sovietology were clearly subject to accusations that they—closest to the entity—had not predicted the USSR's collapse. Some might counter, not without justification, "neither did Gorbachev!" But it was not unreasonable that on new and unfamiliar post-Soviet territory they might seek some new conceptual frameworks with which to comprehend novel realities and potential lines of development (even though it might well be argued that democratic transition theory had not so much predicted the processes with which it dealt as explored them).

As I suggested earlier, the Soviet-Russian instance may "fit" less well with democratic transition theory than some parts of emergent Eastern Europe, especially Hungary and Poland. Poland was an institutionally exceptional state, never completely "Sovietized," arrested, as some might put it, at the New Economic Policy (NEP) phase of communist development. Poland had a private farming sector, private small trade and artisanship, and a strong, independent church. Poland and Hungary both had been, for a long time before the rules began to change in the Gorbachev era, the most liberal Soviet-bloc states. They had arrived at this point by quite different routes, but by the mid-1980s—whatever their formal Soviet-model political architecture—their domestic polity-society relationships revealed patterns that were authoritarian more than totalitarian, even in the modified, post-Stalin sense of the latter term. Herein, it seems to me—as well as to many others—lies part of the analytic-interpretive problem: Theories of democratic transition were theories of transition from authoritarian regimes, not from totalitarian regimes, however weakened, debilitated, and directionless the latter might be at the time of their demise. The USSR, in a sense to be explored further on, *was* totalitarian; its transition took off from a different point than those of Argentina, Brazil, Greece, Spain, Portugal, and the luckier parts of Eastern Europe. In 1991 Przeworski argued—referring to Eastern Europe and not, I think, intending to include the USSR—that many of "the obstacles typically confronted in building democracy and transforming economies ... are the same everywhere, for they are determined by a common destination, not by the different points of departure."[3] Surely there is something in his words, but I lean at the outset rather more toward the notion that the terminus a quo assumes a greater weight than the terminus ad quem when we are dealing with postcommunist states, and especially postcommunist Russia.

USSR: Totalitarianism, Liberalization, Perestroika

The USSR whose preservation Gorbachev sought to achieve—through "acceleration," then restructuring (perestroika) of its domestic economy, the "democratization" of its political process against the background of vastly expanded bounds of vertical and horizontal communication (glasnost), and a revolution in foreign and security policy including withdrawal from the East European external empire—was a totalitarian system. It was not, to be sure, totalitarian in the unalloyed sense of Stalin's time or in the sense any longer of full, active conformity to the Friedrich-Brzezinski six-point model (official ideology, a single, mass party typically headed by one leader, terroristic police control of the population, a state monopoly in mass communications and military force, and a state-controlled command economy)[4] but in a modified, attenuated sense.

Comisso described a new theoretical approach to totalitarianism, one primarily applicable, I believe, to the East European reality. The concept was redefined "from a description of reality into a tendency or an ideal type."

> Totalitarianism was consequently redefined from a description of the actual political system to a tendency that Leninist parties aspired to but were necessarily unable to realize in practice. Political life in communist systems could thus be described as how an organization with a totalitarian ideology adapted to a necessarily nontotalitarian situation. …
>
> … As a theory, the "new" totalitarianism provides a far more nuanced interpretation of life in socialist systems than did the older version. It can accommodate and explain changes in the pattern of rule, the rise of social movements, the impulse for and frustration of attempts at economic reform, the switch from "moral" to "material" incentives and the consequent emphasis on improving supplies of consumer goods, the party's willingness to tolerate as much diversity as it could co-opt. At the same time, it highlights the ideological barriers to the party's apparent unwillingness to abandon its claim to control state and society even as the reality of that control increasingly declines.[5]

If we allow for some Soviet exceptionalism in the realm of social movements (not tolerated until Gorbachev) and in the tolerance of co-optable diversity, the components of the new theory are no mean description of Khrushchev's or Brezhnev's USSR. The theory works better than its older version because the older version, although a solid description of life under Stalinism, was less so held up against the modified realities of post-Stalinism. What Gorbachev inherited—the Brezhnevian stagnation—was a totalitarianism in tendency, ambition, and ideology. It was modified, weakened, and tempered by a mix of corrupt neotraditionalism,[6] of partial state-society understandings that were implicit and one-sided and increasingly failing in the observance but still not entirely mischaracterized as a social contract,[7] and of other trends and factors. For all of this, there was a systemic totalism that was more than and different from authoritarianism.

The end of the USSR, then, coincided with the end of a totalitarian order—how? Here, the stimulating treatment by Rasma Karklins,[8] it seems to me, points the way to understanding. She applies the Friedrich-Brzezinski "syndrome" to post-Stalin totalitarianism, which was already a net of terroristic police control (which the authors of the syndrome later modified to "a system of terror, whether physical or psychic"), and puts less emphasis on "one man, the 'dictator'," (no one after Stalin was quite the dictator in the same way); otherwise, she emphasizes the main characteristic of a syndrome—if the pieces are mutually supporting, the modification of one will affect the others.

Implicit in the syndrome model was that the dictator, or leader, understood that totalitarianism was a syndrome and thus was impervious to tinkering but extremely vulnerable to more serious modification. Explicit in Karklins's argument is that a leadership mistake in this regard is possible and that Gorbachev made one in that he did not understand that he had inherited a syndrome. To summarize her argument, glasnost began the process by ending the critical government monopoly control of the mass media. The flood of information, contention, and debate "drastically changed what Soviet citizens knew, and this influenced what they believed, valued and trusted." Glasnost rapidly destroyed another element of the syndrome—the official Marxist-Leninist ideology. Absent the ideology, the regime lost its claim to a mandate to rule; the Communist Party of the Soviet Union (CPSU) was shorn of its leading role, which was defensible only in terms of that ideology. The move away from repression had been very much part of the Gorbachevian design and resulted in a populace less afraid of reprisals from the government. When, late in the game, "the regime reverted to repression in Tbilisi, Baku, Vilnius, Riga and finally Moscow," injecting violence into what was already a changed situation, it created a backlash rather than imposing stability: Thousands were in the streets, too many to be managed by police methods. Beyond this, "any deterrent effect is more than counterbalanced by the catalytic effect of regime violence at this late juncture. Because protesters have come to expect that the regime will not use repression, they feel betrayed and outraged when it occurs, and protest even more."[9] In such circumstances, the altered realities of August 1991 deprived that month's attempted coup of essential support: The process of erosion had gone so far that the coup leaders could not convince sufficient numbers that they had a right to rule, could not refer to any credible ideology that gave them that right, and could not therefore credibly call upon the military to employ force on their behalf. The USSR was finished.

Karklins's argument from the logic of the totalitarian model, then, is unconventional: Far from not allowing the possibility of change, totalitarianism as a syndrome is implicitly subject to change: "the undermining of one regime trait would have consequences for other traits," and thus "the totalitarian model always suggested a domino theory of democratisation." Conversely, the fact that the basic structures of the Soviet system, the house Stalin built, endured all those years through Khrushchev and Brezhnev places earlier changes in perspective, suggesting that "pre-Gorbachev adjustments in regime policy were not truly systemic."[10]

Gorbachev's radical liberalization, then, was different from anything before in Soviet history. It set in motion processes familiar in the democratic transition perspective, at least with respect to the weakening and windup of the old regime. Established political actors miscalculate; new actors, hence, can emerge to challenge; a process once started assumes its own dynamic. Political action from below becomes less costly, more variegated, as repression from the top slackens. Elites who begin the game with a certain set of rules and parameters wind up playing by new rules they did not decree, contending over matters they initially ruled off the table. As Przeworski put it, "Liberalization is inherently unstable."

> Since liberalization is always intended as a process controlled from above, the emergence of autonomous movements constitutes the proof that liberalization is not, or at least is no longer, a viable project. Street demonstrations are the demonstration that the most sacrosanct of authoritarian values, order itself, has been violated. ...
> ... These indeed are the alternatives: either to incorporate the few groups that can be incorporated and to repress everyone else, returning to the authoritarian stasis, or to open the political agenda to the problem of institutions, that is, of democracy.[11]

Thus, Gorbachev set out with liberalization in view but without a clear idea of the possible consequences: "There is every indication that the CPSU and its leader intended to retain a monopoly of political control." Gorbachev had plenty of power, reposed in the general secretary of the Central Committee of the CPSU. He was "powerful enough to manipulate the members of the old regime throughout the period of transition," and although as leader he had "controls over popular forces, he also [was] strong enough to weaken those controls."[12]

Gorbachev, then, was the agent of Soviet totalitarianism's destruction. He set the process in motion; once in motion long enough, it assumed its own dynamic, no longer controllable. For the monolithism of the past, he substituted a vision of "'socialist pluralism' ... based on the premise that social pluralism could coexist with the one-party state."[13]

In the event, it could not. Some leaders in the opposition understood the dynamic better than Gorbachev. Late in the game—at the Politburo meeting of January 30, 1991 (the availability of Politburo min-

utes is, of course, courtesy of the fall of the system as well), the Uzbek
party leader Islam Karimov criticized Gorbachev for his voluntaristic use
of the power of the general secretary and for the consequences to the
system and its leaders.

> It was possible, Mikhail Sergeevich—I will allow myself to say this—not
> to begin perestroika in 1985. It was possible to live quietly, as they say,
> and in the period of stagnation, to reform slowly. It might not have been
> necessary to stir up enormous masses of people. All would have gone
> on as it had, and you would have prospered, and we would have pros-
> pered. And there would not have taken place any kind of catastrophe.[14]

One might take issue with Karimov as political prophet of what would
not have happened had the USSR been left undisturbed, but as critic of
the consequences of Gorbachev's moves, he seems right on point. It may
be some commentary on the practicalities of political realism of a nondemocratic sort that Karimov, in 1995, still rules in Uzbekistan, whereas
Gorbachev is a private citizen of the Russian Federation.

Two sentences from Karklins summarize her verdict.

> Evidently, Gorbachev failed to foresee the consequences of his policies
> of regime liberalisation, because, like many Westerners, he did not see
> the Soviet system as totalitarian and therefore dichotomous to other
> systems. He envisaged the Soviet regime on a continuum with demo-
> cratic regimes and tried to make it more liberal while at the same time
> retaining its core traits.[15]

Hers, then, is a view that draws on totalitarianism to explain why Gorbachev's liberalization, deeper-cutting by far than any earlier, opened up
the abyss; she also uses the outcome to demonstrate, retrospectively,
that the Soviet system was totalitarian.[16]

The elements of the transition scenario that emerged in the later
Gorbachev period were more the kind that herald the failure of the liberalization project than the sort that mark the road toward democracy. The
old system fell and was dismembered; what was to follow, what was
available to build on by way of institutions, habits, and so on was an entirely different matter.

The collapse of the Soviet megastate was largely peaceful, but it was
a collapse more than a transition. The early December 1991 meeting of
the heads of Russia, Ukraine, and Belarus to announce the formation of
the Commonwealth of Independent States concluded a deal cut among
leaders with varying claims to speak for their peoples (Yeltsin's was by far
the strongest by way of popular election as Russia's president earlier in
the year). This was no pacted transition, no negotiating process engag-

ing an incumbent national elite and elements of its opposition to construct a new form of government. Nor was pacting common at the level of the republics; they were launched into shaky independent statehood.

The public was quite uninvolved in all of this—not, by itself, a fatal defect. Pacting implicitly involves the restriction of broad and undisciplined mass popular access to the process lest it be overwhelmed. And had the end of the USSR involved ruler-challenger negotiations, whom the two sides stood for would have been hard to specify (just as, later, the constituencies of various political parties in the new Russia would be unclear). The August coup had failed not so much because those who opposed it were backed by a politically aroused public ("partisans of democracy rose up to stop [the coup] while the rest of Soviet society passively looked on"[17]) but because it failed to garner any real base of positive support. Four months later, the Soviet Union was buried at a funeral few attended, its end

> crafted, not by representatives of the state in concert with a political opposition and private groups, but by public officials alone, working for the most part behind closed doors. The compact reached was one *among governments,* meaning by this time the cooperating republican governments. Nongovernmental players were not welcome at the table and were informed of what had been decided only after the fact.[18]

The fall of the USSR was unprecedented. But then, the USSR itself had been unprecedented: a totalitarian order eroded but until the mid-late 1980s strong enough to defend itself; an industrial civilization that was backward in most sectors, misdeveloped in its branches, built on principles not simply non- but explicitly antimarket, and inhabited by a population literate and skilled but lacking the consciousness and competencies needed in a civil society. Economic crisis impended; institutionally, there was yet little on which to build the beginnings of a market economy, and the commitment to democracy might be sorely tested by the upswelling of discontent, pain, and anger that dismantling the heritage of the command-administrative economy could bring. Yet it was to the goals of democracy and the market that Russia had been committed by its leaders.

Russia: Shaping a New Polity

The past, distant and more recent, had not been particularly kind to those whose tasks were now the creation of stable democracy and a functioning market. With regard to democracy—including by implication regular competitive elections, consent of the governed, or civil society, and rule of law—a long historical tradition of autocratic and totalitarian centralism and of an overstrong state versus a weak society, as well as an imperial tradition, lay heavily on the new Russia emerging from the wreck of the USSR.** Over the shorter haul, Russia began 1992 with a president popularly elected in 1991 but with a parliament (Congress of People's Deputies and Supreme Soviet) elected in 1990 under less than the best of circumstances. It was a country with no party system to speak of or other mediating structures sufficient to bridge the space between a state looking to change its ways and a society disoriented by the maelstroms of change that had washed over it in the past few years. The political legacies of the final years of the USSR were further amplified by the continued existence of the massive industrial-bureaucratic apparat of the old command economy (branch ministries might have been abolished, but all the factories, farms, and other enterprises that once answered to them still endured) and of the CPSU apparat itself (the party might have been abolished, but the people—often moved to posts in state administration, especially at regional levels, still remained) and with them a massive tangle of old connections, networks, and interests with which Yeltsin and his government would have to reckon.

** This is not the place to review differing views of Russian history over the *longue durée.* But even if national-historical views that emphasize deep-rooted differences among states and civilizations may be seen in some quarters as analytically weak (or even politically incorrect), it is worth emphasizing, in my view, that Russian state history is, on the whole, profoundly undemocratic. A premature political centralization under the thirteenth–fifteenth-century Mongol domination, amplified by the autocracy established by Ivan the Terrible and the further impact of Peter the Great, against the later background of territorial expansion from the original Muscovite state made for something profoundly different from what the West European states with their own tangled histories would achieve by way of state-society balance by the late nineteenth century. Only in the later nineteenth–early twentieth century, between Alexander II's liberation of the serfs in 1861 and the onset of the great war in 1914, might it be said that Russian political evolution seemed headed in a new direction, away from autocracy and toward "civility." It is not a matter of the Russian imperial and Soviet states not working—massive collective efforts, of which Russians were surely capable, led to wars won more often than lost, to territorial expansion, and to economic development impressive by any standard. But these collective efforts were not the sum totals of millions of voluntary activities; they were exercises carried out under despotic, often brutal, rule. For many, Russia's greatness was thus the result of endurance and obedience to unlimited authority. Thus nostalgia for such greatness could be very dangerous in the context of a new, disorganized, and *smaller* post-Soviet Russia seeking its own future and its place in the world.

One cannot help but be struck—at least I cannot—by the sheer amorphousness and indeterminacy of the Russian political scene in early 1992. Under the hopeful surface of a consensus backing a new president and a set of economic moves radical in nature if not quite deserving of the label "shock therapy," one looks in vain for the forces, groups, parties, and organizations that in other scenarios of transition took shape to succeed—or even fail. The problem, then, is to characterize the reality of the political order that existed from late 1991 to, at least, the crisis of September–October 1993.

In this connection, the concept of peaceful revolution—as situation and as ongoing objective—elaborated by Michael McFaul seems most apposite.[19] Peaceful revolution involves attempting and accomplishing "a simultaneous and rapid change in both the polity and the economy without the use of force"—a phenomenon rare and "comparable to but distinct from both violent revolutions and transitions to democracy." Like the democratizers in Latin American and southern Europe, the Yeltsin regime claimed the creation and consolidation of a democratic polity as an objective. Unlike them, it was "simultaneously undergoing a fundamental transformation of its political and economic system" and thus was engaged in a revolutionary transformation.[20]

Latin America and southern Europe had it simpler in the sense that their however-flawed market economies gave shape to "ordering principles of the socio-economic system" that were not challenged in the political transition. McFaul quotes Guillermo O'Donnell and Philippe Schmitter on the "one fundamental restriction" such transitions had observed: "The property rights of the bourgeoisie are inviolable."[21] Obviously, no such bourgeoisie preexisted the breakup of the USSR or could have taken shape in the instant of historical time since to undergird any "stratified and well-articulated" civil society by defending its interests against those of other groups and the state.

Revolutions, as opposed to transitions, do destroy political and economic institutions, but revolutions are rare and typically violent, altering realities "without the blessing of the ancien regime." Yeltsin had not come to power through violence (though one might argue that the failed violence of the August 1991 coup had, by effectively ending the USSR's prospects for survival, propelled him into power as the leader of an independent Russia). Nor, to restate points made previously about the end of the old USSR, had the new Russia arrived at its domestic political order of January 1, 1992, through any scenario in which "political uncertainty is reduced and managed by negotiated compromises [and] basic functions and boundaries of state institutions ... negotiated, bargained, or 'pacted' between the old rulers and the new democratic challengers before the polity is expanded to accommodate wider contestation." There was political uncertainty aplenty; there were old-regime interest groups, courtesy of the unwillingness to use force to abolish them, and a scarcity of strong new interest groups. Hence the new Russian government "could neither rely upon a resurrected civil society nor bulldoze into place a new set of classes and social organizations." It faced at the outset a sticky situation in which "old social units had better defined interests and greater resources than did nascent classes and social groups."[22]

Democratic transitions do not, then, clear the political field; they establish an expanded set of players and modify in important ways the game rules. Revolutions do, and the winners are then free to create a new political, economic, and social landscape on that same field.

> Russia's post-Soviet process of building state institutions falls somewhere in between these two modes of transition. Like other revolutionaries, Russia's new leaders sought to create a new polity. In this endeavor, they had few beneficial institutions to hold over from the Soviet system. At the same time, because Russia's revolution was peaceful, many old Soviet institutions, both formal and informal, had not been destroyed. Nor have the status and roles of those institutions been redefined in a transitional pact. Although many Soviet institutions had been decapitated or stripped of their original mandate, the "guts" of these institutions survived, often with new missions. At the same time, the essential new institutions of a democratic polity, such as a constitution, an independent judiciary, an elected parliament, or political parties were either weak or non-existent.[23]

Thus, McFaul's cogent characterization of Yeltsin's Russia, although not exhaustive, is comprehensive enough, avoiding doctrinaire optimism as well as the totalistic pessimisms of Russia as a mafia state, on the edge of the abyss. More important, peaceful revolution makes room for political opposition to market economic policies, whether emanating from old-regime interest groups anything but democratic in orientation or from broader societal resistance to the pains of the market that is able to make itself heard because of democratic channels. In this regard, it provides a potentially useful corrective to optimism born of a mix of the best wishes for the victims of decades of Soviet-type systems and tendencies perhaps to be too creative in conceiving alternative phasings of democratization and marketization scenarios.[24]

The Labor Problem: Governing and Regulating

The peaceful revolution required new institutions not only to fill out the as-yet-sketchy structure of democracy and to make Russia a "normal," civilized country (although this motivation should not be underestimated) but because the government's program of economic change demanded them.

Such was the problem of labor. The strategies hatched in late 1991 by Yegor Gaidar's economic team—the core of the cabinet—would hit hired labor hard. Formal government decontrol of the vast mass of retail prices would come on January 2, 1992—this on the heels of already unprecedented inflation in 1990 and 1991. The plants in which the vast majority of goods producers worked, especially those that were medium- and large-sized, were still owned by the state, but the state no longer really controlled their directors, who could now set their own prices, exploit monopoly status, and search for ways to avoid taxes. The new government was also trying to wean the plants away from dependence on the state as the consumer of their output. "State orders," the late-Gorbachev substitute for the traditional plan directives, were down, leaving producers confused; they soon sought credits and subsidies in their place. Managers, in some ways, now had more power over their workers, at least potentially. Workers, however, also had the potential to apply more muscle in dealing with managers, since the state no longer stood above the managers as a repressive mechanism.

Still over the horizon, controversial but clearly central to the government's long-term strategy, was privatization—the state's divestiture of its ownership of almost all production units. An opening to small-scale but often immensely profitable private enterprise had come under Gorbachev in the late 1980s with the licensing of cooperatives, leasing arrangements, and so forth. But outside Moscow and St. Petersburg, stores, restaurants, and service enterprises were still overwhelmingly in state hands, as were industrial plants. The former would be easy to privatize; indeed the process, with all sorts of none-too-clean deals, was already under way. But the critical matter was the factories, mines, and enterprises where blue-collar Russia, in its tens of millions, worked.

How and to whose benefit would privatization take place? Could foreigners now become owners, flashing ready cash in the face of a hungry government? Would yesterday's Soviet managers somehow contrive to become the new owners themselves, converting power into property? What, then, might happen to workers? Would workers be dealt into the privatization process, getting equity themselves? Should the factories indeed be sold at wholesale prices to the workers?

If some combination of managers and workers was to take ownership of the wealth created by the people over seventy years of socialist toil and sacrifice, what of the rest of the people who had labored in their own ways to make the economy possible? What of teachers, doctors, and intellectuals? What of soldiers and the police? The organizations in which they worked were not privatizable in any meaningful sense, as were factories. Were they to be excluded? If not, how were they to be dealt in?

Readers familiar with the topic will understand that the issues just raised lay out major issues of privatization as they appeared in late 1991 and early 1992. Many of them would be largely resolved, however controversially, by autumn 1994. They receive attention in Chapter 5. For now, it need only be noted that the 1991–1993 period that is the main focus of this work was not to be significantly affected by any broad new patterns of management-labor relations as a result of the government's large-scale privatization.

Thus, the Yeltsin-Gaidar government, committed to getting the state out of its inherited role of provider-employer-proprietor (if no longer micromanager) of the Russian economy, would nonetheless be forced, for a while, still to be all these things. The reformers—Yegor Gaidar as economic czar, Anatoly Chubais as point man on privatization plans, Aleksandr Shokhin as labor minister, and Boris Fedorov, soon to become finance minister—could see the exit door through which they wished to push the state, but they were not yet on its threshold.

The problem was to drive toward the market while managing the social costs of the economic transition politically. If labor proved militant and unruly, if managers proved oppressive or resistant to the new conditions the government's strategies imposed, all the worse for the new economics. Painful problems were anticipated; if Russia's was to be a peaceful revolution, the government would not be in a position to suppress them at the outset. Well-meaning in a general sense, its leaders ran, after all, a weakened state apparatus. Whereas in certain areas they would be accused of excessive neoliberalism—relying on a variety of economic institutions to rise spontaneously—in labor relations they were forced to be activist. They could not assume a hands-off posture, as the U.S. government does in so much of employer-labor relations. Their chosen path was corporatist.

Corporatism: Choices and Chances

Before I move on, it is necessary to examine at moderate length the matter of corporatism, its variants and their meanings in other systems and some of the whys and wherefores of its adoption in Russia.

Corporatism, in Schmitter's oft-quoted 1974 definition,

> can be defined as a system of interest representation in which the constituent units are organized into a limited number of singular, compulsory, noncompetitive, hierarchically ordered and functionally differentiated categories, recognized or licensed (if not created) by the state and

granted a deliberate representational monopoly within their respective categories in exchange for observing certain controls on their selection of leaders and articulation of demands and supports.[25]

This is a comprehensive and rather demanding list of attributes, an ensemble of characteristics compatible with a variety of regime types that are different in party systems, ideologies, degrees of political mobilization, and public policy. Corporatism is thus not synonymous with an organic state or authoritarian regime. Its obverse is pluralism,

> wherein the units are unspecified in number, and fall into "multiple, voluntary, competitive and non-hierarchically ordered" categories, and are neither monopolistic in "representational activity," nor specially licensed, recognized, "subsidized, created or otherwise controlled" in their selection of leaders or interests to articulate by the state.[26]

Despite the differences, corporatism and pluralism are about the same thing—interest politics—and, in the context of modern societies, work from a common set of basic assumptions about the political world. These, to summarize Schmitter, turn mainly on the growth of formal, associational modes of representing interests, a greater functional differentiation of interests with greater consequent conflict potential, a higher profile in politics for administrative staffs, specialized information and expertise, and an expanding scope of public policy with greater overlap of public (governmental) and private decision arenas.

Corporatism, thus, means "a lot to do." If a historically less-than-democratic Argentina has a corporatist profile, so do Germany, Sweden, and other democracies. But the United States, rather clearly, runs more decidedly to the pluralist mode. Corporatism is not necessarily repression; pluralism is not anarchy.

Russia made the corporatist choice—and under pressure. There is no implication that Gaidar or other advisers chewed over descriptions like Schmitter's and decided for corporatism against pluralism. The choice was obvious given the institutional deficit Russia faced in late 1991 and the nature of the labor problems anticipated. Pluralism is Madisonian, emerging from thinking on Federalist lines, and the problems that sort of thinking defines as critical are not the problems confronted even by would-be democrats to whom, realistically, the problem of order imposes itself as more of a priority. Perhaps Gaidar and some of his early team were in their hearts political Madisonians, as they were neoclassical in their economics. No matter—they were in a situation where very little could be expected to operate automatically, where what was at issue was precisely "economic objects purposely obscured in the neoclassical [economic] model," including, as Randall Calvert notes, "the specification of property rights, the maintenance of a medium of exchange ..., the enforcement of contracts," and the like.[27] These fundamental problems and others are assumed by the neoclassical model to have been solved already, allowing economists to move onto what for many of them have been the more interesting concerns. The Russian cabinet in 1991 was nothing if not aware that such issues were problematic in the real-world setting of Russia and that without their resolution, many other anticipated issues were beyond settling in a peaceful but revolutionary manner. With respect to some areas, as noted previously, policymakers trusted too much to spontaneous generation, but in the realm of labor relations, they felt themselves forced to be "neoinstitutionalist," to build toward the institutions they needed. The corporatist design would provide both an initial institution and a context, it must have been hoped, in which to work toward agreeing on other institutions (taking institution here to imply both organizational structures and the understood game rules) that would affect employers, hired labor, and the government itself.

To the designers, late-1991 Russia's map of potential interests and organizations must have resembled Schmitter's set of pluralist adjectives—"unspecified," "multiple," "nonhierarchical," "not specially licensed"—and in that context suggestive of an anarchy that might be exploited by those who were friends of neither democracy nor the market. Thus, the order a successful corporatist recipe should deliver would undergird democracy, giving structure to the contention of interests. Democracies in operation were not purely individualistic.

> Individuals do not act directly in defense of their interests; they delegate this defense. Masses are represented by leaders; this is the mode of collective organization in democratic institutions. ... Interest associations acquire the capacity to act on behalf of their members because they can coerce these members, specifically because they can sanction any individuals or subgroups who attempt to advance their particular goals at the cost of the collective interest.[28]

As these words of Przeworski's imply, even democratic pluralism contains elements that fit into corporatist interest representation, a point that Schmitter recognizes as well.[29]

Whereas the first choice of Madisonians would be pluralism rather than corporatism, the room to exercise such choice was limited in Russia. But in that hopeful, however non-Madisonian, environment, did not a corporatist design carry the risk of simply extending the authoritarian-totalitarian traditions that were part of history's overburden?

Here it is well to take account of a distinction Schmitter makes between state and societal brands of corporatism and the conditions—economic, historical, political—under which one or the other has emerged. The characteristics of corporatism enumerated earlier do not explain themselves. How did they evolve? Was the number of units limited by deals cut among them or by deliberate government restriction? Were these units singular by way of some prior competitive elimination or, again, because of state intervention? Were they compulsory via contractual or social pressure or because the state so decreed? Were noncompetitiveness, hierarchical ordering, and functional differentiation all products of prior struggles, pacts and turf division among the units themselves, or in each case did the state determine these matters, acting on the units from above? Similarly, recognition by the state can be a matter of something imposed from below on the state by the realities of the situation or it can be "granted from above as a condition for association formation and continuous operation"—two very different things. Representational monopolies and the controls on how leaderships are selected and interests articulated can also emerge from interunit dynamics or from the "asymmetric imposition" of state power.[30]

A corporatism that emerges from the predominantly interunit dynamics, a kinder and gentler variety, is labeled "societal"; one that is born of the state's intervention is "state" corporatism, the tougher type. In the first, the "legitimacy and functioning of the state" are dependent on the activity of the corporate units; in the second, those units are state creations, themselves dependent on a state whose "legitimacy and effective functioning [rest] on other bases."[31] Writing in 1974, Schmitter found the first of the types represented by Sweden, Switzerland, the Netherlands, Norway and Denmark, and arguably by some emergent properties of the United Kingdom, West Germany, Canada, France, and even the United States. State corporatism was exemplified by Portugal, Spain, Brazil, Chile, Peru, Mexico, and Greece. The types of corporatism, then, were associated with rather different sets of political arrangements and had different origins.

The common problem—stated very generally—to which the corporatization of interest representation arrangements was the solution "related to certain basic imperatives and needs of capitalism to reproduce the conditions for its existence and continually to accumulate further resources." This problem presented itself, concretely and historically, in two very distinct ways.

> The decay of pluralism and its gradual displacement by societal corporatism can be traced primarily to the imperative necessity for a stable, bourgeois-democratic regime, due to processes of concentration of ownership, competition between national economies, expansion of the role of public policy and rationalization of decision-making within the state to associate or incorporate subordinate classes and status groups more closely within the political process.

What is described here, then, is a gradual process in politically rather fortunate states that also tend to be financially rather well off. It is a process with which social democrats might have little quarrel, libertarians and neoconservatives somewhat more, but which sounds peaceful and gradual enough that the drift is likely to go largely unremarked until it is well along.

> As for the abrupt demise of incipient pluralism and its dramatic and forceful replacement by state corporatism, this seems closely associated with the necessity to enforce "social peace," not by coopting and incorporating, but by repressing and excluding the autonomous articulation of subordinate class demands in a situation where the bourgeoisie is too weak, internally divided, externally dependent and/or short of resources to respond effectively and legitimately to these demands within the framework of the liberal democratic state.[32]

In a nutshell, "the origins of societal corporatism lie in the slow, almost imperceptible decay of advanced pluralism; the origins of state corporatism lie in the rapid, highly visible demise of nascent pluralism."[33] The latter, in process and outcome, is obviously a "nastier and poorer" form than the former.

Indeed, Schmitter finds the ideology, such as it is, of state corporatism best expressed by the Romanian Mihail Manoilesco's writings of the 1930s, which anticipated the later concept of "external dependence" and described an "institutional-political response to a particular process of transformation [of] the world political economy and its attendant system of international stratification. ... Its 'dominant cause' lies in the relations between *peoples*, rather than between *classes* within national units." For Manoilesco, this response presented in those interwar years a radical nationalistic

> demand for restructuring the international division of labor and its distribution of benefits. Peripheral capitalist nations are becoming increasingly aware of the disparity in returns generated by the exchange of raw materials and foodstuffs for the manufactured goods produced by the advanced, earlier developing economies and are beginning to implement new national economic policies, especially ones aiming at import-substituting industrialization and control of foreign trade.

State corporatism, then, was to work in the service, as the instrument, of an ideology of "defensive nationalistic modernization from above."[34]

Let by-now-wearying readers be aware that I am almost done with explicating and summarizing "Schmitter 1974"—many no doubt have seen many of the quotes before (such being the fate of classic articles)—but that I need to carry on a little further.

Schmitter develops a list of elements that seem to correspond to the top-down forcing of state corporatism on interest representation in national contexts, one somewhat more specific than some of the earlier characterizations.[35]

1. peripheral, delayed-dependent capitalism
2. awareness of relative underdevelopment
3. resentment of inferior international status
4. desire for enhanced national economic and political autarky
5. extension of state control through regulatory policies, sectoral planning, and public enterprise
6. emergence of a more professionalized and achievement-oriented situs of civil servants

Acting to solve these problems can thus generate a state corporatist order. Further down the line, relating to what would emerge as the democratic transition enterprise, there arises the matter of how state corporatism might turn into societal corporatism. Such an institutional shift, as Schmitter put it, had "yet to be made peacefully and incrementally." The transit seemed to depend upon the existence of a set of characteristics adding up to a "liberal-pluralist past."[36]

1. a history of autonomous organizational development
2. authenticity of interest representation
3. protracted encounters between classes and sectors that acquired distinct self-images and loyalties and a measure of mutual respect
4. competitive party and parlimentary arenas to which wider appeals could be addressed
5. a previous pattern of relative noninterference by the state, which extended its role only gradually and then usually at the request of organized private interests

It might be asked how likely it is that peoples blessed by these elements of the "good polity," the civil society, could wind up under state corporatism at all. Schmitter seems a bit unclear on whether these were what pushed the fortunate toward societal, and away from state, corporatism or whether they constituted a legacy, somehow suppressed, that state corporatist polities endowed with them could later use to evolve in a societal direction.

In any case, countries "locked into state corporatism at an earlier stage of development" will have hard going with any such transition. Schmitter, in 1974, finished with a projection. "It is difficult to imagine a politically continuous transformation toward societal corporatism; rather, one suspects that the state-corporatist system must first degenerate into openly conflictful, multifaceted, uncontrolled interest politics—pluralism in other words—as appears to be happening in contemporary Spain."[37]

Contexts: Soviet Past, Russian Present

It may seem that we have come far afield from the world of the decaying USSR or the shaky new Russia launched on the road to democracy and the market as 1991 drew to an end. That is certainly the case; it is also, to a degree, the point.

Before I move on to the next chapter and begin to put some empirical flesh on the bones already outlined—that the Yeltsin (Gaidar, and so on) government would opt for a corporatist mechanism to regulate government, labor, and employer relations—let us review the USSR and Russia 1991 against the background laid out by our consideration of Schmitter's exposition of the various facets of corporatism.

First, the whole history, tsarist and Soviet, that predated Yeltsin's Russian Federation as independent state was one wherein the state had possessed immense power versus society and any of its units—power well beyond what it took to push peripheral, late capitalist societies into the straitjacket of state corporatism. Only late tsarism had showed clear signs of development toward real capitalism (in an economy still mainly statist) and the development of any kind of real bourgeoisie. The USSR was largely a classless but inegalitarian society.[38] The state order created by Lenin and Stalin was totalitarian—a hypertrophic, repressive state beyond the conception of authoritarian-state corporatist elites. Corporatism did not enter into the equation. The economy and its institutions were nonmarket, antimarket; there was no capitalism for the polity to seek to save or promote.

What does ring somewhat familiar is the description of the impulse that drove weak, peripheral capitalisms to state-corporatist means and the six-point characterization of that impulse. Even if we allow for the commitment to "world revolution" (and thus to a certain aggression!), was not Stalin's "socialism in one country" a program of defensive nationalistic modernization undertaken under noncapitalist auspices? Was not the building of the USSR as a system driven by an awareness of underdevelopment and a resentment of Russia's inferior status directed toward political and economic autarky and promoted through state control so massive as to be totalitarian?

This totalitarian order, this iron cage that made even state corporatism look rubbery by comparison, though rusted badly by the early 1980s, was Gorbachev's inheritance, as noted earlier in discussing Karklins's interpretation. He inherited as well a population of hundreds of millions of people whom rational-choice theorists might have seen as each acting to maximize outcomes in an environment of corruption, shortage, and queues as a substitute for bidding prices higher and as restricting effort at work and attempting to control, informally, the shop floor. If rational-choice theory was "undersocialized," the corrective probably lay in viewing those Soviet actors in their millions as "embedded," in Mark Granovetter's term, in whole webs of relationships of patronage, dependence, and reciprocity shaped by the larger economy and polity and in viewing the sociological relationships, in turn, as reflecting the institutions—as political scientists might prefer—that were part of what embedded people in those regularities of behavior[39] that made for the low productivity and failing incentives but still provided the familiar context for the muddling through of late Brezhnevian stagnation.

Gorbachev sought to break through all this—but while retaining the party-state and socialism. He failed utterly. It fell to Yeltsin and his allies, thus, to try to build (or manage a transition to) democracy while creating a market economy on the basis of a population whose resocialization away from modes of behavior and expectation embedded in old relationships and old institutions had only recently begun. It was a daunting task. The economic transition agenda was made all the more difficult by the weakness of the state and by its commitment to democracy in the context of peaceful revolution. One need only look at the list of characteristics facilitating societal corporatism to find an enumeration of what neither tsarist Russian nor Soviet polities had been about.

From this unpromising base, Russia set out toward democracy and the market via a path of societal corporatism. That the whole design might work in the short term was a lot to expect. Russian democratizers rose from a heritage and context different from those of Latin American military juntas. Veterans (however now "reformed") of old Leninist ruling parties or ex-oppositionists might be more prone to division on economic issues, specifically, than the staffs of former caudillos. And the latter had "barracks to retreat to." It was not clear that late-socialist radical reformers or postsocialist marketizers had such boltholes or would be able to moderate their interventionism when market failures arose. Such failures, as Comisso argued, evoked political intervention in developed market economies and constituted respectable reasons for doing so. If Russia's leap into the market with such a weak institutional base was, as it seemed, bound to produce such failures, might not the new anticommunist elites wind up doing precisely what the old ones had done?[40]

It is not a bad question, and the answer would, again, imply something about how well the new societal corporatism might work. It is unlikely that the government, for all its rhetoric of "social partnership," underestimated the opposition it might face or was unrealistic about the kind of partners that would be easiest to deal with. Similar to Przeworski, it probably calculated that economic reforms "can progress under two polar conditions of the organization of political forces: The latter have to be very *strong* and *support* the reform program, or they have to be very *weak* and *unable to oppose* it effectively." Thus the government's alternatives were "either [to] seek the broadest possible support from unions, opposition parties, and other encompassing and centralized organizations or [to] work to weaken these organizations and try to make their opposition ineffective" (emphasis added).[41] Over the years 1991–1993, it might be said (and the government would) that it had tried the first; those who did not like the government's line would, from the outset, accuse it of doing the second. And in spring 1994, a Russian deputy finance minister would tell the author that, in essence, both were correct.

It is time, then, to turn to the story.[42]

2

Searching for Consensus: Corporatism's "Shakedown Cruise," 1992

WITH THE FAILURE OF THE AUGUST 1991 coup attempt, the USSR's fate was sealed, and the Russian Federation, along with the other components of the old state, launched on a trajectory toward independence. "Russian" politics of a post-Soviet variety thus began, but on the basis of both the heavy heritage and the mounting wreckage of the old Soviet system. This chapter, then, deals with labor politics and attempts at corporatist management in the early phase—from late summer 1991 to the end of 1992. In this period, the hopes and objectives of the marketizing, reformist core in Yeltsin's cabinet were to confront the countering forces of bureaucratic survivals in the old "official" trade unions of the Soviet period, in an industrial lobby rooted in heavy and defense industry, and in the fears and apprehensions of a Russian majority ill prepared for change. The treatment through much of what follows is essentially narrative: There is, after all, a story here that engages institutions, organizations, and personalities in one corner of a large political arena. And we no longer deal with the secretiveness of the old Soviet media but instead with a flood of (not necessarily reliable) information from free but very partisan media and from political actors at various levels ready to talk but with their own agendas to advance. It is not a very well known story and still includes gaps. It might be called, as well, a cautionary tale, although the lessons of such may be more evident to observers than they seem instructive or applicable in the minds of players in high-stakes political games. At the end of the chapter, I draw away from the tale to make some tentative conclusions about 1991–1992 on the basis of the thoughts and questions introduced in Chapter 1 on the building of democracy and the market and on the utility of corporatist organizational tools in carrying out these tasks in the Russian context.

Prelude: The Echoes of August

Whereas the coup's outcome, and Gorbachev's subsequent resignation from the general secretaryship and the CPSU itself, ended the party politics of the old style, which had constituted a rear-guard opposition to reform, the path Yeltsin and the reformers trod was littered with two old institutions that would not disappear: the VKP (Vseobshchaia Konfederatsiia Profsoiuzov, or General Confederation of Trade Unions) and the FNPR (Federatsiia Nezavisimykh Profsoiuzov Rossii, or Federation of Independent Trade Unions of Russia).

The VKP was, in fact, the old All-Union Central Council of Trade Unions (AUCCTU). It had adopted its new name at its eighteenth congress in October 1990, by which time the "All-Union" modifier was sounding anachronistic given the drift of the USSR toward, at a minimum, some looser form of federation under a new name. FNPR had been born in fall 1989 out of the old AUCCTU structure, which had—like the Communist Party—hitherto lacked a specifically Russian Republic organization. In late 1990 and in 1991, both organizations, facing the government's increasingly radical reform plans, kept up a constant refrain of defending workers' interests and an insistence that these not be sacrificed as Russia moved toward the market. They found plenty to complain of in the various plans presented by Nikolai Ryzhkov, then Valentin Pavlov, from the government side, as well as in the more radical variants that marked the last year of Soviet power.

Though still dependent on the state, which had backed its dues-checkoff privileges and provided the large funds it administered as the government's delegate in the area of social insurance, FNPR (and VKP, though the latter was quickly losing its relevance as the old state moved toward breakup) was now also independent in the sense that it or its leadership made its own politics, took its own line. There was no longer the overall party hegemony that kept state structures and official trade unions in line, and FNPR could now be simultaneously claimant on, and critic of, the state.

Yeltsin's rise to unchallenged leadership in the Russian Federation in 1991, especially after his June popular election, complicated the situation of the old unions. His July 1991 "departyization" decree, although aimed at outlawing CPSU organizations in enterprises, used broad language, and Yeltsin had to reassure FNPR chair Igor Klochkov that the decree was not aimed at outlawing union organizations at plant level.[1] Whether mollified or not by such reassurances, the union continued to express concern that workers' and union rights relative to those of employers had been eroded by the 1990 changes to the state enterprise law, whose original 1987 version (politically, an era's remove from the world of 1991) had provided for elections of managers and other elements of worker control. With the failure of the August coup, the looming certainty that the future held the end of the Soviet state and the Russian government's commitment to a market economy, FNPR assumed a tougher attitude, declaring "unity of action" days for October 21–26.[2] Yeltsin, on October 16, promised that the government would consult with labor unions before taking any major economic or social policy actions;[3] but he also accused FNPR of acting in a monopolist manner reminiscent of the old AUCCTU.[4] The Yeltsin government of late 1991, with Yegor Gaidar in charge of economic policy and moving in the direction of a shock-therapy policy for 1992, was interested in extracting itself from the owner-manager-paymaster role in the economy as the beginning of a move toward a referee role between the interests of labor and those of the yet-vague category of owners-employers. Some sort of organizational recipe wherein the government would find itself dealing with partners rather than dictating to (and thereby taking responsibility for) subordinates suggested itself, some form of corporatism. Given the realities of an economy still largely state owned, corporatism might have been more a pious wish than a real program, but the stage was set for a solution that would include a trilateral body to deal with the many problems labor politics was likely to present in the rapidly approaching future.

Trilateral Corporatism: Design and Conception

Some thought had been given, earlier in 1991—as the bonds that held together the USSR gave way to concepts of a new, looser, "confederative" union—to the need for new, explicitly multilateral mechanisms to regulate labor relations. These were reflected in documents signed between the USSR government and those of the union republics;[5] additionally, in 1991 the then-USSR government indicated in the more or less traditional discussions on the socioeconomic aspects of the 1992 economic plan with the official trade unions that some of the emerging "employers'" organizations would be included.[6] At the same time, observers of the labor scene, anticipating stresses of an extreme sort in the economy, worried about whether the government could anticipate any partner on the labor side with sufficient control over its membership to conclude durable pacts and maintain mutual respect.[7]

Despite (or perhaps because of) the anticipated problems, the charter for the trilateral commission was, as such things go, brief and general: a Yeltsin presidential *ukaz*, "On Social Partnership and the Resolution of Labor Disputes (Conflicts)," dated November 15. Published on November 19, it appeared among a welter of other presidential and government decrees of the same date in *Rossiiskaia Gazeta.*[8] Its span, from minimum wage levels to deliveries of petroleum beyond the borders of the Russian Republic, was an indication of the overload the Russian state faced as it prepared for the end of the USSR.

The first point specified the annual concluding of general agreements at the national level among government, the trade unions, and the employers, specifying the obligations of the diverse sides in areas of "employment of the population, the gradual increase of social guarantees for citizens, the social defense of the most vulnerable groups of the population, the preservation of the growth of incomes of workers according to the degree of stabilization of the economy," and so on. This was a seemingly tall order.

A second point was aimed at annual "trilateral branch wage agreements" in various sectors of the economy; these would take into account the "mutual obligations" of the sides in "organization, pay for work, social guarantees, the hiring and dismissal of workers, securing the increase in the effectiveness of production, strengthening of labor discipline, the prevention of labor conflicts, and also the observation of the interests of the workers in carrying out privatization." It was proposed that such agreements should aim at securing what looked like irreconcilable objectives—at "observing economically justified interrelations between growth in wages, taking into account the reform of retail prices and growth in the volume of goods produced." But such agreements "should not worsen conditions of work or social guarantees established by legislation."

The fourth point called for establishing, in a two-week period, a commission to carry out these major tasks. It would draw on government, unions, and employers to define its legal status and procedures. This Russian Trilateral Commission for the Regulation of Social and Labor Relations emerged as the RTK.

The how of establishing the commission was unspecified, and two weeks was hardly a long time. In December, reference had been made at the FNPR plenum to a union draft of an agreement among the government, the Congress of Russian Business Circles, and the Council of the FNPR.[9] No other organizations were mentioned. Press coverage of whatever deliberations were then taking place was thin to nil. By late December, some progress could be deduced from a report on the organization of the labor side. Klochkov of the FNPR told a correspondent of recent "intensive exchanges of opinion" regarding the composition of the commission. Agreement had been reached that FNPR would participate on the labor side, along with the Sotsprof union federation and "other parallel union structures."[10] This meant that the FNPR, having sought a monopoly on the labor side, had not succeeded. It also meant that FNPR and the generally pro-market reform Sotsprof—an organization combining workers from state and nonstate sectors, very close to the small (but influential in Yeltsin's cabinet) Social Democratic Party, and destined to become the bugbear of FNPR—would sit on the same side of the table in uncomfortable proximity.

The inside story of how the labor side was assembled gave some interesting clues to how various parties viewed the trilateral commission during its creation. The short time available to form the commission (one source indicates that the period was not two weeks, as in the document, but only one week[11]) was partly attributable to the fact that FNPR had participated in the preparation of the presidential decree, aiming at monopoly on the labor side. The Congress of Russian Business Circles had similar ambitions on the employer side (although, as an organization related to banking, finance, and trade, it represented the employers of what were still quite small workforces). This was of little concern to FNPR, whose demands and complaints from the beginning would target the government directly.

Labor Minister Aleksandr Shokhin and his deputy, Pavel Kudiukin, had, however, other ideas, looking toward broadening participation on both labor and employer sides, and encouraged other unions—notably Sotsprof—and employer organizations to caucus among themselves and come up with recipes for apportioning representation. Among the independent unions, only Sotsprof had shown from the beginning a desire to participate in the trilateral commission—the others apparently viewed the presidential decree and the RTK as potential avenues for government interference in union affairs. Thus, the first round of horse trading was between FNPR and Sotsprof. With the initial notion of a trilateral assuming ten members to a side, FNPR claimed nine places for itself, conceding one to Sotsprof. The latter's counteroffer was six seats to FNPR, three for itself, and the remaining seat for other unions that might later decide to join the RTK. By this time, other unions were growing more interested; at one of their meetings, organized by Kudiukin under the auspices of the Social Democratic Party, the proposal emerged that each trade union federation should get one seat. Since most unions were nominally federations, FNPR, despite its greater membership, would be reduced to one seat. It was having none of this, and realistically, this proposal was a nonstarter. The final resolution involved expanding the number from ten to fourteen places: Nine seats for FNPR and three for Sotsprof would preserve the numbers each had originally sought; one seat would be added for the Independent Miners Union (NPG) and one for the civil aviation union. This left FNPR, on the labor side, short of the two-thirds majority needed on each side to deliver that side's consent to any RTK decision. The resolution of the proportions for labor representation also explains the fourteen-to-a-side eventual structure of the RTK itself, which was not the product of any prior conclusion about maximum feasible effective participation but an arithmetic response to the ad hoc settlement of the union-side representation issue. The participation of a member of the government side (Kudiukin) in mobilizing organizations to demand a place on the opposing labor side might take some aback. But given the state of politics in Russia at the time, there was nothing really remarkable about it, although this would not save such moves from criticism by those—like the FNPR—whose interests were hurt by them. The government was obviously at this time not interested in conceding a monopoly to FNPR on the labor side even though the latter, with its legacy of more than 60 million members, was quite ready to claim it.

The late-December FNPR plenum also set the stage for what would emerge as a pattern of labor posturing. The union promised "constructive dialogue" with the government, but Klochkov, looking toward the January 2 price liberalization, complained that "for a long time already no one has controlled prices" and claimed that they had increased five- to eightfold in 1991 (a clear overestimate). Endorsing the idea of trilateral consultation, though in a manner suggesting that the idea of a commission had not yet been broached in a decree, Klochkov sketched a scenario that was to prove in some ways overblown but in other ways prophetic. "If constructive proposals [and] demands of the trade unions expressing the interests of the people of hired labor are to be ignored as 'populist,' 'provocational,' or 'speculative,' then it remains to us to use the proven methods of struggle—the organization of mass demonstrations under the slogans of the trade unions."[12]

Deputy Prime Minister Gennadi Burbulis, and Shokhin as well, spoke at the December FNPR plenum as guests. The former gave some indication of the gulf between the radical alarm with which the Yeltsin team viewed the economic situation and the FNPR's acceptance of the market, but with social protections that would seem bound to hamper arriving at it. Asked if the government really thought that the confrontation of strong trade unions and a weak economy was dangerous, he replied, "We don't simply have a weak economy, we've got no economy, and strong trade unions don't threaten us because we don't have them, either." Burbulis allowed that union complaints that the government had not managed a "dynamic, compact and consequential dialogue" with the unions had some merit and promised that he would eliminate shortfalls in this area; but he challenged FNPR to rid itself of "the notion that the interests of the workers are dearer to you than they are to us."[13] FNPR, as it would turn out, was not inclined to oblige.

Social Partnership: Conceptions, Reservations

How the trilateral mode of social partnership would work, what it meant in the context of a Russia in a process of rapid change, was not, obviously, clear at the outset. Both the public reception of the idea and the early comments of experts (even some who had been relatively close to the process of formulation) indicated that the ideas and procedures would have to find a place in an unruly politics.

The FNPR newspaper *Rabochaia Tribuna,* in a February four-part series, vented some of the confusion and fears. Some contributors to the discussion focused on the implications of what seemed to be the state's abandonment of its managing and employing role in the economy. "Workers are becoming the slaves of new bosses," as one put it, and there was the risk that property would go to the rich—this was not justice. Justice required that factories go to the labor collectives that worked in them. They could work off the value of the property over five to ten years. Another participant cited the danger that deetatization might involve the state giving away national wealth at ridiculously low prices: The large Raspadskaia mine had been valued at only three days' worth of its coal output if that output were priced at world levels.[14] What, such people seemed to be asking, was the government doing? Had it thought through its own program? Did it have any conception of how its moves might affect the population?

Others focused their criticisms more on the trilateral mechanism itself. Social partners, presumably, were equals in the RTK context; yet the government, in its sphere, had let prices rise to levels "inaccessible to the majority" while imposing taxes that threatened to "literally freeze productive activity," demonstrating a lack of any social policy.[15] Why, too, was the chair of the RTK—Burbulis—a government official? Why not three cochairs, one to a side? And who would speak with a distinct voice on behalf of employers when in February 1992, 90 percent of the workforce worked in the state sector?[16]

Such structural concerns were the ones that informed the commentary of labor specialists. Civilized, trilateral labor relations were desirable; but the attempt to build them would introduce something very new in Russia, whereas developed Western economies were at home with such arrangements. In Russia, employers tended to hide behind the government's back. The government, even this one committed to change, might find old, bad habits hard to break. Despite its interest in having non-FNPR unions on the RTK, in its recent dealings with unions on the coal-industry branch tariff agreement, it had negotiated with the independent miners' NPG but had then signed the agreement with the FNPR-affiliated NPRUP (Independent Trade Union of Coal Industry Workers) the old official union![17]

Russia, then, neither practically nor theoretically ready for trilateral partnership, was nonetheless trying to construct such a mechanism, necessarily from the top down; yet the quality of labor relations also depended a great deal on the state of affairs at shop-floor level.[18] Indeed, given the unprecedented situation in the economy as a whole, regional variations in circumstance, the different conditions in sectors and branches of the economy, and the essentially unique circumstances in relations between bosses and workers in individual plants, there was a strong possibility that RTK deliberations might have little connection or relevance to the grass roots.

There was risk as well in the political pulls operating on the unions. FNPR was, in many senses, a survivor organization of the old regime—however it chose to deal with or deny that fact. NPG, Sotsprof, and some others, however, had been forged in the atmosphere of 1989–1990 "rejectionism" directed against the old USSR government. Yeltsin's government was, in a sense, theirs too. But whereas government as government might try its best to ease the pains of reform, government as employer was embarked on a course that biased it toward ignoring that pain. FNPR resistance might be expected, but what of the others? One analyst predicted "a contradictory, if not schizophrenic, condition in the democratic labor movement. Supporting the reforms, it should be an ally of the government. Being a movement of workers, of hired laborers, it is [the government's] adversary."[19]

Defending the labor side of the table, unions could have little real notion of how well they could control or deploy their members in coming months. FNPR had its huge inherited and generally passive membership. The new independents had more committed members, but how might they behave as economic circumstances grew tougher? Workers were being asked to go against what might seem their natural tendencies, "to support the completely alien goal of creating favorable conditions for the unhindered development of entrepreneurship … including private enterprises with hired labor."[20]

And yet "only a fool or an outright liar serving a rotten system" could fail to see that the "alien goal" was in the long-term interest of workers as well as others. Russia, under "the abnormal, unnatural conditions in which [its] economy finds itself as a result of utopian experiments," needed unions, however unnatural the orientation might seem in normal conditions, to "struggle for the establishment of a free market economy, for the freedom of entrepreneurship, of commercial activity, etc." Some workers might understand this; most did not, to put it mildly. The results of opinion surveys indicated that "many do not have a clear understanding of what is meant by a market economy."[21]

An additional complication was that large numbers of highly literate, highly skilled workers who had been mainstays of support for democracy and backers of Yeltsin before the Soviet collapse were in sunset industries—yesterday's favored military plants, for example—that would have to bear the brunt of much of that government's economic reforms. Reluctant, thus, to back the forces they had worked with before January 1992, they were also reluctant to throw in with yesterday's antagonists, such as the FNPR, even though these were set to protest any factory closings.[22] All this was a great deal for the RTK to handle.

Social partnership and corporatism were thus introduced into a Russian context not in order to maintain a market economy or even to preserve a weak and threatened capitalist order by imposing state-corporatist controls on labor. In Russia, most of what corporatist policy was supposed to regulate was either very new or did not yet exist. Understanding this was not hard for analysts; as two put it, the labor movement had emerged in the West after the "capitalist choice" had been made. However it had been made, the fact itself had pointed out clear tasks for the Western labor movement.[23] In Russia, first principles were still a matter of dispute; big questions had not been authoritatively taken off the table. This would make hard going for a trilateral mechanism.

The Sides and the Players

The RTK started meeting at the beginning of January. There was nothing secret about the commission, but coverage of its deliberations tended to be brief and in all not very informative.Possibly the first time the roster of members was publicly listed was three months into its operation. In an April 1992 issue, the weekly *Ekonomika i Zhizn* published the full text with collective signatories of the 1992 General Agreement.[24] The text was preceded in the newspaper by a somewhat odd-sounding preface, indicating that it was being published at "readers' request." (No provisions, evidently, had been otherwise made for its publication even though by the standards of the time and its flow of decrees, declarations, and laws, the agreement was not an overly long one.)

Who, then, were those who sat at the table? On the state's side, the list was distinctly ministerial.

M. I. Alekhin—First deputy minister of social defense of the population

S. V. Anisimov—Minister of trade and material resources

Iu. M. Arskii—First deputy minister of ecology and natural resources

V. V. Barchuk—First deputy minister of finance

P. M. Kudiukin—Deputy minister of labor and employment

V. M. Lopukhin—Minister of fuel and energy

A. A. Nechaev—Minister of economics

A. A. Titkin—Minister of industry

A. P. Ustiuzhanin—First deputy minister of agriculture

A. G. Fonotov—First deputy minister of science, higher schools, and technical policy

A. B. Chubais—Chair, State Committee for the Administration of State Property

M. A. Shapkin—Deputy minister of justice

A. A. Shevchuk—Deputy minister of transport

A. N. Shokhin—Deputy prime minister and minister of labor and employment

The government's fourteen representatives, then, covered a broad but logical range of portfolios. On the output side of the economy, critical sectors that would constitute choke points in case of unrest were represented by Lopukhin (energy) and Shevchuk (transport), as well as by Titkin with the general industry portfolio. These three sat atop pyramids of enterprises and associations that employed massive numbers of people, raising the question of why they were not on the employer side. Finance (Barchuk) and the new Economics Ministry would play important roles in the dicey transition to the market that lay ahead. Nechaev, the economics minister, was a marketeer generally in the Gaidar mode.

Players on the administrative side were typically very much Yeltsin team members, promarket and committed to change. Given his deputy premiership, Labor Minister Shokhin would often chair commission sessions in Burbulis's (frequent) absences. His deputy, Kudiukin, once a prosecuted and imprisoned intraparty dissident in the late Brezhnev years (when he was a junior researcher at the Academy of Sciences high-profile Institute for World Economics and International Relations [IMEMO]), was also a Social Democratic Party activist and connected to the independent Sotsprof union on the labor side of the table.[25] Anatoly Chubais, the ministerial-level "privatization czar," would exercise critical functions in that role throughout 1992–1994 and find himself the continuing center of controversy over policy. (He would also prove to be the most durable of the reform core of the early-1992 cabinet, surviving into early 1996, as first deputy premier with general responsibilites for economic policy.)

The fourteen commission members on the labor side represented a mix of the FNPR—and its branch and regional unions—and new, autonomous unions not affiliated with the old structures.

A. D. Vasilievskii—Chair, Union of Workers in Local Industries and Communal Service Enterprises

V. S. Goncharov—Chair, Tula Regional Trade Union Council

A. S. Davydov—Chair, Union of Workers in the Agro-Industrial Complex

K. D. Krylov—Secretary, Council of the FNPR

M. M. Kuzmenko—Chair, Union of Health Service Workers

B. G. Misnik—Chair, Union of Mining and Metallurgy Workers (PGMR)

V. I. Romanov—Deputy chairman, FNPR

V. A. Torlopov—Chair, Komi Republic Federation of Trade Unions

G. A. Trudov—Chair, Union of Heavy Machine Building Workers

A. A. Malinovskii—President, Interstate Federation of Unions of Civil Aviation Flight Personnel (FPALS)

V. E. Mokhov—Cochair, Republican Coordinating Council, Sotsprof

D. A. Semenov—Cochair, Republican Coordinating Council, Sotsprof

A. A. Sergeev—Chair, Independent Union of Miners (NPG)

S. V. Khramov—Cochair, Republican Coordinating Council, Sotsprof

Of the labor side, then, the first nine listed were FNPR: Krylov and Romanov from the central administration (the latter number two to Klochkov), five heads of branch unions organized on the old "industrial" principle linking workers and managers in a given branch, and two—Goncharov from Tula and Torlopov from Arctic Komi—representing the regional organizations that had also been part of the old AUCCTU structure. By the end of 1992, one—Boris Misnik of the PGMR—would lead most of his members out of the FNPR in a controversial defection; the pilots' FPALS would operate with increasing independence of FNPR.

Sotsprof, an umbrella organization linking workers in state and nonstate sectors and including some smaller business owners was, despite its original title ("socialist" [later changed to "social"] trade unions), a progovernment supporter of market transition and reform. Its three representatives constituted the bulk of the independent faction on the labor side. It claimed, in 1991 (therefore, USSR-wide at the time), to include 200 organizations with a combined membership of about 250,000.[26]

Aleksandr Sergeev chaired the NPG—the independent union of coal miners (Nezavisimyi Profsoiuz Gorniakov) based explicitly on the "craft" principle and limited for a time to coal-face (primarily, therefore, underground) workers—one of the sturdier offspring of the mobilization of the coalfields that began in the hot summer of 1989. Though in numbers smaller than the FNPR union of coal-industry workers, it commanded more loyalty and attention from its voluntary membership. Finally, the airline pilots' union, although small in number of members, represented a critical occupation. Later, it would be joined by the militant Federation of Air Traffic Controllers Unions (Federatsiia Profsoiuzov Aviadispetcherov, or FPAD).[27]

Government, labor, and "business," then, completed the trilateral of corporatism. The term typically used for the third side was *predprini-*

mateli (rabotodateli), which literally translates as "entrepreneurs (employers)," though the latter word derives from its roots, "work-givers," and may reflect a somewhat different shading than the French-derived English "employer." Neither "businessmen" nor "entrepreneurs" fits too well, as a roster heavily weighted in favor of state enterprises would show:

Iu. A. Bespalov—President, Union of Producers of the Chemical Industry

L. I. Vainberg—President, Association of Joint Enterprises, International Unions and Organizations

A. V. Vasilev—President, Association of Exchange Structures of the Agro-Industrial Complex; chair, Russian Agricultural Exchange

N. I. Golovanov—Vice president, Rosavtodvor enterprise

A. V. Lisurenko—Chair of administration, Russian State Association, or Rostopprom

V. V. Piskunov—President, Association of Industrial Enterprises of Russia

G. M. Savtsov—Vice president, Rosavtotrans trucking enterprise

M. Z. Iurev—President, League of Industrialists and Goods-Producers of Russia; general director of the Soiuzinterprom production union

V. P. Kolmogorov—Vice president, Russian Union of Industrialists and Entrepreneurs (RSPP)

P. I. Neumyvakin—President, Russian Bank League

G. Iu. Semigin—Chair of administration, Congress of Russian Business Circles; president, Russian Financial-Industrial Group

V. M. Skachkov—Chairman, executive committee, Confederation of Entrepreneurs' Circles of Russia

P. T. Drachev—Vice president, Union of Leaseholders and Entrepreneurs of Russia

N. A. Shuliateva—President, Union of Small Enterprises of Russia

Employers, then, were a mixed bag, and rather grandiose titles offered little clue to their actual nature. The first eight represent what were at the time still large-scale state enterprise categories either in production or, in the case of Golovanov and Sovtsov, road transport and infrastructure. Among the latter six, Semigin, Skachkov, and Drachev are more clearly from the emergent private sector. Kolmogorov, of the RSPP (Russian Union of Industrialists and Entrepreneurs) sat at the table as the representative of the premier "industrial lobby" organization, which was rooted in large state enterprises, especially the defense sector, and had large numbers of workers. Organized in 1990–1991 as the USSR Scientific-Industrial Union (NPS), recast on the Russian Federation level by its head, Arkady Volskii, the RSPP would in various ways seek to play a major role in the centrist opposition to Yeltsin's economic policies in 1992–1993. Among those on the employers' side, Vainberg, Iurev, and Piskunov were also members of the RSPP's executive board.[28]

Employers, then, covered the gamut from large state production complexes with massive (over)employment rosters and consequent sensitivity to the application of any stern financial discipline to smaller private employers in production and services. Although those in financial services might well be among the new rich, they were not the employers of large labor forces or likely to become such. The large state enterprises would not always go against the government; much would depend on the government's willingness to support them while in transition and on the prospects they perceived for profitable privatization. The smaller private employers would not always be uncritical in their support of a marketizing government, since that government would find it very difficult to craft taxation policies and procedures that could please emergent business interests.

The fourteen-to-a-side trilateral thus amounted to 42 members, plus the government-appointed coordinator—not a large group given the difficulties of the market transition and the tensions that were to be anticipated. However, it was a large number to handle serious business in a context of rules and procedures that were new and unfamiliar and to a rather large degree yet to be defined. The membership was also large enough that a quorum could be assembled for each meeting—these were all busy people for whom the RTK was important but not necessarily central to their pursuits. (The problem of size was complicated by the fact that the enabling statute for the RTK specified that each member was entitled to a full-time deputy, making for the possibility of a sit-down of eighty-four people from three sides.[29])

There is an unavoidable—and accurate—impression of hurry, patch-up, make-do in all this. When one compares Russia's launch of a trilateral mechanism as a way of constructing a societal corporatism with the examples of trilateralism in the developed West, one is struck by how little one context resembled the other.

A rich literature on trilateralism in the West is replete with its own acronyms and its own catalog of national-scale organizational participants and how they emerged from smaller interest-promoting voluntary associations on labor and employer sides. Indeed, any discussion of what one (rather enthusiastic) writer called "capitalism's most optimal face"[30] in the context of a country or countries must soon get down to bodies like—in the United Kingdom—the Trades Union Congress (TUC) and the Confederation of British Industries (CBI). The latter, though dating only from 1965 (well into the saga of British capitalism) and founded "through an amalgamation of preceding lower-tier associations," was linked by 1966 with the TUC and the government in over fifty formal advisory bodies, through which tripartite consultation "at the very highest level of national decision-taking soon found itself institutionalised as the regular order of the day." Beyond "critically curtailing Parliament's power," trialteralism had the effect of reducing "all former practices of bilateral intervention—the 'interest groups'—to a virtual trickle."[31]

Structuring a trilateral mechanism, then, is a process aided by the preexistence of real associations, engaged in advancing conflicting interests in their own spheres of the economy, that can be combined into larger bodies under government prodding or approval. It would be hard to characterize the FNPR or the new, nonofficial trade unions, to say nothing of the newly minted organizations on the employer side, as meeting these specifications.

Nor, in operation, has trilateralism proven a panacea. Whereas, in mature political democracies where there is no question of the authenticity of elections, the alternation of parties in power, trilateralism may make for a smoothness of process, a conventionalized interaction of employers and owners, labor and the state (as with the TUC and CBI in the UK and at the national level in Germany's metalworking industries the two giants IG Metall and Gesamtmetall on the labor and employer sides, respectively), it has not proven particularly light-footed in dealing with changing market conditions or good at job-creation.

Western Europe has not managed to avoid, since the 1980s, levels of unemployment once thought inconceivable. Cyclical and structural issues are involved. In the late 1970s—hard times in the United States—trilateralist Germany

> was held up for emulation by Americans who admired such various and vaunted aspects of the West German economy as a low inflation rate, labor-management cooperation, an extensive social welfare safety net, state promotion of industrial restructuring, and banks that planned investments in companies by careful scrutiny of long-range goals rather than short-term glances at the "bottom line."[32]

But by the mid-1980s, some Germans looked westward to a U.S. economy marked by things seemingly lacking at home; "job creation in high technology, nourished by bountiful funds from venture capital firms and fostered by close relations between research facilities loosely affiliated with major companies and engineers from elite universities."[33]

Whether it gets things "right" or not—or right frequently and long enough not to discredit itself—trilateralism as a mode of societal corporatism rises out of and concerns itself with problems of mature industrial capitalism in its varied national manifestations. It reflects a broad measure of consensus on the what and why of that economic order's problems, and on the how of dealing with them. The Russia in which the RTK was established—a misdeveloped, noncapitalist industrial economy operating, barely, in a context of fundamental and controversial political change—might look with hope and envy toward countries with those problems, but it could hardly expect to be numbered among them in the near future.

Functioning trilateralism raises its own recurrent questions, especially of the balance at any given time between the interests of worker and employer, labor and capital, and whose side the government supports.[34] The global economy's premium on competitiveness will lead (neo)liberal economists to condemn featherbedding, wage and benefits "creep," job preservation, and other prolabor tendencies as reducing the flexibility of an economy. It is not remarkable, in turn, that defenders of labor's interests see in such criticisms of long-established procedures and their outcomes the threat of "flexibility without solidarity."[35] Labor in advanced Western economies sees its market position deteriorating in a changing arena of world economic competition, where "continuing high unemployment encourages employer efforts to relax the 'rigidities' imposed by central bargaining and to exploit labor's market weakness to 'restore flexibility to a bargained economy' through the reintroduction of market pressures into neo-corporatist arrangements."[36]

Again, despite some partial similarities (Russia in 1991 still labored with overemployment bequeathed by the inefficient Soviet economy but feared the coming of unemployment; Russia had problems with its competitiveness in the world economy but these problems were in fact so severe that it was barely a player at all), what impresses here is first, the tendency of many writers on Western trilateralism to use the word "crisis" for situations that from the Russian perspective, reflect problems only the fortunate encounter. Second, again, the gulf between the problems of managing interest conflict to which trilateralism has emerged, in many Western countries, as a response and the different problems of building a capitalist economy on a base like Russia's necessarily raises major questions as to the utility of trilateralism in easing the problems that accompany the latter process. Given these reflections and what they imply, I turn now to that process.

The Trilateral: Open for Business

As 1992 dawned, the former daily of the old official AUCCTU union, *Trud,* reported rather laconically that the RTK had held its first meeting[37] and gave no details. In view of the January 2 decontrol of retail prices across a broad front in partial imitation of Leszek Balcerowicz's 1990 shock therapy in Poland, the RTK could hardly avoid becoming the forum for complaints about present exigencies long before any stable procedural rules or discussion of long-term problems could be initiated.

Klochkov, in an early January interview, said that the union was for reform but against poverty and a "lumpen-egalitarian" approach. Dialogue was critical; in its absence, the FNPR would know "how to react" to an arrogant government. FNPR was no longer a government tool, an old-style official union. The price increases looked like governmental arrogance; by the middle of the month, FNPR members of the commission complained to Yeltsin about price increases they saw as totally unregulated, even on goods where some controls had been promised. Effectively, they accused Gaidar of bad faith and demanded that he be "brought to responsibility."[38]

Fairly or foully intended, the taxing of the government with breaking promises on pricing policy would become a constant refrain. The government was a ready target, but it is hard to see how it could have, in any case, controlled prices or attempted to do so without bringing on other forms of disaster. Inflation, after all, had been running at unprecedented levels in the old USSR in late 1991; consumer prices had nearly doubled during that year. Whether the Yeltsin government could have anticipated that retail prices would rise over 2,000 percent for calendar 1992 and what it might have done to avert this while continuing on the road to the market is also unclear.

Skyrocketing prices provoked short protest strikes, especially among the "salariat"—educational and health personnel not normally given to militancy but hurt by the downside "stickiness" of their own modest compensation as directly state budget-funded personnel (as opposed to many production workers, whose managers simply raised prices to fund wage increases). By late January, such strikes, plus FNPR negative reactions to various aspects of the government's proposed draft of a general agreement for 1992, gave the "social partners" plenty to handle.

The union had already threatened protests earlier, for January 17; *Izvestiia,* clearly on the government's side, as it would generally remain throughout the year, noted some of FNPR's demands, including an expanded list of price-controlled foods and "full indexing of the population's income" and observed that none of the demands had been "thought through from the standpoint of the state budget's capabilities."[39]

The newspaper quoted a combative Klochkov: "If we are forced to … we will name the specific people we do not want to see in the government. If the government does not compromise, it simply won't be allowed to function."[40]

This was union bravado, and not the last time such threats would be made. FNPR threatened a two-hour warning strike for January 27, which it claimed could involve 60 million people; this was averted, ostensibly by deliberations within the RTK. The business weekly *Kommersant* reported the deal without details (and oddly giving the impression that the RTK had been organized to deal with the threat) noted that the government was finding it hard as well to deal with unions not part of FNPR, implying wrongly that much of the education and health worker white-collar militancy was driven by such unions.[41] Concessions on the government's side settled, for a time, the teachers' and doctors' demands, heralding a pattern that would become rather common. Patterns were also emerging in the small drama of the RTK's own internal operations. On the government side, one recurrent refrain was that the commission was not "the government." Burbulis, who chaired sessions of the RTK in its early days (though Shokhin, the labor minister then, was its major architect[42]), referred to it as a problem-solving context in February;[43] Shokhin, stressing its crisis-prevention functions, denied that it would function as a fire brigade to deal with situations already gone critical.[44] Burbulis, after the commission had settled a March outbreak of labor problems in the Kuzbass (see further on), emphasized that all three sides had "acted as arbiters empowered by the state" in the matter, in line with the (hopeful) image of the government as the neutral "third party"—the corporate referee.[45]

The RTK was not much of anything to judge by some early accounts. A *Rabochaia Tribuna* journalist sympathetic to its FNPR proprietor reported on a February 11 meeting: "Many chairs" were empty. Among the missing were Burbulis, Shokhin, and the FNPR's Romanov. On the agenda was discussion of the draft law on collective contracts and agreements. Debate centered on which of these two terms should come first in the law's title! The meeting was interrupted, the assemblage told to clear the room in thirty minutes because another "more important" body had to meet in the same place. Then Shokhin entered, straight from a meeting with Yeltsin, to announce that the Vorkuta coal miners had declared a prestrike condition. Yeltsin wanted the RTK to handle the problem. So, off the members went to Vorkuta; "sign up, whoever is going." The reporter wrote, "I want[ed] to see how the commission [would] straighten out what, up to now, presidents and premiers could not."[46]

The Reluctant Fire Brigade

The commission obviously was called upon to be the fire brigade its inventors had declared it was not, and conflagrations seemed to be a constant. Clearly, neither Sergeev of the miners' NPG nor Torlopov of the FNPR regional council for the area could speak for the miners of Vorkuta. And it was precisely the government those miners wanted to see, a government that had earlier given in to the coal miners' wage demands. The government, although it talked tough, showed signs of readiness to buy labor peace—at least in sectors it viewed as critical—with a basically capitulatory approach. The RTK, if anything, provided in this context yet one more mode of approach to the government, one more channel through which labor could advance demands—though it often disregarded it. From early on, it was also clear that traditional state-industry interests with large workforces would dominate the employer side of the RTK; the truly independent entrepreneurs' organizations were weaker, newer, and tied to much smaller labor forces typically doing very different sorts of work. (This was true even though, in proportion to the percentage of the total labor force they employed, state-sector employers were underrepresented on the employer side of the RTK table.) These "employer" interests were in no way compromised by government softness on militant wage demands. Indeed, as cash shortages would arise in the coming months due to the inadequate capacity of the state's printing presses to cover rapidly rising wages with the requisite rubles in a cash economy, state employers and their workers would find a touchy and very common cause against the government.

In a February interview, Shokhin pointed up some of the problems from the government's viewpoint.[47] Allowing that no such body as the RTK could be expected to enjoy easy going in such times, he insisted that government-labor relations still could not be allowed to become a matter of "street fights." For the unions, he implied, the main issue thus far had been inclusion at the RTK's table itself: The FNPR had reached for a monopoly; the other unions had, in opposition and seeking access, staked their counterclaims. (Government support of non-FNPR unions in this regard might seem one more brick in the edifice of what the FNPR would define as the government's unremitting opposition to it, but other unions on the commission, including the miners' NPG, had shortly before criticized the government side for not only a general antiunion position but for favoring the FNPR in a manner detrimental to them.[48])

But if one concern was whether the labor side included all the trade unions it should, another—equally or more important for what Shokhin wanted to convey—was whether trade unions and their leaders really represented the interests of workers. Unions gave lip service to the necessity of the transition to the market, he complained, while laying on the table proposal after proposal in logical conflict with that transition—broadening the list of goods to be sold at fixed prices, for example. Higher wages were another union demand, but this demand was unaccompanied by any proposals as to how the government might find the wherewithal to accomplish this aim. Presumably at issue, especially for Shokhin, were the pay packets of government employees themselves—

"budget-financed" personnel. Rather naively, he seemed to expect that union honesty here would require proposals for wage increases and explicit union endorsement of higher taxes to finance them. With the unions mute, he observed, the government had to act on its own and thus bear alone the criticism of entrepreneurs threatened with the burden of higher taxes. Shokhin also mused on the situation of the government as it dealt with unions in a new context. On the whole, it was better for government, and easier, to deal with fewer rather than more unions, but only

> under conditions where those unions and their leaders are able to reach agreements with their members. [If they cannot], if union heads cannot demand from their members the observation of any sort of game rules, but are only translating their demands to the government, then there will be no normal mechanism of social partnership. The strength of social partners is that, if they have already agreed, then they guarantee the observance of these conditions, whether they are a trade union center or an association of entrepreneurs.[49]

Since so much of the workforce was still state-dependent—either state-employed and likely to remain so or state-employed in material production and thus (over the long run) privatizable but still dependent on the state as paymaster, subsidizer, and perhaps monopoly purchaser—the government had no choice but to be an interested party as well as an arbiter in the labor-relations arena.

March: Troubles in the Kuzbass

Such was certainly the case in the Kuzbass coalfields in March. (See the more detailed coverage of these events in Chapter 3.) Large January pay raises to miners and auxiliary coal-industry personnel had driven prices in the region sky high; those outside the branch could not keep up. Some strike activity commenced March 6,[50] with the threat of an unlimited regionwide strike on March 10 unless a government delegation came before that date. Behind the demand was the regional FNPR affiliate—the Kuzbass Federation of Trade Unions (KFP)—acting mainly for non-coal-industry people.

Labor was not, however, united. The Kuzbass workers' committees, tightly linked to the independent NPG, denounced the whole business as an anti-Yeltsin "provocation"[51] and called upon workers in the region not to support the KFP.[52]

The RTK agreed to send a delegation, and the KFP postponed action until March 12.[53] Shokhin emphasized that this was a trilateral delegation, a response of the RTK, not the government, coming to ascertain how widely the region's working people supported the strike call.[54] The delegation met with local representatives at Novokuznetsk on March 13, though it is not clear that it met with representatives of the KFP, which was pushing the strike.[55]

It might well have been tempting to Shokhin to make such an end run around his local irritants. The strike threat petered out, its dynamics never totally clear. Anti-KFP and anti-FNPR forces claimed that the strike had failed because of the lack of genuine local grassroots support.[56] The government had not been brought to its knees, but on March 18 Shokhin indicated that it had proposed new wage increases from April 1 in the budgeted sector, where so many of the aggrieved worked, as well as other adjustments.[57] The government had, in fact, conceded on a broad front.[58]

Only the government, in effect, could. It had, effectively, set the high mining-industry wages by way of major subsidies to this planned-loss sector. It was the only source of a wage adjustment for budget workers as well. There is no real indication that the labor component of the RTK delegation, whether FNPR or NPG, played any independent role. It was not, on the evidence, a matter of government capitulation to strong unions; if anything, the antistrike Kuzbass workers' committees looked locally stronger than the FNPR.[59] It seemed to be more a matter of the government taking a reasonable approach to understandable demands in hard times—just as it would have to deal with pressures to constantly increase the minimum-wage level. But all this could and surely would have been done in the absence of the RTK.

"Success": The 1992 General Agreement

Aside from the fire-brigade tasks thrust upon its government side, the RTK in its early operations focused on reaching a general agreement, which was perhaps its main rationale. This was accomplished, more or less, on March 25 and was announced to the popping of champagne corks. The qualification is necessitated by the refusal of several of the FNPR representatives to sign on that date, before consultations with member unions could be held (emphasizing thus the "truly" federative nature of the FNPR). The FNPR had been critical of government proposals throughout the process.

Early in March, it had denounced the current draft as a "government document" that cast harsh price increases in "rosy hues," that said little about protecting employment at a time when women college graduates in Vologda could not "get jobs as cleaning women," and that presented privatization targets in the form of "planned indicators dear to the heart of bureaucrats." Though later in the year when the government did establish a voucherization program, FNPR often criticized it, for now the FNPR was adamant about this and other demands. But the union would not walk out. It would stay at the table and continue to fight while rejecting any compromises "to the detriment of the toilers."[60]

FNPR kept up the attack on the government's undertakings to the IMF, which it would always see as mistransposing social and economic priorities. It castigated government plans to free energy prices, avowing that such had the potential of wrecking the economy. Still disgruntled over the allocation of seats to the independent unions, FNPR made a target especially of Sotsprof, which "backed the government in all things." Was it appropriate, it asked, that Deputy Labor Minister Kudiukin, who sat on the government side of the table, was also a member of Sotsprof's insurance fund board?[61] Thus on March 25, only eight of the fourteen labor representatives signed the General Agreement—all the independents, but only three members from FNPR.[62] This thus fell short of the two-thirds of each side rule for the RTK ratification process. FNPR deputy chair Romanov referred to a consultation session scheduled for April 2 as a reason for not signing, as well as to substantive matters on which the FNPR found itself opposing the government.[63] The FNPR newspaper published on March 3 a variant of the General Agreement more to its liking,[64] but on March 2 its leaders did recommend signing the agreement, with something of bad grace, while again criticizing the government for "interference" in union affairs (the government newspaper *Izvestiia* had on March 27 prematurely reported the agreement as reached[65]).

Klochkov reflected on the whole process several days later in what could only be called a mixed review.[66] FNPR remained dissatisfied with the agreement, and with the government. One of its assessments returned to the theme of a government obsessed with cold figures, insensitive to the social dimension.[67] The union wanted to continue price controls on some critical goods and foods; the government, however, wanted wholesale liberalization whatever the consequences. Shokhin was ridiculed for having suggested that unregulated prices for some goods might be lower than the current levels, which were distorted by monopoly and supply bottlenecks—that workers then might, indeed, demand price liberalization themselves. The union had agreed to a no-strike provision but reminded the government that this applied to issues covered in and agreed upon in the document and did not exclude labor action on issues not so covered, including the worsening cash shortage that was beginning to put promised wage payments increasingly behind schedule. Here, strikes would be fully legal, union sources warned.

For all the criticism, the 1992 General Agreement was rather remarkable for the number of commitments the government had made. Financing for retraining, job creation, and unemployment benefits had been promised. As it would turn out, FNPR doubts that these could readily be squared with the government's promises to the International Monetary Fund (IMF) on holding down inflation and the budget deficit were not totally off the mark. The government had committed itself to the establishment of a minimum wage, to be reviewed quarterly, with similar reviews of pensions and other benefits. The unions, for their part, had made no commitments to restraint in their wage demands. Employers had promised that they would avoid mass layoffs and factory shutdowns, but this promise appeared to tie the government to them and vice versa: Without credits from the government, state-sector employers could not make such guarantees. In effect, they were betting the government would not have the courage or would not be so foolhardy as to impose hard budget constraints or bankruptcies, and the bet was to prove a good one.[68] Neither would the government keep all its promises—neither the RTK nor the unions, FNPR nor independents, could compel it to do so.

The Cash Crisis

Evidence of a cash crisis first emerged in the growing problem of the cash supply. Prices were rising rapidly; though lagging, wages were rising too, at a pace exceeding the poor adaptive capacities of the cash-emission system. Wages by late spring were at levels astronomical by the standards of only two years before (though by 1995, these new sums, too, would seem laughably low). Plates to print the new, larger-denomination notes, necessary now that people were paid in the thousands and tens of thousands rather than in hundreds of rubles, were still lacking. Workers in many areas—especially those such as the coalfields where pay was extraordinarily high—were falling behind, waiting for literally bales of rubles to be delivered while galloping inflation rapidly eroded the value of the anticipated cash. Local governments in the Kuzbass and in Cheliabinsk lacked the cash to meet even their more modest budget personnel wage and salary obligations: As of May 8, when the issue was raised at an RTK meeting, they were 10 billion rubles in arrears. Local governments and unions united to protest government "inaction." The RTK decided to send a delegation to the Tiumen oil-producing area, where the cash shortage, combined with rising consumer prices and low procurement prices for oil, were also creating an explosive situation.[69] Burbulis assured the FNPR's Romanov that in early June immediate steps would be taken to cover the cash arrears in the hardest-hit areas and to meet the demands of railroad and transport workers similarly affected and that the government would clarify at the next commission meeting how it would moderate the social effects of planned fuel price increases.[70]

Gaidar, as deputy premier and the government's point man on the economy, had to address both the cash problem and the enterprises' running up massive mutual webs of debts and credit, producing reduced quantities—at raised prices—of the same old goods rather than attempting to manufacture something salable. Gaidar criticized this practice as "stupid and irresponsible" at the RTK meeting on June 3—a session at which he also indicated, however, that the government would make some credits available.[71] He addressed himself to an interviewer soon after, sounding alternately hard and soft. To be avoided were "injurious decisions—such as immediately writing off all enterprises' debts and reducing interest rates, which will make the situation almost hopeless." As for the enterprises, "Let them buy what they need. They have nothing to buy it with? Then let them sell their output. If it won't sell, let them cut their prices. They don't want to? But otherwise there is no market. Do they expect the government to give it to them? On credit? At privileged interest rates? We can't! Of course, we will gradually issue more credits."[72]

Still, the cash crisis was a critical matter and one that affected people in the here and now as opposed to the constantly deferred threat of unemployment. Gaidar, for all of the tough rhetoric, was sensitive to this. But he was also concerned that such crisis response had become a constant governmental burden with little sharing of responsibility among its social partners on the employer and labor sides; it was the government, as he put it, that was now "taking 'fire brigade' measures."[73]

Finally, the economist and advocate of budgetary toughness gave his reading of a situation that was, on the one hand, still keeping factories open and workers employed but, on the other, leaving the government tied out of fear of a social explosion to supporting the inertial motion of production for employment's sake—the latter supported by a legislature quite resistant to the sort of tough market logic he stood for. A law on bankruptcies had died there, which meant that "enterprises producing output that nobody wants or offering their goods at excessively high prices are continuing to operate in the same spirit." The same factories insisted, simultaneously, on debt writeoffs, new credits, and curbs on inflation, all of which Gaidar condemned as "economic madness, an impossible task."[74]

Coalition Politics: Labor and Employers

Gaidar the economist, the architect of shock therapy, was by now somewhat submerged by Gaidar the deputy premier. The space between the two was greater than what had separated Balcerowicz the economist from Balcerowicz the finance minister in the different, more consensual—or tolerant—politics of Polish shock therapy two years before. Thus, madness or not, the pressures to issue credits, to muddle onward, to do nothing to disturb and much to maintain the fragile situation, would continue to be felt from both labor and employers. Two days after union and employer sides had come together to formulate positions on plans for energy price increases and wage arrears, the FNPR's Romanov criticized the government for ignoring the consequences of its actions at the May 29 commission meeting.[75] On June 9, Gaidar and Shokhin accepted a set of joint recommendations from the FNPR and the industrial-lobby Russian Union of Industrialists and Entrepreneurs (Rossiiski Soiuz Promyshlennikov i Predprinimatelei, or RSPP) at a meeting with Klochkov and Aleksandr Vladislavlev, cochair of the RSPP. These included tightened controls over banks to guarantee the delivery of cash—even on a daily basis—to enterprises; goods sales at intraenterprise distribution points for temporary chits in the absence of cash; and similar-purpose accounts for pensioners at retail shops where they could be registered and buy on credit. The sorts of measures one might expect from actors formed in the old command-administrative economy were also rational responses to the emergency of a severe shortage of banknotes in a cash economy.[76] This shortage emerged only three years after the old Soviet economy had faced what seemed to be a massive problem of "suppressed inflation" due to a huge cash "overhang." Big labor—FNPR—and state-sector management could readily get together on such issues. But even the emergent private-sector employers had complaints about the marketizing government.

In an April interview, RTK member Gennadi Semigin, of the Congress of Russian Business Circles (representing "150 insurance companies, 150 exchanges, 700 commercial banks, and 500 individual enterprises"), shared some of his views. Siding so often with the labor side was, as he put it, good for business. Social disruption and disorder would, if allowed, spell the end of entrepreneurship. Workers and employers "needed stability"; this was far preferable to "bigger profits now." The government, as Semigin saw it, was not less concerned with stability, but it "has a fetish—financial stabilization."[77] This it was pursuing to the exclusion of a concern with encouraging investment and other necessary components of social stabilization.

Semigin faulted Labor Minister Shokhin for taking a simplistic view along the lines that all the unions wanted was higher wages and all business wanted was lower taxes. Not true, argued Semigin, saying that employers raised wages themselves and looked for tax help for enterprises undergoing military-to-civilian conversion and for those that produced mass consumer goods. But the government was trying to divide business and labor, and whereas it failed with the former, its partial success with the latter—the FNPR-Sotsprof confrontations—had helped it little. Business, in spring 1992, should be seen neither as a delayed Russian version of rough-but-robust early-twentieth-century capitalism nor as the enlarged version of the "cooperative" sector of the late 1980s grafted onto the Soviet command economy as part of Gorbachev's perestroika. It was more complex, it needed "literate" economic policies on the government's part, ones that would take into account more than financial stabilization. His Congress of Russian Business Circles, Semigin complained, had put together a set of proposals in late 1991, anticipating the initiation of social partnership. Gaidar had enthused about some of them, but when 1992 began, none were adopted; after that, "we got what we got." Without some government policy changes, summer 1992 would see "a collapse of industry," and the autumn would "not be an improvement, as Boris Nikolaevich [Yeltsin] says, but full clinical death."[78]

Some of this, certainly, was public relations directed at labor itself. Semigin and the congress had been the first private employer organization to show an interest in the yet-to-be-established RTK (at the point when FNPR was arguing that it should have a monopoly on the labor side—one may assume a certain collusive quality in their relations). The kinds of operations he represented employed relatively few people (whom the FNPR would hardly be seeking to organize) but were also still probably nearly incomprehensible ("making money out of money") to most of the workers represented by FNPR. Nor, at this point in Russia's disorderly nascent capitalism, were sharp practices and weak business ethics anything rare. Even before the massive and heavily publicized growth of the mafia, *biznes* was tough stuff. Semigin spoke thus for what wished to be seen, at the least, as a financial community, a responsible collective citizen concerned for the society as a whole, for "hired labor," the common folk, social order, and good government in the present and future.

In June, the FNPR stepped up its attacks on both the government and the trilateral mechanism. Reviewing five and a half months of its work, the FNPR criticized "the work of the commission, or more exactly, its lack of activity," and noted the frequent absence of a quorum even at meetings scheduled to address important issues.[79]

A *Trud* article blamed the frequent absence of government representatives (rather than the other two sides) for quorum shortfalls and noted that even Burbulis and Shokhin seemed to lack the clout to compel broad enough governmental attendance to get work done. The article seemed to question the basic relevance of union participation in the RTK (saying that Sotsprof as a rule supported "any" government proposal) and pushed for an activation of unions at the plant level to struggle for good agreements and wage arrangements as privatization impended. Walking in the corridors of power, it seemed, was not doing the unions very much good.[80]

Government, then, and not employers, remained labor's main enemy in the FNPR's view. So the FNPR proposed an alliance with the employers, Klochkov on June 16 offering to form an "assembly of social partnership" with the employer side.[81] (The FNPR newspaper, *Rabochaia Tribuna,* had been copublished with RSPP since May 19.) A June 19 report specified a first meeting scheduled for July 8, indicating that consultations had already taken place and that the FNPR's offer was unlikely to be rejected.[82] On July 8 the Russian Assembly of Social Partnership (Rossiiskaia Assambleia Sotsialnogo Partnerstva, or RASP) was founded in Moscow. This was strictly an FNPR-RSPP affair. RASP would not seek to block reform but to create an effective partnership as an alternative to "class struggle"[83]—though it had not been these two partners who had been struggling with each other. RASP's foundation was a move "forced" on labor and management by government monopolism and "general legal nihilism."[84] *Rabochaia Tribuna* headlined its story "Two Partners Remain," leaving out the third, government, which had acted as "a traditional autocrat, enriched by Bolshevik experience." Even by the permissive standards of Russian political invective, this was a bit over the top as a characterization of the Gaidar government: Whatever one thought of Yeltsin's past, Gaidar, Chubais, and Shokhin scarcely fit this profile, especially when its source was an organ backed by old apparat types like Klochkov and Volskii. Nevertheless, the Gaidar government had been born as a cabinet of economists whose line FNPR rejected, whereas the interests of labor and "seasoned," "sober" industrial management coincided. Volskii stressed the need for "practical" work; Klochkov hailed the industrialists' readiness to assume "responsibility" for the economy and the workforce.[85]

What was RASP? What did its founding amount to? More event than organization, it was best seen as an expression of the commonality of interests and positions of large-scale state-dependent industrial managers and the FNPR, arrived at a time when the industrial lobby seemed to be on the rise as an organized political force and the government to be standing still or retreating on critical elements of its own earlier economic-transition agenda.[86]

This weakening had been in evidence for the better part of three months. Yeltsin himself had hinted at the possibility of opening the cabinet to experienced managers just before the Sixth Congress of Peoples' Deputies (CPD) session in April. Shock therapy had not worked to control the money supply and reduce inflation to a tolerable level; nor had it evoked—save for the imports and luxury goods that only the new rich had access to—any real supply-side response. Pressures were strong, then, on a government that could not point to a broadly perceptible economic success in any major sector.

These pressures came less from the public than from the leaders of the RSPP and other industrial lobby organizations, the FNPR (which had, on the whole, less clout on these questions), and segments (especially rank-and-file engineering and technical personnel) of the labor force united in the Union of Labor Collectives (STK), a nonunion body rooted in military industry that coordinated its work with the directorial bodies of the industrial lobby. (The STK was accorded consultative status with, though not a place on, the RTK, by the latter's statute.[87] More detail on the STK is presented in Chapter 3.)

Volskii pushed, at the Sixth CPD, for strengthening the links between the former Soviet republics, now the member states of the Commonwealth, and for a managed transition to the market with selective state support (credits, orders, etc.) for critical industries. Some industrial lobbyists also called for the division of the new Ministry of Industry into subministries supervising industrial branches—strikingly reminiscent of the economic organization of the USSR. Added to these suggestions were hardly veiled threats, which Volskii seemed fond of making, that directors could bring the workers out into the streets (implying that the FNPR was not capable of doing so). Volskii tended to blow hot and cold, sometimes issuing this sort of threat, sometimes striking a statesmanlike pose as spokesman of a constructive opposition of seasoned managers (he was being talked about as a potential prime minister), but in 1992, he generally blew loud.

What these forces and organizations were asking for in the context of a managed market transition would have obviously maintained much of the legacy of the old command economy in sectors where doing so would be expensive without really promoting the behavior modifications among managers, workers, and employees that were a necessary part of the transition. As Philip Hanson and Elizabeth Teague put it, "The development of such an alliance between workers, engineers, and managers would reflect a tendency clearly present in the state industrial sector for enterprises to act like little welfare states with the aim of protecting their labor forces' living standards rather than maximizing profits." Those same enterprises "that make up the bulk of Volskii's constituency, however, are dinosaurs whose prospect in a real market environment would be dim."[88]

But dinosaurs tend to be big and, consequently, hard to ignore. In early May, the cabinet did open, and three industrialists entered: Viktor Chernomyrdin, gas industry head who had just turned the ex-gas ministry into the state joint-stock company Gazprom; Georgi Khizha, from a defense-industry background; and Vladimir Shumeiko, ex-manager, deputy parliamentary speaker, and president of the Confederation of Unions of Entrepreneurs of Russia, a smaller industrial lobby.

Was it "bad" to compromise with dinosaurs? In technical economic terms, yes; in political terms, when the concern was the preservation of future possibilities of reforms hard to pursue immediately, not necessarily. One analysis along this somewhat optimistic line saw the breakthrough policy pushed by Gaidar and the economists as failing for the same reasons that the more modest Soviet-era reforms had failed: They had not successfully engaged the middle echelons of the elite, the industrial bosses, in the process. Khizha, Shumeiko, and others like them were not the worst of the old Soviet managers. They were instead among the best and most adaptable and had been frustrated under the old regime. Perhaps, then, a liberal-centrist cabinet coalition was possible and could provide stability. Parliamentary speaker Ruslan Khasbulatov had, according to this version, been sufficiently impressed with the cabinet opening to encourage regional legislative bodies to cool their opposition to the president and cooperate more with local representatives of presidential authority.[89]

Perhaps, further, an optimist could have felt that the cabinet opening was a politically cagey move, a way of bringing industrialists "into the tent" in order to get them to share responsibility for tough measures of whose necessity they might yet be convinced. (In the short run, optimists seemed to have gotten it wrong; but over the longer run, into 1993–1994, Chernomyrdin and Shumeiko did seem to be convinced, albeit gradually, that some things had to be done.)

But in the immediate aftermath of the cabinet's augmentation, the industrialist centrists seemed to be riding high, and speculation focused on the political ambitions of the lobby, especially on its leader, Volskii. Organizational moves followed swiftly. At the end of May, the RSPP had spun off a political party in its own image—the All-Russian Renewal Union, or Obnovlenie. A month later, this body joined with Nikolai Travkin's Democratic Party and Vice President Aleksandr Rutskoi's People's Party of Free Russia and with the New Generation–New Politics parliamentary faction to form the centrist Civic Union (Grazhdanskii Soiuz) bloc.[90] Soon after this, RASP was founded.

Civic Union, which would remain visible throughout the year and into 1993's crisis and elections and which appeared to be a major political force, would pose an ostensibly broad-based constructive opposition to the policies and practices of Gaidar's team of youngish reform economists ("boys in pink trousers," not "experienced managers"). Civic Union pushed for priority government support for critical state industry in order to fend off Russia's deindustrialization and its relegation by the world to the status of large-scale resource exporter.

FNPR, though evidently invited, did not join Civic Union directly;[91] but Klochkov indicated in July that FNPR was seeking a party or bloc with which to ally.[92] The union was interested "only in the socio-economic aspects of ... cooperation" and went beyond the RTK and the factory floor to explore a parliamentary-electoral partnership. "We are," Klochkov said, "interested in rendering support at any level of elections to those candidates who adhere to the social policy of the trade unions." Creating RASP had been, in his words, an "intermediate stage" in this process but one that had revealed, in the government's conciliatory response, the power that the unions, in organized concert with employers, possessed. FNPR's search did not conclude in formal marriage to any political partner, however, and RASP was not to be heard of again.

Routinization of Futility?

A political sideshow of a sort, the RTK was neither powerful enough to become the major forum for arbitrating the intractable problems before it nor quite marginal enough to be let go without fueling the government's antagonists' fires. The visible political dramas of the spring cabinet reshuffle, the growing confrontation between the parliament under Khasbulatov and the president, and the economic-political grievances that at the end of the year would see Yeltsin stripped of the special powers the parliament had voted him in late 1991 and forced to sacrifice Gaidar and install the industrialist Chernomyrdin as the new premier all tended to cast the mantle of obscurity over the commission. Still, its operations and problems were a kind of index of the problems that drove many ongoing political conflicts at the highest level.

Personnel shifts changed some of the RTK players. Burbulis left the cabinet to become an adviser to Yeltsin, out of the direct line of political fire, and with this move gave up his role in the RTK. Shokhin left the Labor Ministry to take the cabinet portfolio on foreign economic relations. His successor, Gennadi Melikian, found himself in a situation similar to Shokhin's in a context hardly altered since January. As he put it, in the arena of social partnership, the government was supposed to judge between labor and employers, but "the employers are not owners but hired employees of the government."[93] There was no paradox, then, in the two-versus-one pattern of RTK political wrangling, in which the government alone acted as a restraining force on the upward spiral of wages—a job, he put it somewhat plaintively, that employers did on their own in the West. But sounding somewhat centrist-industrialist himself, he stressed the minimal level of unemployment versus the earlier dire projections and expressed support for a policy of selective help to enterprises. This was, ultimately, a financial-budgetary rather than a social matter; all factories could not be helped. But an overall policy of harsh denial and forced closures would generate joblessness at levels socially and politically unacceptable.

Government policy, however thus moderated, could not satisfy FNPR. In September, the union federation focused on what it deemed—correctly—the government's attempt to deprive it of its (largely government funded) welfare functions. The social insurance fund, whose administration was one of the central functions of the old AUCCTU and now of its FNPR descendant and which had been often criticized by the government, was by a presidential decree in August to be placed under government control (even though, reportedly, Melikian had communicated to Klochkov in July some government softening on this issue[94]). Klochkov reacted in the RTK: "We are categorically against it. We regard it as an offense against the interests of working people and we will not allow that part of this money to be taken away from them and sent to mend holes in the budget. There are plenty of those, of course."[95] Thus Klochkov criticized the government for budgetary holes while ignoring the fact that FNPR's social insurance fund represented a claim on that budget, thus creating such holes; nor did he entertain the notion that if the decree stuck, the government would presumably assume the social insurance obligation as well as the funds.

Klochkov and the FNPR were not entirely paranoid in this regard. From spring on, the government, with support from Sotsprof and the miners' NPG, had been attacking this legacy of official trade union monopoly. In June, an attempt had been made to put the fund under a commission including FNPR and other union representatives, with a majority of the seats going to government representatives. No action had been taken, and the constitutional court was left to grapple with the issue. After the founding of RASP, Melikian also made some apparently conciliatory moves on this matter toward Klochkov.[96] The issue was not likely to go away: Funds flowing from the government, plus the accumulated resources and properties of FNPR, represented an inheritance that could not but make it a target. In November, the St. Petersburg Entrepreneurs' Forum sent a letter to Yeltsin, attacking FNPR's continuing resistance to reform and calling on the president to declare all the FNPR's accumulated Soviet-era properties state property and place them all on the privatization block alongside the state assets pledged to the mass voucherization process, then about to begin.[97]

From Trilateralism to Bilateralism

In a reprise of its 1991 gambit, the FNPR announced a day of protest for October 24; the substance of its complaints was much what it had been for the whole year. But on October 20, government and the FNPR (not the whole labor side of the RTK) met bilaterally. Labor Minister Melikian led the government side and Romanov, evidently, the FNPR team. The sides agreed to further talks in the format of a "conciliation commission," with the first of those meetings scheduled for October 27. Melikian characterized some of the FNPR demands as "divorced from reality" but signaled an intent to come to grips with others. On state credits for ailing factories, he agreed that "a consideration of market and social factors was required;[98] however, state-imposed price ceilings on basic food items—milk, bread, and potatoes—were rejected.[99] On October 22, Yeltsin and Klochkov met in the Kremlin, expressing support for "expanding constructive contacts between presidential structures and the trade unions."[100] Though there had been some implication after the Melikian-Romanov meeting that the October 24 protest had been postponed for a month, Klochkov reported that he had told a concerned Yeltsin at their October 22 meeting that FNPR unions had contained protests as long as they could and that whatever came on October 24 "would be a grass-roots initiative."[101] As it turned out, the day came and went with no massive disruptions; afterward, Klochkov seemed to be overplaying a not-necessarily-strong hand when he said that FNPR would not support demands that had been heard for the government's wholesale resignation but thought that it would be "enough to replace a few key ministers."[102]

The October 27 conciliation commission meeting did take place; most effort was devoted to questions of enterprise support, defense-industry conversion, and privatization procedures.[103] Whether such was the stuff of drama or not, bilateralism seemed, in fall 1992, to be replacing trilateralism. (It had, in fact, been tried earlier in the year, in the first wave of strikes by educational and medical personnel, when government and FNPR had, quite logically for a matter that involved government-paid budget personnel only, held bilateral discussions as a preliminary to reporting their results to the full RTK.[104])

The government also seemed to be structuring new bilateral contacts with employers. Gaidar, in his role as acting prime minister, led a group of cabinet officers on October 25 to Togliatti for a meeting with "about 60 industrial generals." Taxes, credits, and other aspects of industrial policy were discussed. Gaidar characterized the talks as a step in the coordination of government policy with "the most important representatives" of a major social group "on whom social stability depends" and explicitly connected this with the forthcoming Congress of People's Deputies session, where government policy and personnel would surely be subjected to the now-predictable attacks.[105] The establishment of an industrial policy council was agreed on; Gaidar chaired the first meeting of this bilateral body on November 2.[106] At this meeting Deputy Premier

Shumeiko expressed hopes that the council would supply the government with data and expertise, also noting—perhaps piously or tongue in cheek—that "the Council has nothing to do with politics, especially politicking."[107]

Complaints about the new structures were not long in emerging. After its first meeting on October 27, the government-FNPR conciliation commission suffered a setback in its second scheduled coming together (November 2 or 3). The government had failed to deliver its responses to the FNPR positions by the promised date of October 31. Deputy Labor Minister Kudiukin visited FNPR on November 2 with apologies for the delay, which he attributed to government overload in preparing for the December session of the Congress of People's Deputies. But only two of the seven government team officials showed up at meeting time, and the meeting was canceled with a reschedule date of November 6 at the Labor Ministry—some guarantee that a government-side quorum would be present. *Nezavisimaia Gazeta* held out some hope that this encounter might go off smoothly.

> There has been a fairly fortunate selection of issues to "get the ball rolling": on the one hand, the social consequences of conversion in defense spheres, relieving the lot of which is something the government has been working on for some time even without pressure from the trade unions, and on the other, increasing the minimum wage, an area where it is very possible that compromise will be reached.
>   ... With regard to the general outcome of the talks, they are most likely to go on for a month at least. So "explosive" November will pass by more or less quietly. But the blackmail threat of strike action after 23 November if the talks do not achieve their goal is not causing much alarm in the government because, according to [Kudiukin], "[FNPR] is incapable of stirring the masses to strike action on its own, it can only 'paralyze' by mounting spontaneous disturbances and 'directorial strikes.'"[108]

With respect to proximate goals, however, things were not progressing smoothly. FNPR's minimum-wage proposal involved raising the current 900 rubles monthly level to 3,375–4,000 as of December 1. The government countered with a figure of 1,800 with a further increase to 2,250 in the first quarter of 1993. No agreement was reached; one report indicated that the union had accepted an immediate increase to 2,250 but was insisting on an upward adjustment in December.[109]

Klochkov reflected on the month-long work of the conciliation commission on November 30. Satisfied with agreements on state support for the arms industry and its workers, he was less pleased on the wage issue: Evidently convinced (however grudgingly) that the state budget could not support a 3,375 ruble minimum wage, he wanted an early specification from the government as to when in the first quarter of 1993 it would raise the minimum to 2,250 (making it clear that the government had not yet made the concession implied earlier).[110]

Government-FNPR talks thus ended with neither total agreement nor a complete parting of the ways. It is probable that FNPR had its eye more on the December Congress of People's Deputies session in the hope—not misplaced—that it would produce cabinet and policy changes in line with some of the union's recurrent demands. Veterans of both the tri- and bilateral processes put different spins on their reviews of the experience. Kudiukin asserted that the conciliation talks had been "suggested by three ministries" so that, outside the trilateral, government might find out what FNPR wanted, and he stressed that these had been talks with the FNPR alone, not with the whole labor side of the RTK. The unions, he said—with FNPR clearly in mind—made threats and demonstrations rather than performing real work at the factory level. They had firmly mastered one word: "gimme" (*dai*). FNPR council secretary A. Solovev saw things differently. "The trilateral commission yammers on about these problems. But it is necessary to solve them, right? So FNPR sent its demands to the president of the country, and he obviously decided direct talks would be more appropriate. Let him send our demands to the trilateral commission, let them consider them there. For us the form of talks is not important, but their content, their results." Among the results he was unhappy with was the failure of the government to link the minimum-wage level to the ruble cost of the "minimum physical norm"—the calculated necessary floor in purchasing power–living standard.[111]

Later on, Melikian and Klochkov made joint statements. Tax breaks for enterprise social infrastructure and investment expenses and credits for defense conversion were among the accomplishments of the conciliation commission; the sides had not been able to agree on subsidizing bread, milk, and potato prices or on the share of factory assets that might be transferred free or steeply discounted to work collectives during the privatization process. The sides would continue to meet on unresolved issues and to work toward the 1993 General Agreement. The conciliation commission would soon inform the RTK on the results of its deliberations.[112]

Hardly in the style of partnerly joint statements, though, was a December 18 interview with Solovev of the FNPR council. He accused Gaidar of trying to freeze the wages of budget-funded workers, of delaying the effective payment dates of salary supplements, and of trying to shift responsibility for these to local governments (which were, of course, in various ways denying the central government tax revenues and thus might reasonably be expected to pick up some of the slack even in the absence of laws that gave them major responsibilities for paying budget personnel). The new minimum wage of 2,250 rubles was too little set against a physical minimum of 2,600–2,800 in October. What was "really" needed, on average, was 5,800 rubles per month. The Labor Ministry's argument that such a level was impossible—based on the International Labor Office's principle that minimum-wage levels had to take account not only of physical minimums, but of the capacities of state budgets—was "not convincing." The government's promise to index minimum wages by the second quarter of 1993 was "to be believed only with difficulty." Solovev ended on a class-conflict, populist note, saying that FNPR demands were not the cause of price rises; monopoly producers, many of whom were the "industrialist" allies of the FNPR and the rising salaries of bosses "and the clerks around them" (an appeal to the visceral distrust of office workers by shop-floor personnel who often outearned them) were to blame. Reforms, then, had to "come not at the cost of people but to their benefit. Without such normal social partnership, civil peace in the country is impossible."[113]

Klochkov, finally, reviewed the year of social partnership from the FNPR leadership perspective on December 25. FNPR, he insisted, sat at the table to represent the interests of hired labor in securing a fair market price for that labor. It rejected the government's "harsh" monetarist course, the "pseudoliberal models" it followed. Foregoing for the moment the usual disparaging comments about Sotsprof or the NPG, he protested the tendency (presumably the government's) to divide trade unions into "good" and "bad"; social partnership could not work if unions were not to be treated as equal partners. FNPR's social insurance fund, then, should remain with FNPR: Once one got beyond politics and attempts to separate the funds from the FNPR, as Klochkov put it, "logic and facts argue that a self-managing social security fund under the aegis of the union is now, in the transition period, the most appropriate variant."[114]

Oddly enough, after the various attacks on governmental policy and bad faith and the accusations directed at Sotsprof as a government stooge, Klochkov praised the potential of the trilateral commission. It could become, in 1993, a "pivot" of the system of social partnership; he hoped for a presidential decree on its continuance soon. By this point, Klochkov probably had some inkling of changes that would come in an RTK whose continued existence for 1993 had not yet been guaranteed but that were likely to please FNPR.

Reviewing a Year

At first glance, trilateral corporatism looked like no great success; surely Russia had not, in one year, reached the gentle, sunny uplands of political and civil consensus, had not learned to pull together with a will in a common economic harness. But that would have been too much to ask—and not only of the RTK.

Trilateralism, after all, functioned—well or poorly—within a broader political context. In 1992 that context turned around a growing, increasingly envenomed, conflict between president and parliament. Yeltsin, after having been bounced from Gorbachev's old Politburo, had experienced the remarkable political resurrection that only late-Soviet changes had made possible: He had been elected by a landslide in the Moscow-wide national-territorial constituency in the elections for the new USSR Congress of People's Deputies in 1989 (over a runner-up who, perhaps symbolically, was the director of the ZIL plant that produced the elite's limousines). He had managed, after obvious attempts to deny him the status, to become a member of the new USSR Supreme Soviet, the permanent parliament derived from the CPD. He had been, in effect, elected as the Russian Republic head of state by the new Russian parliament, which had been created by the republic-level legislative elections of 1990. Finally, he had been popularly elected as president of Russia in 1991 in the weeks before the August coup attempt.

Moving, as Gorbachev had earlier, to base his power in Russia on the state-executive structure and strengthening his position after the August coup by a decree outlawing the Communist Party on the territory of the Russian Federation (RF), Yeltsin looked powerful and popular. He had gotten, largely, the cabinet he wanted. But a much-amended, shapeless RF constitution—dating back to the republic-level constitution that followed the USSR's "Brezhnev constitution" of 1977, which was meant, of course, to be a dead letter—could not in any form clearly demarcate the responsibilities and prerogatives of executive and parliament. It tended, if anything, to assign a great deal of clout to the legislature, which in the old times had been a decorative "sapless branch" but which was now something quite different.

Alone among the republics in 1990, Russia had elected a two-tier legislature, CPD and Supreme Soviet, mirroring the USSR structure. The larger body was to consist of 1,068 members. All the seats were elective; no component for organizations such as the party, Komsomol, and the trade unions, which had made up one-third of the 2,250 seats in the 1989 USSR CPD, was designed in. In only twenty-eight constituencies had candidates run unopposed, and in all over 6,500 candidates competed for the seats. But many of the best and brightest from a reform point of view had run in 1989 for the USSR CPD; the Russian legislative bodies produced in 1990 bore much more the mark of provincial bossism, that is, of the state-party apparats of the oblasts and krais. They would not, as economic times grew tougher in 1992, cohabit well with the Yeltsin cabinet of reformers. The men of 1990 did not on the whole speak the same language as the Gaidars and Fedorovs.

The parliament was loud, disorderly. Party and bloc affiliations were weak and shifting; no second-election test of the new Russian democracy or campaigns that might have imposed some coherence on the picture were yet in the offing. Yeltsin had made concessions; removing Burbulis from the line of fire; opening the cabinet in spring to the industrialists Chernomyrdin, Khizha, and Shumeiko, and at the end of the year sacrificing Gaidar, then acting prime minister, and accepting Chernomyrdin as replacement after the parliament refused to renew the extraordinary powers it had granted the president in 1991. All this further weakened a Russian Federation executive branch that was not possessed of a strong state apparatus to begin with.

In this environment, a coordinating body like the RTK was obviously limited in what it could do; the broader political context was one in which great issues well beyond the coordination of social-labor relations were still unsettled. Looking back after the 1993 September–October crisis, George Breslauer located its roots in political circumstances of an extreme sort as much or more than in the personality conflicts of Yeltsin, Khasbulatov, Rutskoi, and others. Economic issues, however tough, were not the emotive core of the conflict; It was "statehood and nationhood"; it was "what kind of a people the people of Russia would be" and whether Russia could survive the fractionation that had killed the USSR. It was also the legitimacy of that execution: The Russian parliament, it needs be remembered, did not in effect vote for the dissolution in December 1991 of the USSR, and there is no reason to think that many deputies were not nostalgic. Jurisdictionally, things were sufficiently unclear that parliamentary-presidential struggles were polarized and unmoderated. The president threatened the parliament, and vice versa, in a winner-take-all politics of institutions wherein the weaker might not survive to fight another day. Thus, incentives for cooperation were weak in 1992 and would grow weaker yet in 1993.[115]

In 1992, chaos was averted—no mean thing. Labor politics within and beyond the organizational context of trilateral corporatism must be seen thus against a background of a politics wherein a none-too-strong government began the year confronting a weaker opposition and throughout the year grew, arguably, weaker while the opposition, though it grew in some senses stronger, became neither notably more policy specific in its criticism nor more effectively organized as any kind of coherent alternative to the Yeltsin government.

Let us go on to the narrower realms, then, of labor politics. Russia in 1992 not only had a different government from that of the old Soviet Union, it had less government, less power located in state institutions to regulate anything. The Yeltsin government thus did not have the where-withal to impose a state variety of corporatism in Schmitter's sense even had that been its articulated intent. It lacked the "other ground" to base itself on, a ground that would have allowed it to impose the range of re-strictions that structure the web of units that will participate in a state corporatist framework. It had, in any case, a different mission than that of saving a peripheral country's capitalism and with it an imperiled bourgeoisie or that of smoothly managing interests in a mature demo-cratic capitalism of the West European sort.

The government could create, or broker the creation of, the RTK it-self. But it could not impose clarity of operational mandate or deliver the resources and authority that could make the commission the unique fo-rum in which the three sides would hash out their differences. The de-sign was one of societal corporatism, but the enabling documents were vague and general. But as this chapter has surely demonstrated, the or-ganizational components of a societal corporatism were not at hand. The needed kinds of organizations, experienced and formed, did not preexist the RTK by any great period of time. Organizations that had a substantial history, such as the FNPR, were not really oriented toward or capable of acting as partners in the RTK context (which is not to assert that the government was fault-free in this regard).

Employer organizations were a mixed lot, to a degree on differing wavelengths. I need not reiterate the lack of major interest conflict be-tween the employers and labor that reflected the persistent nonmarket nature of so much of the Russian economy. The industrial lobby—not unlike FNPR—targeted the government in pursuit of its survival inter-ests, and the deals it sought were more part of the broader presidential-parliamentary politics of the budget, subsidies, and so on than of the RTK per se. The history of the RSPP, its origins as the NPS of the USSR, gave it both an additional grievance and added agendas. Volskii and the industrialists had not been happy to see the old federative state go, and with it so many of the old economic linkages; in some sense, it had to view Yeltsin as a "wrecker." Volskii, as head of the RSPP, pushed consis-tently for the strengthening and maintenance of a "common economic space" within the new CIS borders, a stance that for various monetary, pricing, and other economic reasons placed him counter to the views of the early Gaidar cabinet.

All industrialists—to say nothing of all employers—did not share precisely the same interests, but through 1992 at least major conflicts were not in evidence. Still, the corporatist image of a group or groups speaking for the world of factories, plants, and production associations was somewhat askew in the Russian case for another reason. Decaying since 1990 and now gone was the world of the old branch ministries that had held the industrial world together. Industrial lobby organizations like RSPP were no substitute; factories were really on their own. Some were better positioned than others to exploit the government; some—notably the units of the long-favored military-industrial complex—were pushed into individual survival strategies including low-tech "degenerate conversion."[116]

Managers had their own specific agendas for survival, for particular modes of eventual privatization that would benefit them while preserving selective ties to the state as buffers against uncertainty; they wanted to maximize their maneuvering room while limiting the state's ability to cut the strings of dependence. As Kudiukin put it, the state might still be the owner of enterprises, but it no longer enjoyed the prerogatives typically associated with that status. The problem went back to the late-phase radicalization of Gorbachev-era reforms, which had in 1990 conferred a great deal more freedom of action on managers without changing state ownership and which had been amplified by the January 1992 price liberalization. "Today the boss of a state enterprise disposes of all the rights of an entrepreneur, save property rights, but directly because of their absence he bears practically no responsibility at all (in the present confusion it is even unclear which government organ has the right to dismiss a director guilty of wrongdoing)."[117] It is bosses, not organizations, of whom Kudiukin writes, and in the atomized world of Russian industry in 1992, it was thus at factory level that most of the labor-management deals were cut. Those who spoke for employers at the RTK were not capable of imposing patterns on such deals and thus of speaking for the employer category as a whole.

Nor was there any of the cleanliness of a real corporate design evident on the labor union side. Much of the union action—of both FNPR and the independents—took place, in any case, outside the RTK, as Chapter 3 will show. But within the RTK mechanism itself, there was little of the singularity, noncompetitiveness, hierarchical ordering, or representative monopoly whereby Schmitter had defined corporatism. The reality was a disorderly mix of corporatist and pluralist characteristics that did not gel. The year 1992, to return to another of Schmitter's characterizations, had as much the "spontaneous formation, numerical proliferation, horizontal extension and competitive interaction" of pluralism in interunion relations as any of the marks of corporatism—"controlled emergence, quantitative limitation, vertical stratification and complementary interdependence."[118] FNPR had tried to cling to an inherited monopoly and wanted to remain, as a national leadership, at the top of a hierarchy. It had not succeeded, but it had survived as the largest organization in the Russian Federation. Still, NPG took away some of its members, Sotsprof attacked it, and one of its major subordinate branch unions defected. Labor thus did not speak in the common voice of corporatism and had no agreed-upon rules, principles, and practices to regulate competitive interaction.

The corporatist mechanism was supposed to be the servant of reform—or the government hoped it would be such—but it ran afoul of some inconvenient facts. "Reforms are least likely to advance when political forces—in particular, opposition parties and unions—are strong enough to be able to sabotage them and not large enough to internalize the entire cost of arresting them."[119] Opposition parties in Russia in 1992 were not at issue; the growing but disorderly parliamentary opposition was a block to reform, but not so much as if it had assumed some coherent shape via the discipline of real parties. FNPR was not strong enough to sabotage reform, though it could greatly complicate it; nor, despite its size, was it adequate to the internalization task, which involves an alternative vision, a counterprogram to reform, that the FNPR lacked. The hard cases of market reform come, then, in those situations where "labor is capable of defensive mobilization, but uncertain about its long-term place in the political system."[120] Though FNPR's 1992 record might reveal it to be short on capability, it surely did engage in defensive-mobilizational moves. Its rhetoric was replete with uncertainties about its future in the political system via all the references to the government's intent to do it in, but the point was that it did survive the year.

When still the labor minister, Shokhin had specified the sorts of unions that could function as social partners, in words quoted earlier. Przeworski puts the same set of specifications in more academic language.

> To function as partners, unions must constitute encompassing, centralized organizations and must trust in the good faith of the government. Such organizations must be encompassing: They must associate large parts of their potential constituencies. And they must be centralized: They must be able to control the behavior of their constituents. Finally, they must have confidence in the government: They must trust that the government will not be unfair in distributing the costs and the benefits of reforms and that it will be competent in conducting reforms.[121]

Against such standards, how did FNPR and the other unions stack up?

FNPR, with its huge membership and heritage of universal, automatic membership, was encompassing in terms of bodies, but those millions of individual affiliations were weak. The federation leadership, the Klochkovs and Romanovs, were far from the shop floors. This left FNPR with behavior it would have found difficult to control had the overall wage-and-salary-earner mood been militant; but on the whole it was not in 1992. Instead, as this chapter has shown and as Chapter 3 will show in somewhat greater detail, the FNPR leadership took the opportunity to exploit situations that called for rectification, such as the education and health personnel pay issues, and that government had let arise and otherwise issued the periodic calls to action on the national level that never quite produced the dramas they seemed to promise. Of course, FNPR harped on both unfairness and incompetence but never laid out alternative visions of which personalities would make a better government or what program that better government should pursue. Sensitive to any implication that it was not a real union body and to reminders that the FNPR-AUCCTU links ran right back to the transmission-belt heritage of old, FNPR never really managed to unburden itself of that heritage.

From its single seat on the RTK and in its broader activity, the miners' NPG did manifest confidence in and offer support to the government, and it did control its constituency. But then, this partner got a great deal of what it wanted from the government in wage demands; controlling its constituents was made easier by this fact as well as by the rivalry with FNPR and its NPRUP coal-industry branch union, which made it less likely that NPG members would join with FNPR-driven protests and strike threats in 1992. Sergeev and the NPG could very likely have achieved the same results had they not sat on the RTK at all.

Sotsprof was harder to characterize. Its structure, much less centered than the NPG's, crossed the lines from hired labor to small independents; its tactics involved poaching on FNPR territory where it could to enroll groups of workers anywhere in order to break inherited FNPR representational monopolies even marginally. Its membership was broadly spread, was a body of constituents it needed neither to mobilize nor to control because so much of its mission seemed political in the broader sense. It supported the government. It did, one may conclude, seek to be a burr under FNPR's saddle; one need not sympathize with FNPR's position to agree that its criticisms of Sotsprof were not without a point.

The government, it might be said, fell a bit short of the partner role itself. The government side of the RTK was functionally divided—economic ministries, social ministries, and production ministries with responsibility of a sort for, if not power over, large numbers of enterprise directors who in turn commanded large labor forces. This complicated the government's search for its own voice, one that in any case was sometimes hard to hear given the proclivities of major players on the government side to absent themselves from RTK sessions. And that voice could not have been a totally consistent one because government policy was not consistent. Shock therapy as a mix of declaratory and real policy had been the watchword from January 2 on; but the response to the industrialists in the cabinet, the "no ... no ... well, yes" line taken toward demands for industrial subsidies and debt bailouts, bespoke a readiness for political compromise even when it seemed to be bad economics. The government's search for its own appropriate role on the RTK was not really successful. It was neither fortunate enough to find disputes of a sort it could referee as a social partner, nor institutionally strong enough to pursue the sorts of policy with which 1992 had, at least in rhetoric, begun. Ultimately, in the sideshow that was the RTK, the critical underlying problem was the same as the one that underlay the "high politics" of economic transition. A new government committed to political democracy had come into power before the critical social and economic building blocks of liberalism, including organizations of *homo economicus* on the employer and labor sides, had emerged. In the West, especially the West of liberal corporatism that Russia sought to emulate, the emergence of such interests and to a degree their organized representation had preceded the development of democracy.[122] The new government of Russia was less fortunate: Its political burdens included the creation of those building blocks—a Herculean task. In their absence, there was plenty of matter for vigorous political contention but little of the sort that any corporatist mechanism could regulate.

3

Disunited Front:
Trade Union Politics and Conflict

SHIFTING FROM THE CONTEXT OF THE RTK to the broader stages of
labor politics, we enter a complicated landscape. The year 1992 was no
clean slate. Behind it lay history remote and recent—improved living
standards and then stagnation under Brezhnev; the growing turbulence
of politics and the further souring of the economy and its drift into crisis
under Gorbachev; and the final, dizzying crash of the Soviet state.

Thus, questions posed as far back as 1990 were still relevant. Wher-
ever the labor "movement" was heading, it had, as one Russian analyst
put it that year, to reckon with varied raw material: Some rejected the
past and reposed hopes in the future, but others, though they had gotten
nothing substantial from the Soviet regime, still felt "attachment to the
'values' of guaranteed poverty and politico-ideological sameness." The
official unions that in the Soviet twilight claimed to care for the workers
cared, as a critic put it, in the same manner as the timber ministry cared
for trees. The new Russia was setting out from a stressful departure
point. Material living standards for much of the lower strata had improved from 1964 to the mid-1970s; as it went into later Brezhnevian
stagnation, the USSR was not Albania or North Korea. But these improvements and the slump that followed had made many "carping,
skeptical." Both material and nonmaterial demands had grown in the
later Brezhnev and the Gorbachev years, and they had not been met.[1]
Phenomena variously denominated as the "new worker," who was more
educated, more skilled, and harder en masse to manage with tools fabri-
cated in Stalin's time, or as a quiet revolution that during the long Brezhnev period had changed Soviet society structurally and psychologically
without major alterations in political or economic institutions were a
legacy that Gorbachev's failed government and state had passed on so
abruptly to Yeltsin's.[2]

In the immediate pre-August coup period, matters had already
moved well beyond the business of socialist renewal. As Leonid Gordon
and Eduard Klopov read the situation, the 1989 coalfield strikes that

launched much of the independent labor movement had taken place in a socialist context, but that had now been superseded; in the last programmatic desperation of late 1990–early 1991, the USSR had turned "toward the market." Now, in 1992, that was the new Russia's direction. The independent, non-FNPR unions had risen under "late socialism," and now faced new and potentially disorienting times. Poland's Solidarity of 1980–1981 had, too, been a political combatant in a socialist context. Reemerging in late 1988, it had borne the weight of a "pacted transition," but by late 1991 it was confused and divided over Polish market economics and the results of shock therapy, suggesting what Russia's independent unions might face.[3]

Some earlier critics of the Gorbachevian phasing of reform had raised the question of whether the new loud but underinstitutionalized democratization had given voice to too many who stood in the way of market reform, whether (in scenarios that combined Pinochet's Chile with China under Deng Hsiao-Ping) the former might not be suppressed for a time to get on with achieving the latter. For the democratic element of the trade union movement, resistance to such moves in post-USSR Russia seemed essential. If the new unions such as NPG and Sotsprof might be expected to see some of these problems, to attempt at least to strike a balance between politics and economics, it was more difficult to tell how the party- and state-subordinated heritage of AUCCTU, VKP, and FNPR might play out.

The AUCCTU's successor, VKP, held its second plenum in April 1991, less than two weeks after widespread strikes had greeted Gorbachev's long-delayed state-mandated price increase decrees. VKP effectively ignored the strikes, taking no position on political demands the strikers had raised. The April 20 government-VKP Agreement on Labor and Socioeconomic Questions, even at that late date, showed no conceptual departure from state socialism with its elements of "parasitism" and "levelling."[4] Could FNPR, then, function in or accept the new, post-August Russian context?

The stakes were historic. Logically, as two veteran labor analysts put it, four possibilities—democracy and market, market without democracy, democracy without the market, and "none of the above"—stood before Russia. The first would be best but hard to achieve; the second might work but would leave in power much of the old nomenklatura. The third looked a utopian-socialist project and the fourth, "relapse."[5]

Unions new and old working in the context of a reformist USSR government that pursued market socialism might have felt, at least, that they were in a somewhat familiar environment. But the USSR was no longer. The Yeltsin-Gaidar government might on the whole have found it easier to pursue long-term goals had there been, for a time, no labor unions at all. But such was not the case.

First Moves

On January 2, the first day of the new economics, consumer prices exploded. Expected but not experienced by any living Russians previously and not really cushioned by the experience of 1991's inflation, the new numbers evoked sharp responses. FNPR protested on January 7: Prices for main foodstuffs were up eight- to tenfold according to its estimates. Klochkov demanded social guarantees that decisions on the decontrolling of the remaining administratively set prices be a matter for joint government–trade union agreement and threatened a day of demonstrations on January 17 if the government failed to act.[6] It would become a familiar, and worn, refrain.

On January 9, the government confirmed that coal mining would continue to be subsidized with 21 billion rubles allocated for the purpose. Miners' pay would be raised and indexed in some fashion to inflation. (The roles of the FNPR coal-industry union and of the independent NPG miners' union in securing these arrangements would later become controversial.[7]) It was no solution. Miners all over the former USSR were edging toward strike action, seeking, inter alia, rights of disposal over a share of the coal mined, this to be sold at prices near to or at world levels to customers of the miners' choice. Such measures seemed a way out of the trap of the laughably low domestic procurement prices that necessitated subsidies.[8]

In Vorkuta, auxiliary coal-industry workers struck on January 9 at the Yur-Shor mine over the widening disparity between their pay and the higher wages of coal-face workers; settlement came on January 13 with a retroactive raise. In this, the FNPR-affiliated Independent Trade Union of Coal Industry Workers (Nezavisimyi Profsoiuz Rabotnikov Ugolnoi Promyshlennosti, or NPRUP), uniting pit workers and auxiliaries, bosses and rank and file, made the running, not the NPG—though the latter would go along.[9]

In the Kuzbass coal basin, which had a militant tradition the equivalent of Arctic Vorkuta's, representatives of the local workers' committees were seeking a meeting with Yeltsin about the impact of reform measures while expressing confidence that the local situation was under control despite rising tensions.[10] But by the time a delegation headed to Moscow on January 20, talk of a general strike on the 25th, supported by the pro-government NPG, was widespread. Even in this favored area, price increases were rapidly outpacing any compensation the government had been able to deliver.[11] The delegation included not only NPG officials but the pro-Yeltsin local head of administration, Mikhail Kisliuk. The problem was regional as well as sectoral. Yeltsin and Gaidar met with the delegation on January 22,[12] responding positively to their demands for serious talks on new wage agreements to be opened by the January 25 scheduled strike date.

Action was swift. The government had grown used to favoring coal miners, and it wanted their political support. If the ruble cost of that support was to be higher than originally estimated, so had prices risen faster in January than any calculations Yeltsin's government had made— or at least made public. On January 24, after talks that included the government, the FNPR coal union, and, to a lesser degree, the NPG, a tripling of the miners' minimum wage was announced.[13] For a time this raise, which meant that in January 1992 miners were receiving in the neighborhood of a hitherto unheard of 14,000 rubles monthly,[14] would quiet the coalfields. But delivering the cash to cover those raises would prove difficult. By March 20 one mine in Mezhdurechensk would strike not over wage levels but over the "impossibility of getting paid."[15]

A pattern was emerging. In generally hard times, some sectors had it harder than others. The government that cried poor would meet economic demands, militantly presented, from sectors that were important and that offered it political support. It would ride out the wrath of those branches less critical to the economic base and thus create regional equity issues in areas where favored and ignored lived cheek by jowl. Workers in other potential choke-point sectors such as transportation and workers geographically close to the favored extractive industries were driven by the "demonstration effect" to present their demands. Railroad workers in Vorkuta and Inta delivered an ultimatum to the government, demanding a meeting to include representatives of all the unions in the polar Komi region to resolve "social protection" problems that were severe because of the climate, isolation, and costs of transporting food and goods into the region. The alternative was a rail shutdown.[16]

On the national level, on January 15 FNPR attacked Gaidar for failing to implement Yeltsin's commitments on prices, labor disputes, and the new social partnership.[17] Picketing of the government headquarters followed on January 16,[18] and as promised, on January 17 demonstrations took place under FNPR auspices in a number of Russian cities.[19] It is not clear whether the response was, in FNPR leader Klochkov's estimate, encouraging; and he was not likely to be so candid as to say. A two-hour work stoppage was reported as under discussion for January 27.[20] All this was outlined starkly against the recent past, the old scale of wages. The minimum wage in January was 342 rubles—by the standards of 1989–1990, not bad pay, but against the accelerating inflation of 1991, the year of collapse, very little indeed. FNPR called for an increase to 1,000 rubles by March 1, claiming that 90 percent of the population now fell below the poverty line.[21]

In this world of minimal rubles, far from that of miners and others with clout, lived long-suffering medical personnel. Their FNPR-affiliated union mounted a strike threat for January 25 (or January 29—sources show some confusion).[22] Not only pay but funds to keep the starving medical sector going as the government sought to cut costs were at issue. As a union official put it, "The medics' pay raise is simply ludicrous and puts them on the poverty line. ... If the government does not accommodate us, it will be telling the people honestly that it does not guarantee everyone free medical services."[23] The government came to grips with the medical union on January 24, authorizing an increase as of February 1 and further reexamination of salary issues and assuring the protestors that the Supreme Soviet would seek ways to increase the general funding. This did not immediately end all strike action, but a February 29 report indicated a settlement. The increase would give doctors a base salary of 1,150 rubles (still a derisory amount, and hence the union official's reference to a raise to the "poverty line"). Some hard currency would be dedicated to the import of medical supplies.[24]

Especially sharp was the plight of those in nonfavored sectors who lived in regions where coal workers dominated the local economic profile. The Yeltsin government had not let prices soar in the manner of Poland's more genuine shock therapy of January 1990. But most consumer prices had been decontrolled, and government enforcement of the controls that remained was weak. In most of Russia, regional governments were responsible for those controls but could also provide subsidies according to their resources and inclinations. Retail trade in food and goods was now in effect free; prices rose to dizzying heights without as yet much supply-side response. In the coal regions, miners' huge wage boosts drove the local price spiral ever higher, leaving those who were not so well paid further and further behind. In the Kuzbass, the January militancy had produced increases across the board for all those employed in the coal industry. Underground workers with seniority enjoyed wage scales of 15,918 to 17,650 rubles monthly; directors got 27,485. Cleaning women in the mine offices received only 2,324 rubles monthly, but this was, obviously, more than a doctor's salary![25]

In Vorkuta in February, a coordinating council of strike committees emerged that was based on directly state-paid "budget" personnel. First Deputy Prime Minister Burbulis went to the region and promised—not very realistically—that the government would try "to find resources to bring the pay of workers in spheres of the economy subject to budget funding into line with the average wage in the coal industry."[26] By the end of the month, the head of the coordinating council reported that the government would allocate the funds necessary, noting as well that nonminers had seen the coal miners' raises as "disproportionately high."[27]

In Vorkuta there was little direct evidence that miners, especially NPG supporters, had any strong feelings pro or con on raises for other categories of workers and employees. They had aimed at absolute wage levels, not at some multiple of the compensation of less-favored branches. In the Kuzbass in March, the picture would be somewhat different. There, local workers' committees and the NPG, linked to coal-face workers, would confront FNPR and groups whose grievances it sought to exploit over broad political and intersectoral labor concerns. The Kuzbass "March troubles," seen briefly in Chapter 2 as an RTK agenda item, deserve extended treatment here.

March 1992: The Kuzbass Crisis

The Kuzbass-Kemerovo oblast had experienced massive coal strikes in July 1989.[28] Although it is true that the NPG had been born in the Donbass in October 1990, Kuzbass activists had played a major role in the process. It had been in the Kuzbass town of Novokuznetsk in May 1990 that the Confederation of Labor (Konfederatsiia Truda, or KT) had been founded to unite nascent independent labor unions and activists in opposition to the FNPR's parent, the official Soviet AUCCTU. The support of the KT, however, was drawn at that time almost totally from the militant coal miners.[29] Kuzbass had the coal; it therefore had power in both Gorbachev's late USSR and Yeltsin's new Russia. It was, as a radio commentary of March 3 indicated, a region with the wherewithal to bargain with the center. "A treaty [has been] signed between the government of the Russian capital and the Kuzbass administration. ... Coal for heating electric plants will be supplied to Moscow as well as metals and chemical industry products. In return, the Siberian residents will get the equipment they need, automobiles, and consumer goods."[30]

But though the miners typically were militant in the Kuzbass, they were *not* the source of the March strike threat against the government. In supposed reaction to the failure of the government to send a delegation to the area, the Kuzbass Federation of Trade Unions (KFP), made up of FNPR unions under Anatoly Chekis, and the coordinating council of Kuzbass strike committees, chaired by Gennadi Mikhailets, announced a strike to involve alternating stoppages in "various branches of industry" commencing on March 5 and a general strike to run from March 10. "Miners support us," said Mikhailets, in what would turn out to be something of an overstatement.[31] The strike was announced just as Burbulis, Gaidar, and others were meeting in Moscow with another cast of characters: members of the Kuzbass *workers'* committees (the descendants of the 1989 strike committees, unrelated to Mikhailets's coordinating council) and the head of administration in Kemerovo, Mikhail Kisliuk, a Yeltsin supporter.[32]

According to an announcement made by Mikhailets, the strike began March 6, and eighty-eight enterprises participated.[33] The same day, the Kuzbass workers' committees denounced the KFP and the coordinating council. The sixfold wage increase being sought (miners had received a threefold increase earlier, there being some confusion about whether they had demanded even more—or less[34]) was not the issue; politics was. The workers' committees warned: "The official trade unions are the last bastion of reactionary communist forces. While ostensibly fighting for working people's interests, as in 1917, they intend to take advantage of the people's grave situation, which is only natural in a period of reforms." The strike agitation was "part of a plan by political revanchists to overthrow the government and limit the president's powers. ... The working people know practically nothing about the populist demands hastily formulated by representatives of the official trade unions. This is a strike by the nomenklatura." The workers' committees counseled forbearance: "Contradictions that arise with this government can be resolved at the negotiating table, without ostentatiously summoning leaders to the oblast."[35]

Yeltsin's ally Kisliuk sounded the same note in a radio appeal to Kemerovo residents to disregard the strike call;[36] strike backers, reportedly, responded with a vote of no confidence in Kisliuk.[37]

Entangled here were intraregional political rivalries of the sort that would emerge in many oblasts in the new politics of Russia.[38] Here, the main players were Kisliuk as the head of administration and Aman Tuleev, chairman of the oblast's soviet and neither economic reformer nor democrat. Typically, if not always, the head of administration was Moscow-appointed and supported the line of the president; the local soviet chairman, "elected" through various combinations of manipulation and democracy at the regional level, was more likely to defend the entrenched local interests in which he was enmeshed. A telegram went to Burbulis on March 6, requesting his presence in the Kuzbass on March 10 (hence the reference in the previous quote to "ostentatiously summoning") to avert a general strike. Tuleev signed it, as did Chekis of the KFP and Dmitri Volkov, the number-two man in the regional administration (and therefore Kisliuk's nominal subordinate). Whether Kisliuk's signature was absent because he saw this move as political provocation or because he had not returned from the March 5 Moscow meeting is not completely clear.[39]

The strike backers' main demand was the wage increase—six times the current level. The workers' committee council, closely linked to the Independent Union of Miners and hence no ally of the FNPR, admitted that the wage disparity between miners and the rest of the workforce and its impact on local prices had been provocative. But the council still urged Kuzbass workers to opt for conference table over picket line and continued to attack the local strike organizers.[40] The latter decided on

March 10 to postpone the general strike until March 12 after receiving a cable from Burbulis promising that a delegation would arrive on that date.[41]

The delegation, however, would not include Burbulis. On March 11, the RTK met in Moscow, discussing a draft of the 1992 General Agreement and also the coming trip to Kemerovo. Shokhin chaired the meeting (Burbulis was reported, perhaps as a snub to the Kuzbass strike organizers, as being absent to chair a conference on "state support to the socio-cultural sphere"[42]) and stressed that the delegation was not solely "governmental" as demanded, but of the RTK and not, in his words, a "fire brigade."[43] The visit was to sort out what in fact was taking place in the Kuzbass. It did seem that such was needed, Shokhin having referred at various points to the miners' demands rather than to the groups actually involved in the strike calls.[44])

But to whom would the delegation talk, and to what effect? Some of what might be expected from the strike organizers' side was provided by soviet chair Tuleev, who had spoken briefly in Moscow on March 10 at a meeting of the communist faction in the Russian Federation parliament. His speech illustrated what a market transition actually meant to many who gave it lip service, as well as the general leanings of established regional elites: Although for the transition, he saw the local situation as "explosive," the government policy as a path to the "abyss," and called for transferring more powers to the regional level, as well as a larger share of tax funds.[45]

Despite the "explosive" situation, the remarkable thing about the Kuzbass general strike of March 1992, in retrospect, is that *it did not take place*. The Shokhin delegation arrived and held talks in Novokuznetsk with workers in a metallurgical plant and a mine, with the regional workers' committee, and with the Novokuznetsk city administration, where Shokhin spoke against "pitting workers against workers." Evidently, neither representatives of the KFP nor the strike coordinating council nor members of Tuleev's regional soviet went with the Moscow delegation to the meetings in Novokuznetsk.[46] The delegation had, earlier in the day, met in the city of Kemerovo with some KFP representatives and expressed its view of matters, accepting that something had to be done to "eliminate imbalances in wages" across some of the workforce, and recorded this in an interim protocol; but strike committee representatives complained that "the commission did not need to travel to the Kuzbass to take such a decision. They got the impression that the commission had been formed to give off hot air."[47]

With the delegation and the RTK promising recommendations to the Russian government on the Kuzbass situation within a month, there was a pretext for the KFP and strike coordinating council to suspend the action. This they did. But in some views, this only concealed the fact that the general strike threats had been "hot air." As one journalist critical of FNPR put it on March 12, this was no matter of a telegrammed promise prompting suspension of an action in progress. No such action had been mounted; the FNPR could not do so. The strike had failed because it "was simply not supported by Kuzbass working people."[48] Beyond some teachers who had sent their pupils home,

> FNPR reported that 20 enterprises in Kemerovo employing a total of 1,700 people staged warning strikes. The FNPR information center was unable to tell workers committees, surprised by the low number of strikers at these mini-enterprises, who exactly was on strike. ... It turned out that the low number had a simple explanation—the 20 enterprises involved were storekeepers unhappy at the consequences of [price] liberalization.[49]

Whatever had happened, then, was no broad-based proletarian revolt against social injustice and an unfair share of reform's pains.

Arrangements had been made to consider the findings of the Moscow delegation and to host a return delegation from the Kuzbass at the RTK in Moscow on March 18–19. Mikhailets, of the strike coordinating council, said the delegation would "raise the issues of concern to us again, and ... try to regulate them at the level of the trilateral commission."[50] Shokhin indicated that the government was proposing both a new April 1 overall wage increase for budget workers, which would help, and some specific "zonal" wage-determination mechanisms for extractive-industry areas.[51] The KFP threat was thus followed by a promise of wage increases. But it would be a long stretch to argue that this would not have come in any case. The Kuzbass had in the past generally enjoyed regional bonuses; the government seemed disinclined to cut the region off. Also, the pattern for the budget-financed sector was emerging as one where the government was making some concessions even if it could not keep pay up to the levels of those powerful industries it owned but now hardly controlled. Moscow, probably, promised little it would not have conceded in any case given that in its budget workers it was dealing with people close to a (very) minimum wage.

March events in the Kuzbass demonstrated several things: First, they revealed further politicization among the trade unions. FNPR and the independents were tangling over more than seats on the RTK; they were divided over the relation of labor to the government itself. Klochkov had not assumed a high profile during the Kuzbass affair, but opponents of the KFP had made it clear that FNPR unions were at the core of the action—old, official, communist unions. The NPG had not been vocal, but the Kuzbass workers' committees, sprung from the same roots, had remained pro-government, pro-reform, pro-Yeltsin, and antistrike. There was self-interest in this politics as well: At this point, NPG's leaders were more inclined than most to see long-term government plans on prices and privatization as likely to work in favor of the coal industry.

Second, NPG's hell-take-the-hindmost pressing of wage demands complicated the government's position. The latter had given in, creating a social justice issue. It then gave in, to a lesser degree, to complaining education and health personnel, but not enough to make them happy. The government was paying some price, if not yet a large one, for securing NPG support. The teachers and doctors, educated people and presumably well disposed toward the government conceptually, could be directed against it in practice by the economic exigencies the FNPR exploited. Although in both the Kuzbass and Komi, coal enterprises established voluntary funds to supplement local education and health pay, this was not a nationally applicable solution.[52]

Arctic April: Tensions in Komi

A somewhat similar set of issues would arise, again, in the far north in April. The Komi Republic towns of Vorkuta, Inta, Usinsk, Pechora, and others would become the locus of claims against the government from both the extractive-industry workers and others outside these critical sectors; the FNPR and rival independents would continue their conflicts as well.

A growing problem was that of the cash crisis. In early April, at the Sixth Congress of People's Deputies, Klochkov had complained that payment of wages and pensions was in arrears in many areas, especially those where large pay increases had been awarded.[53] Government wage concessions were one thing; the capacity of the printing presses was another. In Komi, oil- and gas-industry workers in the Usinsk area set off a strike that began to spread to other sectors (first, a teacher action that closed the schools).[54] Elsewhere in the Arctic, around Norilsk, a strike warning was issued by mining and metallurgy workers, collectively owed 2.5 billion rubles in back pay.[55] The Komi action spread, fed by what locals perceived as delaying tactics by the RTK. The April militancy in Usinsk was an extension of troubles that had surfaced in mid-February. The oil and gas workers had struck, demanding free prices for their product, deliveries of consumer goods and equipment, and other benefits.[56] Commencing on February 15, the shutdown had been halted when talks with government representatives began. Work resumed on February 18, but stoppages had resumed when promises were not honored by March 15.[57] Partly the workers' readiness to strike—virtually simultaneously with the issuing of demands—was driven by perceptions of inequity in the treatment of oil and gas, as opposed to coal, workers. Earlier, Usinsk had not been so squeaky a wheel as had nonmining, budget-funded workers in the Komi coal towns of Vorkuta and Inta; the latter had gotten special funds to raise wages in violation of the government's own guidelines.[58] Now, Usinsk wanted higher wages in the fuel sector and also wage supplements for other workers in the area.[59]

An April 15 report indicated that schools in Usinsk had been for the most part closed for a month; teachers, child-care personnel, and much of the "social sphere" were on indefinite hold in Ukhta, Sosnogorsk, and Pechora. Health services were also affected. A citywide conference of nonindustrial workers announced plans for an indefinite strike to commence on April 29 in pursuit of across-the-board raises that would bring them to the industrial worker average. The Yeltsin government, in the midst of conflict with a hostile Sixth Congress of People's Deputies, appealed for time to consider the demands, setting May 1 as the target. A local coordinating council evidently supported the government in this request, but it went unheeded by many.[60]

Usinsk seems to have been fated to do badly. The government kept delaying dealing with the oil workers; costs to the oil concerns rose, and revenues fell. Other local sectors were affected as well. On May 8, after the government announced yet another delay in dealing with the oil issue until May 20 and with local enterprises out of money to pay wages and in debt 1.6 billion rubles, the oil workers struck again, adding a call for the government's resignation.[61] Militancy, even in an important sector, did not guarantee a government rollover, especially when the Usinsk workers were not, unlike the Kuzbass and Vorkuta miners, organized and vocal supporters of the Yeltsin government's political line. It is time to give the coal sector a closer look.

The Coalfields: Unions and Disunity

Assembling any coherent picture of the mid-1992 state of affairs in labor politics Russia-wide remains, even at this remove, difficult. Spontaneity was evident in the multiplicity of committees, councils, and so on that seemed to arise with such frequency. Yet most of Russia was quiet. The street politics of the neocommunist Trudovaia Rossiia marching in Moscow was an exception, but it was not the metropolitan tip of any national iceberg. People on the whole were trying to cope on individual or household levels. Enterprises were trying to survive; much of their maneuvering was at local levels, not coordinated with some branch administration. In their vast numbers, workers were still members of FNPR unions, but this, to all indications, meant little to them. The coal industry was different, and there the complicated relationships of unions were sharply highlighted.

The NPG had been formed in a breakaway from the official AUCCTU's branch coal-industry union, the NPRUP. The latter was much the larger, but the former's membership was voluntary, not automatic. How would each deal with its constituencies and how compete to gain, or retain, membership? Who could sign miners' wage agreements? Could the NPRUP's numerical superiority be converted into sole status as negotiator?

Certainly, the NPG would not accept this. In January, the NPG had threatened strikes in Vorkuta and the Kuzbass, essentially to force the government to negotiate with NPG and thus set the desired precedent. But it was the NPRUP that invited Gaidar's team to the table. The government came. NPRUP pressed for a wage level five times the prevailing one, across the board for the branch as a whole. The government countered with an offer of 2.8 times current levels. The NPG, after initially refusing, finally joined the negotiations, supporting the government offer and its application to all in the branch (a decision that it would later, as hinted earlier, regret and that was alien to a union that had based itself so narrowly on subsurface workers who were a minority in the NPRUP).[62] There was little trust, and no love lost, between the NPG and the NPRUP. As a *Komsomolskaia Pravda* commentator observed, "The former calls its rivals apparatchiks with their noses in the trough, and the latter in turn calls its rivals political intriguers who recklessly give indiscriminate support to any government decision." The NPG was open about its "[pro-government] political orientation," the NPRUP "narrowly sectoral" in its interests.[63] The NPG's joining in, then, in NPRUP's earlier industrywide demands had created the appearance—moreover, the objective reality—of collusion in getting across-the-board raises for a long "tail" of nonminers in the coal industry and thus had contributed to the sort of intersectoral tensions that the KFP-FNPR would try to exploit in the Kuzbass in March. "The driver of a diesel locomotive hauling freight cars in the mine yard was now earning more than his counterpart who took these freight cars along the main lines, and a female medical orderly at a [mine] dispensary was earning more than her counterpart in a city hospital."[64]

Divisions ran deep as well between NPG and NPRUP over the prospects for the coal industry and its basic economic viability. Miners' clout led to pay increases, but those increases drove the need for yet greater government subsidies. The alternative—freeing coal prices to rise, presumably to world levels—promised havoc across the economy. Neither relatively efficient nor inefficient coal users could afford world prices. An end to subsidies would drive high-cost, less-efficient coal mines to the wall all the more rapidly. The NPG saw market prices at this point as an inevitability, closing some pits as something to be dealt with when it came with some cushion from increased coal-industry incomes via the freed prices. The NPRUP generally stood against price rises that might speed the closure of loss-maker pits, as well as pricing coal beyond the ability of domestic users to pay for it, hence amplifying domino effects across the industrial economy.

To some degree, organizational self-interest was involved. The Kuzbass, the home of the NPG, had what appeared in 1992 to be the best prospects as a productive area and a likely ability to enter the world of the market. In this it was quite different from the archaic, nearly played-out Donbass, equally militant in 1989–1990. But this was 1992, and most of the Donbass was now in a foreign country—Ukraine. The NPRUP spoke for a broader spectrum of personnel across mining regions where-in many mines of lesser evident survival capacity would have to close. (The militant miners in Arctic Komi, in Vorkuta and Inta, however, typically backed the government and its long-term plans even though with recovery costs high and the whole infrastructure a relic of Soviet-era Arctic frontier and convict-labor development, it was impossible to see their region surviving without massive subsidies.) In a sense, the NPG was unrealistic (or opportunistic) in its stance. It favored a future freeing of prices and privatization but meanwhile depended on its massive government subsidies. When the time came for major liberalization of coal procurement prices, it recoiled from the consequences.

The NPG-NPRUP rivalry was fought in a sector of the economy notable for its militancy and rather exceptional in that regard. A large literature on labor and trade unionism notes that miners are typically militant, citing the frequent isolation of mining communities, the solidarity of workers mutually dependent in an industry fraught with physical danger, and so on. These generalizations have not gone unchallenged, but the point here is that the coal unions' militancy—from the massive 1989 summer strikes to the early post-Soviet period—arguably had quite specific roots.[65]

Miners were traditionally well paid; the rubles in their monthly packets were plentiful in contrast to those of workers in virtually all other branches of the economy. But miners lived poorly. Soviet planners decreed quite low procurement prices for coal, making of it a unique planned-loss sector that depended on large government subsidies for its operations, including miners' pay. Unlike many other ministries, then, the coal ministry could not operate—even in the distorted manner of the Soviet command economy—by self-financing. Typically, favored ministries could distribute to their subordinate enterprises financing and materials for housing construction and other infrastructure facilities and guarantee a certain flow of goods to internal retail distribution points in those enterprises. In these terms, the coal ministry, despite the centrality of the fuel to the economy, was poor. In consequence, miners lived frequently in atrocious housing; were underprovisioned in terms of schools, recreational facilities, and other benefits typically provided by employing enterprises; and had much less available by way of food, clothing, and other goods that enterprises in other sectors could provide for internal sale. The coal ministry could not provide.

In 1989 and in 1992—and to the present—industrial enterprises have proven much less militant than the mining sector. The sources of the relative quietude in industry go beyond the fact that the less well paid factory workers generally got more in terms of housing and various goods because their ministries and enterprises had more to distribute in an chronic economy of shortage where access counted more than cash in hand. Nonmilitancy derives as well from the dependence of factory workers on the management's paternalism regarding those benefits: Especially in areas such as positioning on waiting lists for better housing, management can manipulate to its advantage, favoring certain categories of workers over others and denying benefits to troublemakers. Mine directors, with fewer resources at their disposal, could do much less in this regard; miner militancy to a major degree may be attributed to the lack of deterrents in management's hands.

The coal towns of 1992 looked, then, much like the coal towns of 1989—shabby housing, poor infrastructure, weak retailing systems— and looked toward a Moscow government from which they sought relief. For the NPG, stressing its own image as a "real" union, a defender of workers' interests, the stress was on wages, the demand was for more, and the path was the devolution of the mines to private ownership (which miners typically saw as *their* ownership) and the freeing of coal prices; but in the interim, the wage increases would come from government subsidies. NPRUP, as the old branch union uniting bosses and miners underground workers and auxiliaries, went more directly for subsidies in its approach to the government and, in this sense, was more consistent. From time to time, it reminded miners that it was (unlike NPG with its contemptuous rejection of these functions) in the benefits-distribution business and that much of what miners got, however meager, came through its operations. Both unions, though rivals, would find some common ground in precisely the set of particular grievances that drove miner militancy and in the particular circumstances that gave mine bosses fewer resources than their counterparts in industrial plants with which to discipline their workforces.

Teachers and Doctors: Suffering Servants

FNPR seemed to have better prospects for scoring points against the government with the budget-funded service professions. There was frustration aplenty to be exploited among educational and medical personnel. The FNPR sought to do so and on April 20 announced a day of unity across the country.

> In Moscow, bus drivers are demanding a pay rise to bring them up to, no more, no less than 15,000 rubles per month. The average wage of medical workers, on the other hand, is 980 rubles, and their work is no less dangerous or responsible. An all-Russian strike by health care workers is to begin today. Between 20 April and 3 May, medical certificates will not be issued and surgical operations will be carried out only in the most serious emergencies.[66]

The 15:1 ratio of bus driver pay to that of medical personnel reflected part of the Soviet economic legacy—the underfunding of services, even the most "human," and a bias in favor of "essentials" that came to include not only heavy industry but transport as well.

By April 24, varying degrees of strike activity in the medical field had started in several cities, including St. Petersburg. Moscow medics, already picketing the government's headquarters, were threatening action for April 27;[67] a report estimated that perhaps 50 percent of doctors and other medical personnel were striking on that date. Medical care was still being given, but work on ancillary tasks (writing reports, issuing sick-leave certificates) had halted. The Moscow medical workers' local projected a cutback to only emergency care by May 4 and complete cessation of medical service on May 10 if no progress was made toward meeting its demands. Doctors' average base salaries in Moscow were reported as 744 rubles monthly; the members of the doctor-plus-paramedic team that rode in Moscow ambulances earned less combined than the driver![68] The government, trying to limit its own budgetary obligations but forced to countenance demands it could scarcely deny in principle, aimed at a reconciliation by May 1.[69]

It offered 1.8 times the current pay—unsatisfactory to the medics but restated as "not subject to change" by Deputy Labor Minister Kudiukin at an April 30 meeting with union representatives.[70] Protests continued with the medical union demanding an across-the-board increase to bring average medical pay up to the level of the average industrial wage; this implied a 3.0 coefficient rather than the government's 1.8.[71]

The government was tougher with the doctors than with the miners; it was, of course, paying the former, although regional and local governments were supposed to pick up some of the tab. Doctors were not so tough as miners had been. They were generally constrained from denying care to routine patients or threatening a total shutdown, "which for doctors means breaking the Hippocratic oath. For that reason none of the [Moscow] medics are seriously considering taking such a drastic step."[72]

Eventually, the wraps came off a complex package. It included a 20 percent increase in basic medical salaries,[73] a schedule of supplements for various activities and additions to the workload, and instructions to regional governments to channel some of their tax revenues into further increases in pay for medics. Backdated to May 1, the provisions of the May 13 decree would increase the pay of the most work-laden doctors to 2,500–3,000 rubles.[74]

Pay grievances from the education sector were, if anything, more complicated. Primary and secondary education were under local administration; only higher education and certain types of vocational training were financed from the federal budget. The teachers' union lagged a bit behind its medical colleagues, but its demands were similar. In early May, it based its claims on an emergency decree of the RSFSR government from July 11, 1991, that mandated an increase in primary and secondary teachers' pay to the average industrial-wages level and higher-education faculty pay to double that. Shokhin, citing the then-average pay in education as 1,986 rubles (a figure nearly useless because it included the range from kindergarten caregivers to professors), projected that the government might pump that level up to 2,500; Gaidar argued that layoffs of some teachers could finance raises for others.[75]

The FNPR teachers' union was unimpressed. Its head, citing work actions already under way and a possible nationwide strike commencing May 22, argued that the government should find the money and, if necessary, add to the budget deficit; as it was, education was absorbing only 5 percent of the Russian wage fund.[76] In some areas, a local parity principle could be very costly: Kuzbass teachers demanded that their pay be pegged at the level of the average miner's wage, and struck. The local soviet (under Tuleev), agreed to increase the salaries as demanded and added a month's compensation for the strikers. The regional administration (essentially Yeltsin's people) declared this move illegal.[77] It is unlikely that any arrangement could have bumped the pay in question up to the miners' average, but as noted earlier, Kuzbass enterprises did establish voluntary funds to supplement local education and health personnel pay.

The Moscow government, basically taking a position similar to the one it had adopted on the doctors, was not overly forthcoming. Initially (May 12), the proposal was for a 25 percent across-the-board hike (it had been 20 percent for the medics), retroactive to May 1. This increase was, presumably, in addition to a new minimum-wage level of 900 rubles for all budget-sector workers authorized for May 1.[78]

A package was ultimately delivered in a May 13 decree, and like the one for the doctors, it included various supplements as percentages of the new base pay levels for various duties and instructions to local governments to channel more tax receipts into education wage funds. These evidently made for an average 160 percent increase in teachers' pay, versus 170 for doctors.[79]

The government's round with the doctors and teachers concluded with it citing another forthcoming across-the-board adjustment for budget personnel in July and with grudging comments from Klochkov and Yakovlev, the head of the teachers' union[80]—but with little clear about exactly how much teachers and doctors would really earn. Both groups were still subject to local governments' ability and willingness to pay, and their behavior could not be predicted or controlled by the central government. By any calculation (and they are hard to make given the spotty and unreliable nature of data), it is extremely unlikely that the total official compensation of medical and education workers ever rose to equal the average industrial wage at the same time in the same areas. According to an *Izvestiia* report of May 16,[81] the independent 80 percent across-the-board increases for all budget personnel, not just for doctors and teachers, effective May 1, would have meant for education workers an average of 1,360 rubles—up, it is true, from a miserable 755 rubles earlier. But 1,360 rubles equaled only 53 percent of the average industrial pay level of February 1992. In this range doctors and teachers were to remain: October 1992 pay ranged from 50 to 57 percent of industrial pay.[82]

Hardly as militant or as successful in getting what they wanted as the miners, medical and educational personnel nonetheless shared with miners some similarities that drove them to labor actions when factory workers were, in very large measure, quiet. Like miners—and indeed like the bus and trolley drivers who were more successful at getting raises via strike threats—doctors and teachers worked in contexts far removed from large industrial plants with their own distribution systems for scarce goods. Their hospitals, polyclinics, and schools could not provide for them and hence lacked leverage over them. Long poorly paid (although positioned much better than miners for various sorts of moonlighting to supplement base pay), they were forced to compete, with the rest of the nonprivileged population for goods and food in the open-access, street-level retail economy. Their need for rubles was acute, and their alarm in the face of skyrocketing prices and a government that was not inclined to be any more generous to its budget personnel than it had to be was fully justified.

"Organized" Labor: Diversity and Problems

If the state of labor politics at the first post-Soviet May Day was complicated, so was that of the "movement"—a melange of organizations stretching well beyond the FNPR, NPG, and Sotsprof, which have claimed most of the attention here. FNPR included many branch and regional organizations beyond those that sat on the RTK; it did not control them all. Numerous independents with no prior AUCCTU-VKP-FNPR history had emerged as well. Further, organizations formed neither by law nor by charter as trade unions but claiming both to defend hired labor and to advocate general economic and political programs added to the array.

FNPR's national leadership stood at some remove from many regional and branch components. The independence thrust upon Klochkov and others by the USSR's collapse was real enough, but also the Moscow government had no real interest in backing up what had been its pseudounion's national headquarters. Hence, the branch and regional bodies became increasingly more independent of FNPR central. As time went on, central headquarters controlled less, collected less (in shares of the dues checkoff), and could predict less how individual organizations would behave.

Some of those organizations were tougher than others. However real and justified their grievances, the education union and M. M. Kuzmenko's medical workers' union (with its seat on the RTK) had to settle for moderate gains. The FNPR's coal-industry union did rather well by its members. The NPG's economic pressure on the government it backed politically did not hurt the rival, larger organization.

Toughest of all of the FNPR affiliates was probably its Moscow regional organization—the Moscow Federation of Trade Unions (MFP) under Mikhail Shmakov. Proximity to the central leadership in the capital in this case hardly signaled subordination. MFP was pro-democracy but syndicalist in its economic orientation, pushing for the transfer of factory assets to the workers and worker control over production and suspicious both of the cupidity of the old managerial nomenklatura and the government's privatization plans. MFP's "third way" economics dictated as much a combative as consultative stance toward the state.[83] It had rejected social partnership, criticizing the FNPR leaders for joining the RTK and declining the place at the table to which its 5 million-plus members would surely have entitled it. As one of the premier specialists on the Russian labor movement put it, in December 1991–January 1992, the MFP—"the anarchists' stronghold"—had "shifted to demagogy that bordered on the full rejection of reforms," coming close to reactionary and authoritarian "red-brown" forces in the process[84]—at least sometimes.

Among FNPR RTK members, the pilots and flight-crew union (FPALS) under A. A. Malinovskii was given to asserting the independence of a large portion of its approximately 30,000 members, driven partly by the demonstration effect of the air traffic controllers' union (FPAD) in furthering the interests of its members.[85] By the end of 1992, the mining and metallurgical union would depart from the FNPR in an acrimonious divorce. Another important branch union from the old AUCCTU—the railroad engineers (Rossiiskii Profsoiuz Mashinistov–Lokomotivnykh Brigad)—was now independent, not having joined FNPR when the AUCCTU gave way to the VKP.

Independent trade unions with no prior history of subordination to official structures included (beyond FPAD, NPG, and the somewhat unique Sotsprof) many others. Some were regional, others aimed at encompassing broad ranges of crafts and occupations or at snaring individual defectors from FNPR locals in plants. They were often given to membership claims that were appropriately swallowed only after generous salting. Among these were the confusingly similar Confederation of Free Trade Unions of Russia (KSPR), claiming 80,000, and the Russian Confederation of Free Trade Unions (KPSR) with 12,000; two organizations both named Zashchita (Defense) with rosters of 15,000 and 4,000; and Spravedlivost (Justice), a St. Petersburg regional organization of 3,000.

Looser yet in terms of the accuracy of (even small) enrollment claims and strong organization, in all probability, were a number of bodies chartered as trade unions (TUs) that, not unlike Sotsprof, based themselves on both owners and hired labor in nonstate, small, and cooperative businesses. A list follows, with their claimed membership.

All-Russian TU, or Edinenie (Unity)	1,800
Russian TU of Workers in Medium-Size and Small Business	1,300
Union of TUs of Workers in Cooperative Enterprises	200–250
Interregional Confederation of Unions of TUs of Russia	300
Russian TU of Workers of Innovating and Small Enterprises	200
Russian TU of Workers of Construction Organizations and Enterprises of Nonstate Property Forms	200
Confederation of Productive TUs of Russia	150
Association of Free TUs of Small, International, Lease, Joint-Stock, Collective, Cooperative and Other Enterprises (MAKKIP)	120
Russian Union of Free TUs (Solidarnost)	110
Russian Federation–TU of Workers of Joint (*sovmestnykh*) Enterprises	90

Despite the small membership numbers and the general fluidity of the organizational picture, not all of these would disappear, as Chapter 4 indicates.

Finally, broader sociopolitical organizations (not registered as trade unions) that combined claims to defend the interests of hired labor with advocacy and struggle for "this or that path of development of society as a whole"[86] sought a place, thus claiming some of the functions political parties might in other, more stable, systems.

On the rejectionist–Soviet restorationist side, the most visible and audible was the Working Russia (Trudovaia Rossiia) movement and its Moscow branch, Trudovaia Moskva. Antidemocracy and antimarket, it combined old communists and new authoritarian-nationalist forces— the "red-brown" linkage. It grew out of earlier worker-based antireform organizations. First among these was the United Front of Workers of Russia (OFTR), founded in fall 1989 largely with the backing of communist party officials and ideologues. OFTR, despite its pseudocharismatic leader, one Veniamin Yarin, and an *ouvrieriste* agenda that looked as if it might draw support from workers disoriented as the old Soviet economy continued its downslide,[87] never really became a strong force. In the pre-coup summer of 1991, the RSFSR Communist Party brokered, thus, the creation of new bodies of similar stripe—the workers' councils (sovety rabochikh). Overtaken by the collapse of the USSR, OFTR and the Russian workers' councils were joined in the creation of Trudovaia Rossiia in early 1992. Much given to street demonstrations (especially in Moscow) and strident rhetoric under its leader Viktor Anpilov (a leader also of the radically restorationist Russian Communist Workers' Party[88]), it was in the red-bannered forefront of nearly every protest against government policy in 1992 and 1993.

More cohesive as an organization, clearer in a narrower definition of objectives, and ostensibly pro-democracy but, like the MFP, rejecting full endorsement of the market and favoring worker control and ownership of the factories was the Union of Labor Collectives (Soiuz Trudovykh Kollektivov, or STK). Born in 1990 mainly out of large military industry plants in Moscow and St. Petersburg (Leningrad), STK drew on preexisting plant-level organizations, the councils (sovety) of the work collective—also styled as STKs. These latter, established in all Soviet enterprises in the pre-Gorbachev days, were essentially as cosmetic as the old plant-level AUCCTU locals. Even as perestroika proceeded, many remained so. But the 1987 law on the state enterprise had endorsed a certain measure of worker control (election of managers and so on) and hence empowered the STKs. Although this generally mattered little, some STKs in the coalfields in 1989, like some union locals, did stand up for worker interests. In 1990, under growing economic stress and an increasingly clear policy trajectory toward the market and privatization (if only in general terms), modifications were made in the law to remove those worker-control elements; the STKs of what then seemed the potentially profitable defense industries came together to push for worker ownership and to fight against nomenklatura privatization and for their enterprises.[89] Keeping a relatively low public profile, the STK, despite its antinomenklatura stance, made common cause to a degree with industrial lobby organizations. It pressed the short- and medium-term interests in job preservation and enterprise survival that it shared with industrial bosses as it came to face drastic cuts in procurement orders from Yeltsin's Russian government.

Finally, aligned on the government side in 1993 as a pro-democracy, pro-market reform worker organization would be the earlier-mentioned (in the context of the March 1992 Kuzbass crisis) Confederation of Labor, or KT. Founded in 1990 on the local base of the Kuzbass workers' committees but with the participation of representatives from the Donbass and Cheliabinsk and with a dominant role in organizing it played by Moscow intellectuals,[90] the KT, like many new labor organizations, had not been free of internal rivalries and dissension. It had, nonetheless, turned from Gorbachev to support Yeltsin during the late perestroika period. But now, like the NPG and some of the pro-government independent unions, it found itself compelled to take a critical view of economic policies it opposed while remaining politically supportive. Necessarily, thus, its approach was more nuanced than that of a Trudovaia Rossiia and thus more difficult to explain to confused workers. It involved "a loss of clarity and simplicity, which for a significant segment of workers are synonyms for correctness"; the slogans on offer from "the neocommunists and nationalists, demanding the actual rejection of reforms, or demagogically promising to carry them out without a lowering of living standards, [could] appear very attractive."[91]

Some of these organizations would play larger roles than others. Some were "real" and large, others real but small. Some existed perhaps more on paper and were more expressions of hope or opportunism than of organizational accomplishment. All were part of the color mix in the confused canvas of labor politics.

Continuing the Struggle

On May 1, Moscow unions rallied in Gorky Park, demanding that Yeltsin's government set its sights on a social market economy, bar any increases in unemployment, place privatization under working people's control, and, since the government showed intentions of raising fuel prices to world levels, raise labor prices to world levels as well.

All this was tough, but not vague: The MFP typically was direct. But it was economically illiterate and somewhat premature. By no reasonable standard was there much real unemployment yet. Privatization subject to worker control could mean a giveaway to workers or worker veto power over privatization itself, leaving the government the reluctant proprietor. World-level labor prices were, of course, an emotional demand, another way to phrase demands for higher wages to meet prices. FNPR saw full indexation of wages as the answer, ignoring the consequences of escalator-type mechanisms in economies much healthier than Russia's. (The government at the end of 1991 had set itself to maintain a lag of no more than 30 percent between prices and wages.)

The slogan missed the point that there is no world price for labor per se, though there is one for many products. Russia, of course, was not in the world market with respect to the vast majority of its goods. The prices it could charge for its labor, given its products, were closer to third world than to Western levels—a potential element of attraction to possible foreign investors, an insult to many Russians. Hence the sense of outrage and denial from labor unions (as well as industrial lobbyists and nationalists of various stripe) at the notion that the role of supplier of raw materials and low-value-added goods and skilled yet cheap labor might well be for some time Russia's actual niche in the global economy. The economic crisis of transition was a crisis of national status as well.

It is not, of course, necessarily the mission of labor unions facing national-psychological revolutions to explain constraining economic realities to their members. But the various contrasts between world levels of this or that and the situation of Russian workers were misleading, often irrelevant, and likely further to confuse workers who had lost the familiar moorings of their old lives. Russia might not be paying the world price for labor, but then Russia was still not paying world prices for many things, including the fuel it produced and consumed. It could not afford to; it had never done so. In comparison to other workers in Russia, fuel workers were, on average, better paid (when they were paid) by virtue of state subsidies to the fuel industry. In 1992 Russians were not poor because they were paying and absorbing world-level prices for fuel while having their wages held to some low artificial domestic level. To assert this was to assert the inaccurate.

It was also to be demagogic. FNPR might accuse Sotsprof of being in the government's pocket, denigrate the importance of the new independent unions because of their smaller numbers, and assert ever more loudly its own graduation from the official transmission-belt status, but it could not escape attributions of its illegitimacy. These came early and would recur.

"Trade unions—the school of communism"—these are Lenin's words. "The party's faithful assistant" has today begun to replace it in all respects. I'm referring to those who manipulate millions of people. Whenever I hear I. Klochkov, head of the Federation of Independent Trade

Unions, who is often on our television screens, I don't know whether to laugh or cry. Just who is it that is speaking about "the defense of the working people's interests," and presenting the government with ulti-matums by threatening it with strikes? Igor Yevgenievich Klochkov, for-mer Komsomol leader of the Naro-Fominsk Komsomol Gorkom, for-mer first secretary of the Naro-Fominsk CPSU Gorkom, former second secretary of the Moscow CPSU Obkom. All his life he and his ilk have lived in that "communism" which was built for the separate party elite by the rank-and-file members of the party and the trade union. But the point is not in the positions they have occupied but in the fact that they are continuing in the same spirit.[92]

From mocking Klochkov's resume, this critic went on, a bit insensitively, to criticize striking teachers, to call striking doctors perjurers violating the Hippocratic oath, to remind bus drivers that they "get enough." This probably by implication attributed too much effect to FNPR efforts given the modest outcomes for doctors and teachers. But the broad judgment on FNPR was the main point: Its leaders were "not worried about the needs of the working people" but aimed rather "to return the country to the plan-and-allocation economy, to the power of the party-ocracy for whom the trade unions have always been like pageboys waiting for the crumbs from their master's table."[93]

For reformers, the FNPR—the USSR's largest survivor organiza-tion—was part of the inherited problem. Interested as they might be in holding down wage increases and cutting subsidy burdens, the reform-ers were not likely to attack the miners' union (NPG). NPG and the other independents supported Yeltsin and his team on the broader political is-sues, as well as on the plans for privatization and, at this point, decontrol of coal prices.

Another reading of FNPR, from an Interfax news service commenta-tor, gives what might be seen as a more balanced assessment.

With a membership of 60 million, the [FNPR] is the largest trade union organization in Russia. Although it supports the economic reform effort by and large, it fairly often finds itself in opposition to Mr. Gaidar's gov-ernment when attacking the latter's insufficient foresight as to the so-cial repercussions of reforms.

All in all, it is the independent trade unions that produce the most disruptive effect on the economic and social situation in Russia. …

… The government's worst problem in recent months was the [NPG], which used the threat of work stoppages in the coal industry to force the government to more than triple miners' wages. This, together with various bonuses, incentives, benefits and other payments, brought the average remuneration of personnel working under ground to Rb 30,000 a month, which is 12 times more than the nationwide average.

For this commentator, there was, thus, "fault" as well as rational self-interest and exploitation of "market position" and regional clout by the miners of the NPG.

Sterner critics would by and large find the earlier remarks on FNPR's support for reform somewhat misleading or unperceptive; they accepted the reform in principle but rejected from the outset its inevitable, if harsh, short-term consequences. But it would be hard to disagree with the assessment of the contingencies after the April 1992 signing of that year's general agreement between the trilateral "partners." Its workability would depend less on economic developments themselves than on "the degree to which trade union cells at the enterprise level and individual employers will feel themselves bound by the provisions of an agreement signed on their behalf"[94] in the RTK.

The real point was that too many processes were too far beyond the weak regulatory capacities of the new central government. This did not mean real political crisis but rather the ongoing low-intensity conflict whose episodes fill these pages. The government avoided an open fight: Promises might be made and a confrontation thus cooled. The government might then honor the promises only partially and late, saving itself some money as funds promised but delayed declined in value before their delivery. The FNPR, in turn, did not possess the deployment capacity to put its tens of millions into the street.

Managerial behavior, as well as that of labor, presented the government with problems. Internally, with wholesale and retail prices largely decontrolled, factories could charge what they liked. Accordingly, largely monopolist plants raised their prices to buyers, thus compensating themselves for higher prices charged by their suppliers further up the production chain and covering deficits in their income as they produced fewer goods. Factories became simultaneously debtors and creditors; they were unable to pay suppliers and unable to collect from customers. Factories produced, shipped, crediting and debiting one another as long as materials were available, ran up large tabs, and then pressed the government for the credits to cover the web of obligations.

The government condemned such behavior—Gaidar more sharply than most—but it did not force the issue. The central bank, under Viktor Gerashchenko—who was developing at this time the reputation of the world's worst central banker in the Western financial press—and who was subordinate not to the government executive but to the parliament—issued the credits. The bank cared less for the ruble than for the traditional fetish of production, even to the point of subsidizing its "value-subtracting" varieties.

Different were the extractive industries—coal and, to a degree, the oil and gas sectors. Outside the Russian borders, there were buyers for their products. Coal, oil, and gas were fungible goods; Russia's were as good as anyone else's. For the state, energy exports represented hard-currency earning opportunities. For energy producers, there was precisely the same attraction, but only if the government did not, after producers marketed output at world prices, try to pocket the difference between the price realized abroad and the absurdly low domestic prices (less than 10 percent, typically, of world levels). Domestic energy consumer enterprises, of course, were differently situated: The world prices that represented profit potential to the producers were, to them, unpayable. Here, nothing had changed from the Soviet period, and the state maintained controls whose abolition might be good economics but would be extremely risky politics.

By midyear, fuel extractors were calling for the deregulation of energy prices. The oil workers of Usinsk in the Komi Republic were still demanding more in May; budget workers in the area agitated for catch-up increases of their own. The government on May 21 raised budget-employee wage levels "three times," and upped the oil procurement price, but the oil workers wanted "free market prices."[95] The government balked. Yeltsin appealed to oil and gas workers on June 3 to consider the ripple effects. "Expensive oil means expensive bread, milk, and other products indispensable to your families too." Total decontrol would "hit the pockets of ordinary workers in the oil and gas industry and wipe out the value of their wages. ... The situation in the country could get out of control."[96]

Yeltsin sweetened his appeal with references to the prospective increase in prices, credits to be awarded to support the oil and gas complex, and tax relief for energy extractors and added that the "question of covering the wage payment debt has been examined. Despite certain difficulties this problem will be solved as early as this July."[97] It would not be so simple.

The Cash Crisis and the Summer Offensive

Workers in oil and gas were among a growing number who were getting paid late. As a street-level, grassroots issue, this was a volatile one. Gaidar, in a long TV interview on May 18, summarized the situation.

> Beginning from April, there was a sharp acceleration of the present crisis. ... You have earned your salary and because someone has not printed enough money ... it is no use to explain it here. I could be saying that the ready cash is being managed by the Central Bank, that without it I cannot take a single ruble from my own state mint and send it to a certain region. I can refer to the Supreme Soviet Presidium, which has put the brakes on printing the high-denomination banknotes. No one

would be interested. … In June we should be doubling our production of the higher denomination bank notes of R200 and R500 from 64 billion in April-May to between 124–128 billion. This is before we move on to the R5,000 notes.[98]

June and July saw protests over the wage arrears in a number of cities and regions, from factory workers in Sverdlovsk (who demanded that the government work "not for a deficit-free budget but for stabilizing the working people's living standard"[99]) to ambulance drivers in Kamchatka and miners in Rostov.[100] These workers and their families were indeed suffering great hardships.

Beyond them, the more symbolic side of antigovernment labor politics escalated as summer wore on. In July RASP—the Russian Assembly of Social Partnership—had been founded. More bombastic was the summer campaign of the All-Russian Labor Conference. On June 6, over 600 people assembled in Moscow as the All-Russian Conference of Representatives of Labor Collectives, Trade Unions, Strike Committees and Entrepreneurial and Creative Associations. Evidently assembled on the initiative of the Russian Unity parliamentary bloc, strongly critical of Yeltsin and Gaidar, it provided a forum for strident antigovernment broadsides touching on the fears of those who saw yesterday's great power in economic collapse and attributed this to various plots and machinations.[101] The sympathetic coverage in *Sovetskaia Rossiia* gives some indication of the sort of alarmism expressed.

> If present trends continue, the country's national income will fall by 44 percent by 1995, which will greatly exceed the analogous drop in the first two years of the Great Patriotic War. It will prove possible to restore its level only by the year 2012 at best, when the developed countries will have moved far ahead, leaving Russia in the position of a semicolonial appendage of the West, a source of raw materials where the overwhelming majority of the population is on the poverty line.[102]

Fears of semicolonialism were also a favorite theme of the industrial lobby, some of whose spokesmen were fond of the term "Kuwaitization." In this reading, Russia was headed toward a future wherein those well placed in the extractive sectors would, as a sort of comprador class, do very well, enjoying elevated Western levels of affluence while the rest of the population sank to third world levels. The conference ignored the waste of energy and material in Russia's many value-subtracting plants. The government was, simply, "guilty," its "adventurist and antinational actions" placing Russia "on the brink of complete disaster."[103]

The assembled delegates backed the establishment of a permanent body, the All-Russian Labor Conference, that convened in plenum a month later (July 11) and produced a resolution with eleven demands the government was to implement without delay; if it demurred, the same resolution called for forming an all-Russia strike committee to declare a prestrike alert on August 17 and, failing government action at that point, a one-day national warning strike for September 7. The ten substantive demands (the eleventh was for TV coverage) amounted to the restoration of the outputs, if not the structures, of the Soviet economy:

1. price controls on state-sector goods and services
2. minimum-wage and pension hikes with monthly indexation
3. average wages for budget personnel pegged at 80 percent of the industrial wage
4. payment of all wage arrears, indexed 100 percent for inflation
5. repeal of privatization legislation; work collectives to determine fates of plants
6. subsidies for food production
7. suspension of bankruptcy legislation
8. a ban on the resale at profit (speculation) of state-produced goods
9. quarterly indexation of enterprise capital funds
10. credits to state enterprises and organizations at 10 percent annual interest[104]

Points 1, 6, and 8 would have restored elements of the old regime-society social contract (however poorly, in the end, the old regime had honored it) and also create shortages in the traditional sense while giving a boost to the black market. Points 5, 7, and 9 aimed at setting the inherited industrial structure in concrete. Point 10, added to the others, would peg credits at an interest rate that in the conditions of 1992 could hardly be more negative and that would wreck, near totally, even weak budget constraints on enterprises. Points 2 and 3 threatened a wage-price spiral without any controls and would make a hash of the price controls of point 1.

However extravagant the whole, individual points did touch on issues salient to many directorial and labor claimants on the government. Budget personnel (point 3) would do better if their pay were indexed even at only 80 percent of industrial wages; the latter were rising as managers rewarded their workers, leaving government to cover the cash demand generated. Points 1, 2, and 8 all in a sense held out a carrot to lower-paid workers and pensioners on whose resentments and pains FNPR sought to capitalize. Points 7 (though bankruptcies were still well over the horizon), 9, and 10 involved keeping enterprises afloat—something all hired labor would see as a good. Point 5 was in line with the worker control–ownership ideas of the STK and the MFP.

These demands got support from the All-Russian Commodity Producers' Conference, a gathering of antigovernment elements of the industrial lobby that met in August. It brought together 2,000 directors, union leaders, local government and agricultural officials to protest the government's second-stage reform plans, which included the beginning of large-scale privatization. Organized under the aegis of the Industrial Union parliamentary faction headed by Yuri Gekht—who in August 1991 had welcomed the coup—it struck a note harsh and uncompromising; compared with the Industrial Union, the RSPP industrialists, headed by Volskii (who had condemned the coup), looked centrist.[105]

On August 15, another plenum of the labor conference discussed further moves toward mounting a strike action and evidently formed the committee called for at the June gathering.[106] FNPR was not, directly, part of this—not a member organization of the conference, although it did enjoy observer status. The union had, in any case, declared a two-month moratorium on strikes on July 17, which, for what it might have been worth, was out of synchronization with the conference's strike target date of September 7.

What came of the labor conference's strike threat? Nothing much. The lack of results had demonstrated the declining appeal of restorationist rhetoric once taken beyond the hothouse contexts of parliamentary and conference politicking and hinted at a developing divergence of interests among elements of the government's opposition.

Going back to the old economic system, even though nearly everyone could probably specify some aspect of it that had worked to their own benefit, was increasingly seen as unrealistic. As a *Moscow News* writer put it, "The common sense of the masses mustn't be underestimated."[107] *Izvestiia* noted with a measure of ironic contempt that the conference "presented an alternative economic program drawn up by a group of economists whose knowledge has not been tapped by the official organs of power" and judged the elements of the package to be "as populist as they are irresponsible."[108]

Nor was across-the-board programmatic rejection of the government's course, rationalized as concern for social justice and industrial survival, popular with the whole industrial lobby. Its members might share with labor unions and populist politicians concerns about staying afloat, but longer-term prospects and looming privatization divided them as well. *Izvestiia* reviewed the recent events:

> The obvious failure of both the attempts made at the end of last week to create a structured opposition to the present authorities—first at the conference of commodity producers, and then at the All-Russia Labor Conference plenum—is the result first and foremost of the patent lack of correlation between the main interest of the vast majority of the body

of directors and the interests of the parliamentarians who organized both events. The leaders of enterprises, especially those that have already been privatized or are on the brink of privatization, are eager to join in calls for a reduction in taxes, the introduction of indexation of circulating capital, and the suspension of the decree on bankruptcy, but patently do not support the idea of forming strike committees at their enterprises or replacing the government and president.[109]

Even though the FNPR had not assumed a high profile in the conference process, it found itself in late summer under renewed attack from the independent unions. FNPR was a federation with at the time about 112 branch and regional components—a big target. The closest (but not very close) organizational approximation the independents had was the earlier-noted Confederation of Labor (KT), founded in the Kuzbass in 1990.[110] Under the KT banner, independent unions convened on August 22, 1992, avowedly to undermine the FNPR's continuing assertion of a right to lead labor as a whole by proposing a consultative council embracing all non-FNPR unions. The NPG, Sotsprof, the Kuzbass council of workers' committees, and smaller regional unions from Perm and from St. Petersburg came together. The gathering also included the airline pilots' union—now distanced from FNPR—and the militant air traffic controllers' union, FPAD.

The FNPR's monopoly control of the social insurance fund was a major bone of contention. To the government, FNPR was a nuisance, one largely financed, of course, by government transfers. A nuisance deprived of a significant proportion of its resources might be less so, and this (along with the feeling that in "normal" countries, governments rather than labor unions handled social benefits) goes a long way toward explaining the government's intermittent, if stalled, attempts to deprive the FNPR of its monopoly. Klochkov continued to denounce any such move as "against the interests of the working people."[111] And the government was clearly not anxious to assume the administrative burdens of FNPR distributional functions.

For the independent unions, getting a share of the funds and the accumulated properties of the VKP-FNPR was a matter of justice and another blow at the old monopoly. Most independent unions were indifferent to assuming the old distribution functions, but depriving FNPR of its advantage in this area would surely reduce its capacity to hang on to its large but weakly affiliated membership, and with it the monetary inflow to FNPR coffers from the 1 percent of wages automatic dues checkoff in the plants. Still, accomplishing this would be hard: A journalist characterized the situation of the average worker long enrolled in the old official union structure, clinging "out of inertia" to the "former AUCCTU which, even if it would not defend him, would at least pay his hospital bills and give him a pension, and, after plenty of grovelling, would give him a coupon for some scarce product."[112] The social insurance struggle would go on with continued sniping from the opposing sides right up to the September–October 1993 political crisis.

Striking and Meaning It: FPAD in August

Another government-labor conflict with dynamics rather different than the set-piece government-FNPR confrontations involved FPAD, the Federation of Air Traffic Controllers' Unions, whose clout had first been manifested in 1991.

FPAD announced a strike for August 15, 1992; its main demand reportedly was for a doubling of wages[113]—remarkable in the contemporary context because air traffic controllers' (ATC) pay was on the average thirty times the 1991 level. FPAD's potential chokehold had led in 1991 to large raises indeed. In mid-1992, pay levels ranged from 14,165 rubles monthly at small airfields to 27,680 at Moscow's domestic airports. Polar and other regional bonuses could boost these levels—to as high as 39,935 rubles in Irkutsk. ATCs, in fact, had been earning more than pilots until a June-July adjustment brought the latter up to par.

Izvestiia, usually sympathetic to non-FNPR unions, gave the FPAD demands a negative review, characterizing them as "point-blank blackmail."[114] Eighty-one of the 135 FPAD locals supported the strike call, according to an FPAD source on August 10.[115] On the same day, the Russian Federation procurator's office declared the planned strike illegal—based, it seemed, not only on public-safety considerations but also on the union's demand that a new state committee on air transport be created that was independent of the transport ministry and its civil aviation department. *Izvestiia* again characterized this as overreach, as "group egotism and blackmail" by "capricious monopolists."[116] But FPAD remained firm, its vice president calling for governmental intervention from higher levels in the air transport department. A meeting was scheduled with Aleksandr Rutskoi, the Russian vice president.[117] FPAD struck out at media coverage of the pay-raise issue. According to the union, the problem was the government's reluctance or inability to compel regional authorities to honor commitments already made in May and the establishment of a rock-solid minimum ATC wage—a rather high one.[118] In the meeting with Rutskoi the union rejected a call to suspend the strike for a month; a second meeting was scheduled as the deadline neared. Local bodies, on whom ATC pay depended, claimed to lack funds. In some cases, "instead of the promised minimum of 15,000 rubles per month, the controllers currently are receiving only half this amount."[119]

FPAD struck at 10 A.M. on August 15. At many airports, military ATCs took over, receiving mixed reviews on their performance (especially from FPAD's chairman!).[120] The strike ended at 9:35 P.M. the same day with union officials citing pressure from the regular police, the paramilitary OMON, and enraged passengers at Moscow's Vnukovo airport. Later, FPAD's vice-chair complained that Rutskoi's assurances of no reprisals against strikers had been false and threatened that if sanctions followed, so might another strike.[121] FPAD indicated plans to take the government to court over nonobservance of the wage agreement.[122]

By August 25—having evidently gained nothing from the strike action but having inflicted a certain amount of chaos (though it is difficult to imagine how Russian domestic airports could be made more chaotic)—FPAD was requesting Yeltsin's direct intervention and calling upon parliament to investigate the August 15 actions of some officials while also beginning to call for another strike "to protest against the persecution of controllers."[123]

Three weeks passed. Positions evidently hardened. A September 19 report said that FPAD was now demanding base pay of about 50,000 rubles monthly and threatening a strike. Deputy Labor Minister Kudiukin expressed exasperation, accusing the union of "deliberately ignoring the adopted norms and procedures" of dispute resolution and of using "strong-arm methods."[124]

FPAD was dealing with a myriad of different situations in different airports and locales. The old Aeroflot had been broken up, its place taken by numerous regional companies that were obviously not inclined or able to honor nationwide wage agreements. On October 29 FPAD voted, preliminarily, for a November 30 strike. Now, the issue was the prosecution and victimization of controllers and, again, the establishment of a new state aviation committee; there was no mention of 50,000 rubles.[125] As the new deadline neared, a Moscow court declared the new strike illegal. FPAD indicated that it would appeal this ruling but also noted that until November 28 and a final vote, the November 30 strike was not a certainty.[126] Last-minute talks failed even after the union was reported (again) to have withdrawn wage demands; the strike was set for December 1.

On that date, at 9:30 A.M. with thirty minutes remaining to the deadline, FPAD suspended the strike; according to its head, a message from the Transport Ministry outlining "specific steps" to end "criminal proceedings and disciplinary measures" had just been received.[127] But a day later, the ministry claimed that the FPAD leaders had caved in because of support that had dwindled, by the deadline, to the ATC unit at only one airport.[128]

The government had more or less held its ground. Had the union lost? Partially, at least. Although wages remained high and legal prosecution was unlikely, job discrimination and some dismissals seemed likely at many airports, for various real or trumped-up reasons.[129] The governmental spine stiffening may have involved several factors. One was Rutskoi's tough style. (After one prestrike meeting in August, he had said that Vladimir Konusenko, the FPAD head, should leave the talks only "in handcuffs."[130]) Another was the unpopularity of FPAD's actions; it was difficult to make any plea of real economic hardship plausible given FPAD compensation compared to other sectors. Fear of the consequences of a strike in this case may have pushed the government to make arrangements, as before, to replace FPAD with military ATCs. The government had an out of its own: However committed the ATCs were, they were small in number. The government could mobilize substitutes to take their place; it could not, should it come to it, replace Russia's coal miners! The FPAD conflict at least had real issues, real objectives, and a real shape, unlike the ongoing low-intensity conflict in which the Yeltsin-Gaidar government was enmeshed with the FNPR.

October 1992: Anniversary Militancy

As October came, the two-month FNPR strike moratorium declared in August was coming to an end. FNPR now began to prepare another round of October days of protest like those it had launched in 1991. What massive labor protests or threats were supposed to accomplish against a government whose policy was already somewhat moderated is not clear. Through 1992 thus far, after all, FNPR had not been able to deploy large numbers of workers in truly organized job actions. As a *Trud* commentary suggested, FNPR bluster about how the government was trying to drive it out of public life and recurrent announcements of forthcoming muscle flexings hardly conveyed impressions of strength, especially when, at shop-floor level, FNPR locals, to whom the central leadership was paying very little attention, were acquiescing to short-time and lay-off arrangements.[131]

Grassroots weakness and the shop-floor mood were surely in the minds of FNPR leaders in October even if they put a rather brave face on it. In an interview, FNPR deputy chair Vasili Romanov sounded confident of broad-based worker support: "People," he said, "will follow our lead now."

> When we held a poll in August (a very big one, beyond comparison with the data of other sociological services), 99 percent of respondents were ready for collective forms of action, but only 6 percent were in favor of strikes. Now 100 percent are ready for collective forms of protest and a considerable percentage, at least one-third, are in favor of declaring an all-Russian strike unless the government meets our demands after 24 October. The situation is changing fundamentally.[132]

Then, in response to the interviewer's question about "triggering an explosion": "But social tension has reached the limit. We are not proposing spontaneous action and destruction. We are proposing sitting down at the negotiating table for the last time. We are giving the government a chance. Unless it embarks on serious talks, our actions will be harsh."[133]

If only 6 percent of FNPR members had supported a strike in an August poll of unspecified method (earlier, it had been reported that 10 percent of the 10 million workers polled had indicated their readiness[134]), how had it been ascertained that now one-third did? No answer or any comment on the two-thirds evidently unready to strike was given.

One-third of FNPR's 60-million-plus members, could they be delivered, was still no inconsiderable number. Romanov's call to go to the negotiating table "for the last time" was likely aimed at leaving FNPR, as well as the government, a way out. Both sides duly headed for this exit via the month-long process of *bilateral* government-FNPR negotiations outside the RTK (the special conciliation commission noted in Chapter 2). The government thus was spared a general strike and FNPR the embarrassment of calling for one and dealing with the consequences had the call failed.

The Misnik Defection: FNPR's Broken Branch

The hardest hit FNPR took in late 1992 was not from the government or the independents but from one of its branch unions, whose head sat on the RTK—the 2-million-plus-member Union of Mining and Metallurgy Workers (PGMR) under Boris Misnik. As the FNPR leadership was gearing up for its October protests, a plenum of the PGMR voted to exit the FNPR. Misnik criticized the FNPR's "political image," cited his union's agreement with many government policies FNPR opposed,[135] and characterized the FNPR leadership's policy as "effectively geared to abandoning the policy of a market economy and returning the Russian economy into the fold of state control, especially in the spheres of economic links, prices, and wages."[136]

Misnik's bill of particulars was lengthy. FNPR had "all the worst traits" of the old AUCCTU. Sectoral-branch and regional organizations overlapped, and the large (about 100 members) presidium ("80 percent of whom are former party apparatchiks") was too large for policymaking, which fell to a nonstatutory fifteen-member executive committee. "Representatives of local organizations are presented with prepared documents at plenums" in violation of what were supposed to be the rules of a bottom-up labor federation. FNPR policy was "fundamentally unacceptable," since the PGMR "has recently been fighting for a market economy."

> The directors in our sector are no longer running to Gaidar with requests. Questions of prices and pay are decided at plant level: People can see where the money came from and where it has gone. ... We believe that it is possible and necessary to reach agreement with the government and find compromises, and not act like the [FNPR] leaders: Sit down at the negotiating table on 20 October, call people out on the streets to attend protest rallies on 24 October, and return to the negotiations 27 October.[137]

Misnik implied that FNPR had scheduled its one-day protest for October 24 so that it would coincide with the noisy meeting of the "reactionary National Salvation Front" and thus inflate its own apparent scale; he promised as well that now PGMR would make its bid for a share of the funds and functions of FNPR. "We intend to secure full participation in running the Social Insurance Fund, which the bureaucrats are tucking into at the moment."[138]

FNPR hit back. In a salvo in *Rabochaia Tribuna,* it asserted that many of PGMR's local affiliates had indeed participated in the October 24 protests; that some, not pleased by the defection decision, had sought reaffiliation with FNPR; that Misnik, whose rhetoric had been tough as any in the October 1991 days of protest, was now a "turncoat."[139]

Having afforded Misnik space, *Izvestiia* now did the same for Klochkov, who denied that FNPR had scheduled its protest in alignment with the National Salvation Front and then accused Misnik of a sell-out.

> In my view the position of the leadership of the Mining and Metallurgical Industry Workers' Trade Union and the real reason for it are perfectly explicable. The independent trade unions [that is, FNPR] in Russia are gaining in strength now. They make an inconvenient partner for those who do not like to conduct an equal dialogue with the opposition. There are people in the government who benefit from strike-breaking in trade union ranks. It would be more convenient for them to deal with split and weakened trade unions.[140]

The FNPR newspaper then published the dissent of the leader of the Rostov affiliate of the PGMR, who referred to a rule that only a congress rather than a simple plenum of the union could legally vote for disaffiliation from FNPR. He said that no one had listened to his objections. Another union official from Norilsk accused Misnik of arrogance and thanked FNPR for allowing his large local (about 40,000 members) to rejoin as an associate member. As to Misnik more generally, he had indeed sat on the RTK, "only there, as far as I know, he more often supported the governmental than the union side. And so it is in this case."[141]

But Misnik had hardly been a government lapdog on the RTK. Distrustful of the government's intentions in forming a social partnership (as had been at the time the NPG and the Moscow regional union council—Shmakov's MFP—with its syndicalist orientation), he had been a vocal complainant early on about RTK procedures and had engaged in a shouting match with Burbulis across the table.[142] Now he replied in a letter to the FNPR's paper. On the matter of PGMR locals siding with FNPR, the response was, essentially, "prove it!" *Rabochaia Tribuna* operated "in the worst traditions of the Soviet press." Indeed, when PGMR left FNPR, it did not have or claim to have unanimous support for the action from its membership; the decision was made "by an absolute and qualified majority, and this shows real democracy." The FNPR "today has turned into a politicized organization, objectively opposing the course of reform. FNPR is not able … to reform itself internally."[143] Misnik's letter shared space with two pro-FNPR "dissidents." His motivation, they asserted, was political; he was less concerned with FNPR structure than with the disposition of social insurance funds. They accused him of not understanding that a trade union should be in opposition to "any government," whether a "Gaidar government or one dominated by the National Salvation Front."[144]

Finally, a few days later, the *Rabochaia Tribuna* editors gave the official version. Misnik felt FNPR should pursue the path of reaching agreements with the government. But it had, and such agreements had come to nothing. The government accused FNPR of trying to dominate the labor side of the RTK under the mantle of workers' defense. Well, FNPR was by far the largest union; yet government treated it as just "one among many." The government, it seemed, wanted more and smaller unions so that it could divide and conquer. Smaller unions were weaker, likely to get closer to the government and to cultivate "fraternal relations with the Big Boss."[145]

Misnik, then, was an ally of the government—similar to Sotsprof. Politics was behind it all, but politics was not an element of FNPR's activity. Deals between unions and government were suspect unless FNPR made the deals. The Misnik defection would not prove fatal to FNPR. But what had been called his schism had evidently taken out over 2 million members, a number likely larger than the total membership of the independent unions that uneasily shared seats on the labor side of the RTK with FNPR.

The Road Not Taken

The unions had various agendas. The miners (NPG), the air traffic controllers (FPAD), the airline pilots (FPALS), and, by the year's end, Misnik's PGMR were economistic in the Samuel Gompers sense: They wanted "more." They accepted the broad directions of the Yeltsin government and supported it politically while trying to get what they could from whatever combination of government as employer and government as political authority applied best. Sotsprof, with its rather different profile, actively supported the government's political and economic programs— in this respect the recurrent FNPR accusations were not wholly off the mark—while looking to sign up workers in various venues, often by provoking defections from FNPR. In organizing, it enjoyed a certain amount of success, including elements of some of the Moscow subway system workforce, but its main activity seemed to be as a service and legal advice center for would-be organizers of new unions. As opposed to many other non-FNPR unions, it was legally registered as a trade union and could offer itself as an umbrella to potential affiliates—and thus increase its own membership.[146]

FNPR, for its part, kept up its criticisms of government policy, its complaints about the implementation of virtually every reform measure, its calls for the replacement of *some* members of the government, and its demands for various measures to ease the pains of transition that the government could not, really, afford. But in the end, it cannot be said that FNPR ever articulated any clear alternative to the government's policy. It criticized, demanded, and threatened regarding particular issues and policies while avoiding a clear no to the market—the pseudoneutrality noted earlier. FNPR had no larger social project, and labor unions without projects have little to distinguish them from any other rent-seeking group.[147] Such, in fact, was the way the government had treated FNPR—as a rent (advantage, concession, handout) seeker.

There was a project available, which none of the unions adopted wholesale, though elements of it made appearances in the programs of some of them. It was, quintessentially, a third way: an anarcho-syndicalist, industrial democracy, workers' control, democracy-without-the-market recipe for the future. To a degree, it was the project of the national Union of Labor Collectives (STK); it was rather explicitly the project of the small Moscow-based Party of Labor (PT), founded in 1991 by the joint efforts of Shmakov's FNPR-affiliated MFP, the Confederation of Anarcho-Syndicalists, and the Socialist Party (SP)—a small, postcommunist, left-wing but anti-Stalinist body.[148]

Though a nonstarter (at least in the times with which this work deals), the program is worth exploring through the words of some of its advocates because of the fears it points up, the issues it raises about building the market on the basis of a society and economy organized for so many years according to antimarket principles, and the context it provides in which to place the Yeltsin-Gaidar government's early choice of economic objectives. The program offered a critique of the capitalism third-way advocates saw being transferred from the West to Russia, of who was imposing it, and of why it was being imposed. Who, broadly, was the government—after 1991, Yeltsin's but before it Gorbachev's—which in radical economic reform had, in Boris Rakitskii's words, "launched an economic attack on the people and [driven] 100 percent of workers, employees and peasants to the poverty level." In this broad indictment, the government was somehow the instrument of the industrial managers who were demanding tighter restrictions on workers and on democratic processes. Such had been one aim of the August 1991 coup plotters (yet somehow, as Rakitskii saw it, their interests had been taken care of by both Gorbachev and Yeltsin as well).[149]

The signs had been evident. The 1987 law on the state enterprise had included, as noted before, some worker-control elements; by 1990, these were gutted in line with the agenda change to a transition to the market. This was seen as a pretext for the throttling of nascent elements of industrial democracy and for "forcible privatization." The beneficiaries would be the nomenklatura, and the "private owners of shady capital."[150]

Allied with these, however, was a large segment of the intelligentsia—economists and others. The democratic political movement that had emerged under perestroika and glasnost was largely of the intelligentsia. It had little contact or sympathy with the workers and their perspectives. Bourgeois-democratic in aspirations, at least, in its opposition to the old barracks pseudosocialism, it saw capitalist enterprise and hired labor as the alternative, not industrial democracy.[151]

Terms such as "bourgeois-democratic" were, to a degree, labels used as much in a polemic as an analytical sense; there was, after all, plenty to polemicize about. A more nuanced treatment of the various elements flowing into the social mix of the new masters of Russia was that of the veteran labor historian O. I. Shkaratan. Partisans of industrial democracy would have agreed with much of his political map, though not necessarily with his diagnosis of where broader support for anti-industrial democracy came from.[152] In this version, big industrial managers were not, on the whole, on the side of the August coup. But plenty of the old state and party provincial apparat had, since 1987–1988 and the licensing of cooperatives, been engaged in attempting to convert its power into private property rights. State, party, and Komsomol funds were being laundered into the private economy, aiming at the creation of an underground party economy.

These nomenklatura elements, along with the bosses of military industry, were for the market but for a market of monopolies. But they were not the whole of the new rich: engineers, scholars, and scientists had also in significant numbers turned their talents to making money in ways long denied them, in addition to less educated small businessmen and entrepreneurs. These people, unconnected to the old power elites, were neither so well organized nor so rooted in history as the other, nomenklatura, component of the new rich. These latter, in Shkaratan's view of late 1991, derived support from millions of functionaries in the agroindustrial complex who were hanging on to control of this large sector and gradually appropriating effective control of the land itself. Millions of workers in the state distribution system as well, interested in retaining their control over goods of various sorts, resisted any democratization of the economy; and finally, similar millions of functionally illiterate unskilled and semiskilled urban workers had thrown in with the nomenklatura. (It was, presumably, not the latter upon whom syndicalists would seek to found industrial democracy, but their view of the workers as a whole was itself broad enough to anticipate a large lumpen element in blue-collar Russia.)

Why was this all happening? Partly, it was driven by crude self-interest and cupidity, the desire to get rich as manifested in people with the power to alter or exploit situations to their advantage in ways the masses could not. But partly as well, the bourgeois-democratic transformation was driven among the thinking and writing strata by beliefs, conclusions, and positions on the meaning of the past Soviet experience and on the path to be taken toward the future. These visions took little account of what might happen to other strata of the population on that path. Thus the democratic opposition, the experts who could produce in the Soviet twilight the 500-days plan for rapid economic change (and, presumably, the authors of 1992 shock therapy), were insensitive, in fact hostile, to the people.[153] The democrats had taken the outcome of the barracks variety of Soviet socialism as proof that no socialism worked. Capitalism was the needed, decisive turn. Socialist property was one of the legacies of a misconceived quest for utopia, and if it now stood in the way of the future, get rid of it, root and branch. That this would only substitute private for earlier state exploitation of workers was no concern of the democrats.[154]

Despite the critique, partisans of third-way industrial democracy seemed close to conceding that capitalism, however bad an idea, was one whose time had come. In late 1991–early 1992, the bourgeois-democratic line became the dominant concept; it was supported by the new nomenklatura, the emergent entrepreneurial strata, and even by some working people who preferred nonstate employment. Old and new bosses shared desires to shed the obligations of maintaining full employment and were ready to shift to others the burden of coping with the unprecedented problems of the economic transition.[155] Five years of the CPSU's attempts to defend itself had created deep anti-[barrack] socialist feelings among the masses and finally a vacuum that both the humanistic and technical intelligentsia, as well as some "politicized workers' groups," filled with bourgeois-democratic ideas.[156] "Almost all serious researchers are now enamored of the liberal point of view, which is very far from that of the working people."[157]

What was wrong with the bourgeois-democratic program, and what was to be put in its place? The full answer combined two elements. First, it offered a moral critique of the capitalism that was coming with its anticipated injustices; second, it included a pragmatic critique that asserted that the liberal, capitalist, bourgeois-democratic project, whatever its record elsewhere, could not work in Russia, in Russian conditions.

On the moral side, it was a rejection of the economic individualism of the market and market institutions. This was not simply a matter of disgust at "the dirt and amorality characteristic of a period of initial capital accumulation"[158] but the rejection of the principle of "freedom for the strong, support for the weak" (which sounds rather social democratic) as not good enough. The state had no right to remove itself from social protection: "Our fundamental demand is full employment and a state guarantee of the provision of work." The state "must" put an end to inflation. Since, after all, workers had created, had already paid for, the productive wealth inherited from the Soviet past, "we will resolutely oppose demands for any buyouts by working people." The government had no right to get out of consumer production, rather an obligation to stay in to compete with the emerging private sector.[159] Thus "our new theoreticians" needed a firm rebuke, since they were heading in so wrong a direction, "and this after many decades of recognition of the theoretical worth of the labor theory of value by all progressive science in both East and West!"[160]

Russia could not completely copy Western ways; no country can become a reproduction of another. But this seemed to be the direction of Yeltsin's program.[161] Liberal-democratic views that minimized the state's social obligations might work in stable economies, but not in Russia. The state's obligation to secure employment should be legislatively embodied even if this involved the repudiation of recent legislation. The state had to do "what no one else will do."[162]

Second, the critics offered a more or less full-blown defense of a self-managed, worker-control economy cum political democracy. Arguing (rather overoptimistically) from some Western examples of employee-owned enterprises, a theorist for the STK disposed of some anticipated objections: If the labor collectives or owners of plants performed poorly, society would not be called upon to bail them out as the state now compelled it to do. Worker ownership, against many expectations, "may restrain wage increases, especially under inflationary conditions, when it is more advantageous for collective owners to invest their resources in material assets than to receive money that is depreciating in value." Experts from the International Monetary Fund (IMF), the Organization for Economic Development (OECD), the World Bank, and the European Bank for Reconstruction and Development (EBRD) might regard the record of worker management as lamentable, and the connection between industrial democracy and efficiency might not be linear. But this, to its advocates, did not mean that their program could not work. The third way remained open with compelling reasons to pursue it.[163]

However one might characterize the third way (I readily confess my lack of sympathy, along the lines of Vaclav Klaus's observation that the third way leads to the third world), it was a vision that, if adopted by labor unions, would have constituted a project explicitly counter to the government's. FNPR had its reasons—heritage, cynicism, distrust?—for staying away from it; indeed it would be hard to recognize a place for FNPR in a world thus reconstructed. The independent unions had their various points of disagreement and rejection as well, although many of their members—miners, perhaps, especially—would have agreed with some of the premises. But to many, these problems were real. The "democrats"—in quotes or not—were not overly sensitive to workers qua workers. But as some counseled them, they ignored workers only at their own peril. No anarcho-syndicalist, the labor specialist Leonid Gordon warned democratic independent trade union leaders in 1993 of taking too long-term a view, of assuming that "when there is conflict between short-term and strategic interests, it is necessary to give the preference to strategic objectives, to support the government at any price. The call to demand from the government a prohibition on strikes is nearly inaudible from the workers' side, but these are popular among politicians, among them those who were advanced by the labor movement." In the volatile labor movement, taking such a position could "lead to a rapid fall in the influence of the democratic wing and the strengthening of the influence of its opponents."[164]

On its face, Gordon's advice was reasonable enough, and leaders would indeed find it hard not to follow as their members grew more disenchanted. But a realistic view of the roots of such tensions raised the question of how the necessary long-term objectives might find any broad-based support at all unless union leaders and others continued to argue their necessity.

Summing Up

Thus had interunion rivalries and politics taken shape in 1992, a shape that would largely persist in 1993. Matters of principle were involved, but not of explicitly distinct visions. FNPR, really, had no grand vision. The independents in the main had visions—a rough one of a post-Soviet political system and a probably rougher one of a market economy in which their people could make their way. The pro-government, pro-market positions of the NPG leadership, and their relative ability to deploy their membership, was one thing. But, as Stephen Crowley has suggested,[165] miners' understanding of what market and privatization meant was a peculiar one. They were convinced that they had been exploited under and by the old regime and saw in the (antithetical) market an escape; the base of their claim to justice was in fact a labor theory of value that linked the claim to their role in material production—hence their contempt for managers and auxiliaries who produced nothing. Privatization meant privatization for the miners, who could then enjoy the fruits of their labor through charging their own price for coal. Wage work for outside owners and investors was not the future as they conceived it. In a sense, this consciousness had elements of third-way thinking at its core but was disassociated from the communist or socialist labels that had been totally discredited by the Soviet regime, which they now saw as major exploiter and appropriator of their product. Sotsprof had yet a broader perspective, but it was a fuzzy one that combined organizing with political activities, some of which seemingly had little to do with labor.

FNPR was burdened with its old-regime provenance. Try as it might to assert its renewal, it still leaned too hard on its inheritance as an entitlement to dominate. This made it a target for both the other unions and the new government. As we have seen, accusations of bad faith were a constant; strikes and labor actions rarely involved interunion cooperation. For the independents, FNPR was not pro-worker but antigovernment. For FNPR, the independents were pro-government but not concerned with the working class as a whole. FNPR spoke loudly from its majority of labor seats on the RTK, but its message got a tepid reception from its tens of millions of toilers. It still relied heavily on its welfare and distribution functions to retain its membership—and not, on the whole, unsuccessfully. For all of its calls to action, FNPR's strength was perhaps greatest in the large industrial plants that still had some benefits (however reduced) to distribute (however manipulatively) to their workforces—and where, consequently, it was the FNPR organization that did the distributing. Such plants, as we have seen, were unlikely sites for authentic strike action.

The independents had fewer soldiers. But on the whole they were more committed, whether they were small groups that, like the air traffic controllers, performed a critical function and demanded pay in line with its importance or the miners, whose readiness for militant action had to do both with grievances of a glaring sort and management's relative lack of both paternalistic resources and repressive capacity. Members of these unions could be more reliably deployed for the time, but the linkages between leaders and rank and file, given what often amounted to very different understandings of key ideas, were not bulletproof.

There existed, then, no single social partner on the labor side, but recurrent cacophony. On the whole, for government and those on the employers' side with a stake in RTK processes, a weak and internally divided labor side was probably as attractive an alternative as a businesslike one that could both organize and discipline its constituents in classic corporatist fashion.

4

Renewal or Exhaustion?
Trilateralism and Conflict in 1993

BY THE DECEMBER 1992 CONGRESS of People's Deputies session, the Yeltsin government was in retreat; confrontations in the Congress and the Supreme Soviet made for tougher going for the reformists in the cabinet. It was in this context that Gaidar—architect of shock therapy, mainstay of the reformist team since 1991, deputy premier, and for the past months acting prime minister—was sacrificed to antireform forces.

Yeltsin left to the Congress the choice of a new prime minister from among alternatives he named. The post went to Viktor Chernomyrdin, the gas industry's former boss and one of the industrialist trio added to the cabinet earlier in the year. Chernomyrdin was, in background and general public stance, hardly the thoroughgoing marketeer. Through 1993, he would prove somewhat unpredictable: Early on he called for price controls, then abandoned this position; he criticized privatization procedures under Anatoly Chubais without really posing major obstacles to them; and he generally eyed his reformist cabinet colleagues from the standpoint of a former manager of production who had the (presumably relevant) hands-on experience the economists lacked.[1] But in the various conflicts of the year, he would support Yeltsin.

"Getting to Yes" in 1993

Within this more conservative-gradualist economic and political context, so different from the takeoff of January 2, 1992, where was corporatism? The RTK had dropped out of sight in late 1992, such attention as there was being largely devoted to the bilateral government-FNPR conciliation talks. Whether the RTK actually existed in late 1992 and early 1993 was not clear even to the presumably well informed.[2] There was certainly no evidence that a provision of the 1992 General Agreement that work on concluding the 1993 General Agreement should begin no later than October 1, 1992, had been adhered to; it hardly could have been with the bilateral talks going on.

During what seemed publicly at least to be this recess of the RTK, a meeting took place between Chernomyrdin and the FNPR's Klochkov.[3] Gaidar and Burbulis were out of the picture; Shokhin, of course, remained in the cabinet but with the portfolio for foreign economic relations. Deputy Labor Minister Kudiukin, another of FNPR's favorite targets, was on his way out. Under constant FNPR attack for his Sotsprof connections, he was also criticized for his developing connection to the new Moscow office of the Free Trade Union Institute, sponsored by the AFL-CIO.[4]

Good feelings seemed to prevail at the Chernomyrdin-Klochkov meeting: Both, after all, were former apparatchiks, their experiences and outlooks different from the Shokhins and Gaidars. Chernomyrdin's early-expressed positions on price controls via limitations of profit margins, even if abandoned under pressure from cabinet reformists and derision from serious economists, were the sort of measures FNPR had been requesting. According to the government press secretary, "The sides found mutual understanding on a broad range of problems—from inflation and hidden unemployment to ineffectiveness of work. ... Intelligently organized and fairly paid labor plus tough discipline at all levels—there is the formula for resolving Russia's current problems."[5] Behind this boilerplate, as it would turn out, much had changed in the business of trilateralism. The RTK was rechartered—late, it seemed—for 1993.[6] On February 26, it held its first session of the year, ostensibly with a commitment to a less rhetorical, more businesslike style.[7] The FNPR's Romanov observed that a union draft of a 1993 general agreement did not contain the "previous slogans and appeals" and that wages were the main concern for 1993. First Deputy Premier Vladimir Shumeiko, of the industrialists' trio, would serve as coordinator of the RTK. To the FNPR, he surely looked better than Burbulis and might be expected to generate a better attendance record. (Once, after it had been announced to the commission that Burbulis was sick and would be absent, the same day's TV showed him playing on the government team in a football match against personnel of the Moscow mayor's office![8])

Shumeiko insisted on getting results at the February 26 meeting, calling for the signing of the 1993 General Agreement on the early date of March 5. FNPR took credit for getting the government to agree that all its decrees on labor relations should be subject to prior agreement on the labor and employer sides of the trilateral. The meeting ended, nonetheless, on a note reminiscent of the early stages of 1992's shakedown cruise with Shumeiko rushing out "to a rather more 'heated' conversation—with miners prepared to strike."[9]

The RTK survived. But it was not the same body that had sat in 1992, especially on the labor side of the trilateral, and this had much to do with the positive attitude Klochkov had expressed. A very much pro-FNPR piece on the 1993 opening day criticized the 1992 composition on the familiar grounds that it had included "three functionaries of the 'Sotsprof,' uniting people of whatever unknown branches. (Earlier 'Sotsprof' was a political organization.) And it was this trio, with which representatives of the Independent Miners' Union [NPG] as it is called, frequently allied themselves, muddying the water, carrying on long, vacant conversations."[10] But now, Sotsprof was gone. Of twenty-eight seats for "members and their deputies" on the labor side of the 1993 RTK, FNPR now had twenty-one on a new principle of representation that depended on the size of a union's membership. Sotsprof, from its three seats of fourteen in 1992, had "received not a single mandate," and NPG chair Sergeev, out of solidarity with Sotsprof, had declined an invitation to join the 1993 RTK.

This, at least, was the FNPR version of how it had come not only to dominate the labor side in 1993 but to accomplish the removal of its main opponents. How this all had been engineered was impossible to gauge from the contemporary media coverage, which remained thin. (Klochkov was quite right in noting that the RTK's work was "almost uncovered in media of mass information, especially television. ... And people in their overwhelming majority do not know that there is such an institution."[11])

What had actually happened?[12] Essentially, FNPR decided to push for a more strictly (numerically) proportional share of the labor seats for 1993: Given its numbers and those of the NPG and other independent unions, it should on this basis get the veto-proof majority on the labor side that it had lacked in 1992. Kudiukin suggested another principle that, not surprisingly, would have left FNPR with fewer seats. Another suggested compromise involved a formula that would give half the seats to FNPR, the other half to other unions, whose numbers seemed to be growing rapidly. (Not all of these unions were reliable government allies or FNPR antagonists, as had been Sotsprof, NPG, and the PGMR, the latter having left FNPR at the end of 1992.)

But 1993 was a new year with a new prime minister. Shumeiko, detailed to be RTK coordinator, and Labor Minister Melikian were inclined more toward FNPR and its position. This tilt, characterized by one analyst as manifesting the "strengthening of pro-nomenklatura tendencies in the new cabinet of V. S. Chernomyrdin,"[13] signaled a kind of insider deal in the making. With help, or at least benign neglect by the government, FNPR had arranged a meeting on January 18 between its representatives and those of "some other unions"; whether all of its old opponents were included is not clear (see further on). This meeting, it is likely, was the event deputy FNPR chair Romanov referred to months later when he said that in January, FNPR had proposed the Consultative

Council of Russian Trade Unions [Konsultativnyi Sovet Rossiiskikh Prof-
soiuzov]; this was founded, initially, by "representatives of 14 parallel-
functioning trade unions, and later on—another 14."[14] FNPR had thus
collected some non-FNPR unions not represented on the 1992 RTK, several of which resented the three seats that had gone to Sotsprof: These
included the former AUCCTU railroad workers' union that had not
joined FNPR at its founding, the trade union of cooperative medium and
small business workers, and the Congress of Russian Trade Unions
(KRP).[15] A January 20 account reported that sixty trade unions—half part
of FNPR, half not, had met and adopted the proportional principle and
had allocated seats to seven unions (FNPR and six others, generally from
the list just noted but *including* NPG) to fill the fourteen seats. (There remains some confusion about the twenty-eight seats including
"deputies," versus the fourteen, which does seem to be the number both
in 1992 and 1993). According to this source, Sergeev of the NPG was not
pleased with this and, joined by Mokhov and Efremenko of Sotsprof,
Misnik of the miners and metallurgists, and Konusenko of FPAD, exited
the meeting in protest.[16]

The independents so troublesome to the FNPR in 1992 had been
slower to act, apparently assuming that a reactivated RTK for 1993 would
have much the same players as before. They met on January 21—among
them FPAD, the NPG, the unions of seamen and dockworkers, the mining and metallurgy union, and evidently Sotsprof and the pilots' union,
which had also been allocated one seat[17]—and constituted themselves
as a consultative *committee,* nominating their own representatives to the
labor side of the RTK table.

They then appealed to Yeltsin and Chernomyrdin to bar FNPR representatives from sitting at the table on legal grounds. Referring to Article 5
of the Russian Federation law on collective contracts and agreements,
they argued that FNPR belonged to the category of "organizations or organs, created or financed by employers [or] political parties" prohibited
by that article from negotiating in the name of workers. The reasoning
was based on Klochkov's participation in the leading organs of the Civic
Union—itself largely the creature of the employers' RSPP (the Russian
Union of Industrialists and Entrepreneurs).[18] In essence, the independents were touching on the issue of what sorts of organizations could be
legally recognized as labor unions; there were advantages to being so
registered. Sotsprof, despite its somewhat unusual configuration, was so
registered. FNPR had attacked the rationale for this, and now in turn was
targeted by its opponents. FNPR complained to *Trud* about its coverage
of these dealings and threatened lawsuits.[19] But the committee of outsiders was outflanked, and the legal challenge failed. Shumeiko communicated a decision to organize the labor side as FNPR proposed. Of the

core fourteen seats, FNPR unions would have eleven, and one each would go to the KRP, the railroad workers' union, and the airline pilots' union (which had been on the 1992 RTK).

Whether the government now saw merit in FNPR's constant proposals to moderate reforms or decided to let FNPR and its allies dominate the labor side to set them up as blameworthy when deadlocks arose,[20] it would get bad reviews for this move from critics on the reform side in fall 1993 as the country moved toward the September-October crisis and bloodshed in central Moscow. "In January 1993 the government ignored numerous warnings, taking to itself as 'social partners' the Federation of Independent Trade Unions of Russia (and factually the trade-union nomenklatura of the former Shelepinite-Yanaevite AUCCTU, struggling for survival). On September 22 this 'partner' confirmed its loyalty to the Stalinist-Brezhnevite-Khasbulatovite Constitution."[21]

To bring up not only Yanaev, as Gorbachev's vice president one of the major coup plotters of 1991, and before that AUCCTU head, but also the ghost of another AUCCTU head, Aleksandr Shelepin, whose hard-line qualities had been such as to see him bounced from the Brezhnev politburo in the 1970s and sent into political obscurity, was to render a harsh judgment indeed. In this variety of hindsight, Shumeiko, working under a prime minister who preferred to deal with the old-style personalities of the FNPR, "placed his wager on the official trade unions—and lost"; while the new free trade unions, when the government found itself in trouble, "all the same came to [its] aid, like some sort of fellow-democrat. ... Playing games with the FNPR brought [the government] no dividends."[22]

But this was all still in the future. In January, the die had been cast; the government *had* found itself a different sort of partner at the RTK table. One might raise the question of whether the February 5, 1993, decree that rechartered the RTK for the year, a very short statement, actually covered the very-much-altered body;[43] but the independent unions decided against further pressuring a government they still, generally, supported.

Rubles, Conflict, and Social Insurance

Before the events that shaped the new labor side of the RTK, the FNPR had raised another issue in opposition to the government, in the course of which it generated a set of organizational allies whose composition may again help understand something of the state of play in 1993. On January 9, FNPR accused the government of a "preliminary bombardment" in advance of what it characterized as a "general offensive" against the union. At issue was legislation the government planned to introduce in the Supreme Soviet on January 11 to establish the Russian State Assistance Fund and thereby deprive unions of their "right to administer social insurance."[24] The inherited near monopoly of the FNPR and the rubles of the social insurance fund were again at issue. An appeal to the Congress of People's Deputies was drafted and signed not only by Klochkov but by representatives of thirteen other unions and organizations. As the appeal went, "practically all trade union organizations of Russia"—with the exception of Sotsprof—backed continuing union control of social insurance. The relevant provision of the Russian labor code had been challenged three times already by the government and thrice upheld.

Some parliamentary fireworks followed with Klochkov condemning the "attempt of certain definite political circles, making use of parliament, to remove the unions from active participation in the social sphere, [take] from the workers" control over worker resources, and place "all their incomes and social guarantees in the hands of state officials."[25] But the issue, for the time, sunk into the gray parliamentary goo. An enabling law for a new fund was to be worked out by parliament's commission on social policy within three months; FNPR complained that in any case, this same commission had been charged with coming up with a new law by October 15, 1992, and had not managed this;[26] and indeed, "discussions were continuing" on the matter in May.[27]

But what were those unions and organizations whose representatives had added their signatures to Klochkov's in the appeal against the government's plans to strip unions (primarily FNPR) of the social insurance funds and functions? The list[28] is an interesting one.

N. Solovev	Russian Confederation of Free Trade Unions
Iu. Sedykh	Trade Union of Cashier (*inkassatsii*) Workers of the Russian Federation
V. Klebanov	Association of Free Trade Unions for Workers' Defense (SMOT)
V. Krivopuskov	Russian Trade Union of Workers of Exchanges, Commercial, Farming, and Other Entrepreneurial Structures
G. Dominiak	Trade Union of the Aviation Staff of the Russian Federation
B. Kremnev	Federation of Trade Unions of Workers of Civil Aviation
V. Kurochkin	Trade Union of Aviation Service Workers (PRIAS)
Iu. Kosarev	Congress of Russian Trade Unions
I. Khazanov	Confederation of Free Trade Unions
B. Fedorov	Association of Free Trade Unions of Small, International, Leasing, Joint-Stock, Individual and Other Enterprises and Organizations (MAKKIP)

A. Goptar   Independent Trade Union of Military Personnel
T. Shtukina   All-Russian Trade Union (Edinenie)
Iu. Ass   Moscow Union of Collectives and Citizens for People's
                   Privatization

It is surely fair to observe that this list is not thick with names that qualify as household words even for students of the labor scene; it is an interesting mix.

Though FNPR made much of the preeminence its large numbers gave it over other unions (even as it declined, by its own estimates, from 72.6 million members in the beginning of 1992 to 64.3 million a year later[29]) and of the government's obligation to take it seriously because of this, there is no evidence that the other groups on this list represent the numbers, not to mention the clout of the miners' NPG or the 2-million-plus members of the mining and metallurgy union that left FNPR in 1992.

The first striking name on the list is that of Vladimir Klebanov, a name that echoes from the Brezhnevian past of regime versus dissidents. His organization is listed in the original as "Assotsiatsiia Svobodnykh Profsoiuzov Zashchiti Rabochikh 'SMOT,'" which clarifies and confuses to equal degrees. Klebanov emerged to public notice in 1978 as the founder of the dissident labor union Association of Free Trade Unions of Workers in the Soviet Union (Assotsiatsiia Svobodnykh Profsoiuzov Trudiashchikhsia v Sovetskom Soiuze), which was quickly suppressed.[30] In the late 1980s, under the different Gorbachev dispensation, a successor organization—Free Trade Unions–United All-Union Central Committee of Free Trade Unions (Svobodnye Profsoiuzy–Obedinennyi Vsesoiuznyi Tsentralnyi Komitet Svobodnykh Professionalnykh Soiuzov) emerged.[31]

But the affiliated SMOT organization listed on Klebanov's 1993 signature line of the appeal to the CPD raises other questions. SMOT (Svobodnoe Mezhprofessionalnoe Obedinenie Trudiashchikhsiia—Free Interprofessional Association of Workers) was another dissident organization of laborite coloration, founded in 1978 and given more to the publication of samizdat bulletins on labor and social issues than organizational work. It, too, quickly was forced underground, reemerging somewhat reorganized in 1988.[32] I see no evidence of Klebanov's association with SMOT in the 1970s or late 1980s or of SMOT's with any organization in which Klebanov, about whose courage in bad times there was no doubt, was active. After the Soviet collapse, he received little credit for his earlier activities in the 1990s—indeed, he lived quite marginally in Moscow—and his signature in 1993 presumably stands for something less than a large organization.[33]

Among the other signatories, three—Dominiak, Kremnev, and Kurochkin—connected with aviation-related bodies are hard to categorize. The unions are not, seemingly, affiliates of Malinovskii's largely independent pilots' union. Kremnev's seems to be the "remainder" of the old official aviation industry union, and PRIAS a union of technical service and aviation engineering personnel.[34] The armed forces union, headed by signatory Goptar, was revealed later in the year to be essentially a paper organization with a lot of bluff.[35]

The point here is that the non-FNPR supporters of the appeal to parliament on the social insurance fund constituted a peculiar lot. There were too many unions listed to constitute the seven that in a twenty-eight-union reading of RTK representation, direct and deputized might have supplemented the FNPR's 21 seats.

Organizations with grandiose names sprout like mushrooms after rain in the new Russia: Some of those listed may be, essentially, paper organizations like the military union; others may be real but new and, likely, small. Save for those signatories identified with the FNPR, none of the organizations or names on this January 1993 appeal match the list of union signatories to the 1992 General Agreement; nor can it be told who or how many on this list signed the 1993 General Agreement, since the signatories' list does not seem to have been published.

General Agreement, 1993: Trying Again

There was a 1993 General Agreement, though it was not reached by the overoptimistic projected date of March 5. Evidently concluded on April 30 or May 1, its text was published May 7.[36] The document dealt with numerous points and, rather like the 1992 version, assumed obligations on all sides but mainly bound the government. Several provisions—on price controls for drugs and medicines, on certain foods and basic goods, on indexing of savings deposits to inflation, and on defining and adhering to socially tolerable unemployment levels—had the look of government concessions that might be impossible to deliver and therefore, in the short run, would cost the government nothing. Yeltsin had been making the same sorts of promises in public as his government headed for an April 25 referendum with questions on approval or disapproval of himself as president, his economic policies, and early elections for a new parliament and a new chance at presidential elections.

The reference to a limit point past which unemployment would be in some sense intolerable was general. The commitment to a minimum-wage level the RTK would recommend to the government was specific: 4,500 rubles per month minimum wage as of April 1, 1993. It was on these two points that the FNPR-dominated labor side entered its memorandum of disagreement (*protokol raznoglasiia*), published along with the text. The union wanted to set the upper limit of unemployment at 3.5 percent of the labor force and to substitute a minimum wage of 6,000 rubles, henceforward indexed to inflation.

Was the 1993 agreement likely to prove more than the 1992 version, characterized by the FNPR's number-two man, Romanov, as, ultimately no more than a list of "good wishes"?[37] There were certainly reasons to doubt it. The RTK still lacked, after all, a clearly defined legal status, whatever that might amount to in the conditions of Russia 1993. What force, then, had general agreements that were its product? After the signing, Labor Minister Melikian and employer-side RTK member Kolmogorov of the RSPP commented more enthusiastically than did Klochkov, who chose to focus mainly on the unresolved disagreements.[38] His deputy Romanov had, a few days earlier, sounded a bit more conciliatory: "The government has gradually become convinced that our persistence is not obstinacy. And thus, in the work on the general agreement for 1993, the government has related to our proposals in a more tolerant manner."[39]

In the end, looking at the fifty-plus paragraphs of the General Agreement, so many of them involving "prepare proposals," "submit proposals," "work out (rules, systems, procedure) proposals," one could well have concluded that the document laid out paper tasks for the RTK itself more than it established any rules or guidelines according to which, for the rest of 1993, the RTK would regulate anything.

On the Labor Front

Whatever the new composition of the RTK and whatever the reaching of a 1993 general agreement portended for social-labor relations and their regulation, old problems remained, and nowhere more than in the coalfields. A delegation of Kuzbass miners had arrived in Moscow on February 10 to present the government with demands about 1993 tariff agreements and other supports to mining. The regional NPG head, Vyacheslav Sharipov, threatened a strike March 1 if no agreement was reached.[40] Vorkuta, too, had problems. The Vorshagorskaia mine's workers had been on a lone strike since December 1992 over a director who had not fairly divided up Western goods obtained via barter of some of the mine's output. Advantaged in some sense, the polar miners lived in a strange world whose economic base grew less stable as the issue of closing high-cost, low-efficiency coal mining rose on the government's horizon. The problems, although not typical of the grievances of Russian labor, linked issues of economics and subsidy, law and order, central versus regional government powers, and the legacy of the one-factory town. The danger of becoming a city of unemployed miners whom no one in the south wants is very real for Vorkuta. The Komi Republic has taken possession of its oil, gas and timber, but its coal has remained the federal property of Russia because of the unprofitability of mining it. But now, the miners believe, the Russian government has decided to wash its hands of the coal, too.

The economic nervousness is being intensified by social nervousness. The mines, which in past strikes won the right to freely dispose of some of their coal, have used it in barter transactions, and today Vorkuta is saturated with imported vehicles and electronics—more so than any other city in Russia. Wheeler-dealers from all over the country have flocked to these goods like bees to honey. Wholesale thievery has begun, and criminals are hashing things out and dividing up their loot by means of shoot-outs on the streets.[41]

The government was surely aware of these problems. Its rhetoric at the time was leaning toward recognizing the social dimension—the human costs of reform and their political implications. But what might be done was not clear. First Deputy Premier Shumeiko, in a report to the government, had noted problems of growing wage disparities, poverty, and unemployment. With 1992 past, "the potential for achieving financial stabilization by limiting the incomes of the population and of social-sphere sectors [was] basically exhausted"; now, under pressure from the Congress of People's Deputies, the government was "faced with the very complex task of walking a razor's edge: implementing ... social support measures, halting the production decline in priority sectors, and supporting agricultural production, while avoiding the plunge into hyperinflation."[42]

On March 1, some Kuzbass mines struck, but NPG leader Sharipov counseled moderation in the face of government efforts to be responsive, and most suspended the action for ten days; in Vorkuta, more mines went out, mixing with their economic demands calls for direct presidential rule, for a new constitution, and for the abolition of the Congress of People's Deputies.[43]

Thus were big politics and labor politics linked in March. The Congress of People's Deputies was meeting and leaning more and more in an uncompromising anti-Yeltsin direction. At issue was the "facedown by referendum" Yeltsin wanted for April 11, which would put the issues of his presidency and policies, and the general viability of the present constitutional and legislative arrangements, directly to the people. Parliament resisted, the Congress canceling on March 10 the April 11 referendum. The independent unions lined up with the president: The Kuzbass workers' committees and local NPG saw a "creeping coup" in the Congress's actions and threatened strikes; Vorkuta miners struck a similar note.[44] FNPR, without its usual rhetoric, called for respect for the constitution and condemned "political adventurists"—by which it clearly did *not* mean the Congress; the air traffic controllers (FPAD), the pilots' union, and other independents backed the president and the referendum.[45]

On March 20 came Yeltsin's decree establishing presidential "special rule" and with it a new April 25 date for the referendum. The Congress reassembled in extraordinary session; tried but failed (by sixty-two votes) to impeach Yeltsin on March 26; and a few days later grudgingly gave in on the April 25 referendum, relying on various technicalities to fend off the possibility of Congress being forced to stand for reelection.

In the tense times between March 20 and the compromise, FNPR and the other elements of labor divided again. FNPR called for simultaneous presidential and parliamentary elections in the "very near future"—disregarding the rather different circumstances under which the Congress had gotten its mandate in 1990 and Yeltsin his in 1991.[46] The date FNPR proposed was June 27, but this was a nonstarter.[47] The NPG met to back Yeltsin; in Kuzbass, workers' committees and miners backed the president while Tuleev, the local soviet chair, called Yeltsin's move a coup.[48] The Kuzbass NPG registered its opposition to Congress reconvening in its extraordinary session—foreseeing what would be its attempt to depose Yeltsin; national head Sergeev threatened a general coal strike April 1 if the Congress moved against Yeltsin and meanwhile signaled that an economic strike would in any case be mounted against parliament because the Supreme Soviet had not provided by March 25 a schedule of how it would meet miners' demands.[49]

On April 15, Deputy Prime Minister Sergei Shakhrai met with FNPR representatives, on the one hand defending the referendum as "a thousand times better and hundreds of times cheaper than staging rallies and building barricades" but on the other expressing a conviction that simultaneous elections might be advisable; this was not Yeltsin's position, but it was more or less the FNPR's.[50] On April 19, Yeltsin got unambiguous support from leaders of "about 30" non-FNPR unions, representing, according to a sympathetic source, more than 5 million members; at their meeting, they supported the presidential line and called for early parliamentary elections.[51] The following day, Klochkov mocked the meeting and 5 million figure (a likely overestimate), referring to the independent unions as encompassing "several tens of thousands" (a clear underestimate), and warned Yeltsin about underrating the importance of FNPR's 60 million.[52]

The president won the referendum in the sense that the vote favored him, his policies, and early elections to the parliament and went against subjecting Yeltsin himself to such a contingency. The margins were not massive; the requirement imposed by the constitutional court that more than half the eligible electorate, not a majority of actual voters, would be required to compel early elections was not met.

Yeltsin failed to seize any initiative after the vote even though it demonstrated that the FNPR leaders' position carried little weight with the millions of members those leaders never tired of mentioning. As the FNPR "defector" and head of the mining and metallurgical workers' union, Boris Misnik, commented:

> In view of the fact that the [FNPR] lists its membership as 65 million, there seemed to be no way they could lose. But the trade union members (and Russia's voters are almost all covered by trade union membership in [FNPR]) went to the polls and cast their votes in favor of the president and his policy. They clearly do not share their leaders' views. In a decent society the leadership would in such a case as this at the very least hasten to explain, and if their explanations proved unconvincing they would resign.[53]

Regulating Without Resources

Neither political institutions nor resources available to the government were really adequate to channel, discipline, or meet the demands of labor on the FNPR or the independent side. This was a fundamental fact of the situation from early 1993 to mid-1993, wherein deadlock between president and parliament and further cabinet compromises in a centrist direction that could not quiet a parliament that would *not* be quieted virtually guaranteed that nothing lasting in the labor politics area could be accomplished.

Union sniping continued. In Sotsprof's view, the FNPR still served "Leninist ideas religiously. These trade unions always were, are, and will remain appendages of the administration. To remain in these trade unions means to contribute to a delay in reforms." Warning workers to leave FNPR affiliates and offering them help in building "genuine" unions, Sotsprof argued the inevitable crumbling of relics of the old system: "Times are coming when they [FNPR] will be unable to issue vouchers and apartments—you will have to buy all of this."[54]

FNPR harped on well-worn themes that had been standard since Sotsprof had gotten its three places on the labor side of the 1992-model RTK. Sotsprof was linked to the Social Democratic Party of Russia; the 1992 labor minister, Shokhin, and his deputy, Kudiukin, were social democrats and had somehow been selected to enter the government. Sotsprof leader Sergei Khramov and his deputy, Semenov, had jobs in the Labor Ministry. On the RTK, Khramov had "always" defended the government position from the labor side of the table, so that "proposals of the trade union side that were directed at improving the position of workers were continuously blocked."[55]

Weak or strong, the labor side was heavily tilted toward FNPR—an outcome to which the government had, after all, acquiesced, perhaps because it considered FNPR more comfortable than other unions as a social partner. The government's motives are difficult to determine because government behavior in the RTK context was complicated. The government had often talked tough but in the end made concessions to labor. The problem was that having made certain concessions, the government did not actually deliver—and perhaps never intended to. The chairman of the union of retail trade and catering workers identified the "weakest link" as "the lack of a mechanism of responsibility for the violation of agreed-upon terms of social partnership. ... The articles of the 1992 General Agreement on indexation, the quarterly revision of wages and their correspondence to the acceptable minimum income were not fulfilled. Who was responsible for such a serious breakdown? Why, no one!" But "no one," in fact, was the government—the articles the union official referred to were obviously ones where the government's undertakings were at issue.[56]

The government might not honor its RTK undertakings, but it did continue to add the sort of people at cabinet level who favored support, subsidy, and a continued large government role in the economy. The May 1993 appointments of two more industrialists—Oleg Lobov and Oleg Soskovets—to first deputy premierships was greeted by the FNPR-RSPP newspaper in terms that took a clear swipe at reform economists in the Gaidar mode. It congratulated the two and "the government of Russia at the same time: it has enriched itself with two highly qualified specialists, who have a knowledge of life which is not just from textbooks."[57]

But such appointments were not and could not be magic bullets no matter how enthusiastically greeted. The government remained wary of the expense of socially oriented reform and thus was resistant to calls for limiting unemployment to strict, modest figures (Solovev, of the FNPR national board, called again for a ceiling of 3.5 percent unemployment in May[58]). In May as well, the government threatened cancellation of subsidies for imports of butter, sugar, and other food basics that would push prices higher.[59]

After the referendum, political warfare continued over a new constitution with president and parliament offering conflicting drafts as their relations grew even cooler. Klochkov, in an interview and phone-in meeting with *Trud* readers, expressed more criticism of the presidential than the parliamentary draft, his main complaints focusing on the absence of the right to legislative initiative for trade unions (though this was absent from both drafts) and the lack of constitutional guarantees of a set of "socioeconomic rights primarily of the wage worker."[60] In response to a caller from the Novocherkassk locomotive plant, Klochkov went on to characterize the government's "ideology."

> We are greatly worried by the ideology which is taking shape in the government—tightening credit policy, up to and including enterprise bankruptcy and the stoppage of production. In order to fight inflation, some figures believe, let us curtail credit, the indexing of working capital, the mutual offsetting of arrears. ... This is the idea—no credit, let the weak enterprises die. But we can see that not only the weak ones, all would come to a halt one after the other. People would be left without work, without pay.[61]

But Klochkov was imputing to the government an ideology belied by its own performance, and by Yeltsin's own prereferendum campaigning. Credits *had* been issued in 1992 and 1993. The president *had* made some expensive promises—notably a March package tied to a costly living-standard decree.[62] If Finance Minister Fedorov initially had reservations about funding it, by early June he was defending this basket of goodies, denying opposition charges that the government had "resorted to populist measures to win a few more votes" and asserting that the government could cover the projected 13 trillion ruble cost without "printing confetti money" by way of savings anticipated through cutting subsidies for imports, reducing coal subsidies, and allowing oil and gas prices to rise and produce more excise tax revenue and by drawing on an anticipated IMF systemic transformation facility of $3 billion. Even the generally hard-nosed Fedorov was thus not above politics,[63] and accusations that the president had once again sinned by way of economic inconsistency were hard to counter.

The summer would be marked by increasingly venomous recriminations between president and parliament—Yeltsin versus Rutskoi and Khasbulatov. Privatization, moving ahead since early in the year, was one bone of contention. Another was budget politics. Variant budgets, like shuttlecocks, shot back and forth between Yeltsin and the White House. The parliament rejected Yeltsin's relatively tight budgets and the president refused the parliamentary ones, which made a joke of any attempt to stabilize the ruble and promised instead lavish subsidies to addicted industry and agriculture. These conflicts would help bring on the fall crisis; meanwhile, the government again faced problems in the coalfields.

Coal and Miners: Pains of Problem Solving

There were strong reasons to raise coal prices, still ridiculously low by the standards of the world economy Russia sought to enter, and also reasons that coal prices could not be allowed to rise to the levels of a world market whose realities were so distant from those of Russia. Negotiating this minefield, occupied by some of the government's most militant blue-collar political support, was serious business.

The mining sector bled. The government planned to cut subsidies for 1993 from the coal sector's request of 860 billion rubles to about 400 billion (this in a Russian economy where coal was priced at 1,000 rubles per ton but price-decontrolled timber for pit props cost 20,000 rubles per cubic meter—six being required to mine one ton of coal!). Mining enterprises were stuck in the mutual debt-credit web of so much of the economy: The Vorkutaugol association in Komi held 11.5 billion rubles in receivables, 5.6 billion of this owed by the Cherepovets metallurgical plant. But Cherepovets could not pay; it held 56 billion rubles in receivables from its customers. Vorkutaugol in turn could hardly clear its red ink: It owed (a comparatively moderate) 4 billion, the vast amount of this to the railroad that hauled its coal away and was threatening its own strike in protest against nonpayment.[64]

Like so many other problems, this one "could not be allowed" to go on—yet the government's plans were confused, and confusingly communicated. Early leaks in June indicated that coal prices would rise 2.5-fold, by government fiat;[65] but on June 21 Yeltsin reportedly signed a decree providing, ostensibly, for full decontrol of prices effective July 1 and freeing coal from export duties—this with the reported approval of Fedorov, Chubais, and Shokhin. An early report indicated an "enabling" factor in a move that Yeltsin had earlier characterized to miners as impossible due to its radical knock-on effects: "Free" prices were expected to rise over current ones by only 20–30 percent (rather than 2.5-fold), thus staying well below world prices, because "most coal customers cannot simply afford such an increase."[66]

This must have been something of a snap decision, since the fuel and energy minister was reported, as late as a cabinet meeting on June 18, to have asked for the 2.5-fold increase[67] and NPG union head Sergeev was quoted on June 23 as approving of the 2.5 increase but making no reference to any decree freeing prices.[68]

If only so much coal could be exported, if domestic consumers' financial capacities would restrain effective price increases, could the government avoid continued subsidization of the industry? Could the government deny the miners, not having done so in the past? One commentator, sympathetic to the government but sensitive to the many considerations and harsh, forced choices involved, explored the complexities. Releasing coal prices was an earnest expression of good faith to the IMF and other international bodies, but it was also a way of removing "a strong trump card" from the miners. With consumers unable to pay, higher prices set at the mines' discretion would backfire, demonstrating that coal too needed subsidies; miners, however accustomed to being tough in their demands on a government they backed, would become— like the representatives of many other sectors—just "petitioners." This was sad, but it was the logic of events.

> It may seem that this is betrayal of the miners themselves who by their active stance supported the reformers, sent delegates to political debates, and held strikes and meetings. ... And, alas, that will in part be the truth. Indeed, by supporting the marketeers the miners have dug a trap for themselves. But not because the government and reformers are so bad—the development of civilization has proceeded along a path on which demand for coal is declining while expenditure on its extraction is, on the contrary, increasing. Breaking a natural process and denying objective reality means driving our economy into an impasse. Subsidies are like a drug and after a brief improvement in mood there follows a "letdown" after which a bigger dose is needed, and so on endlessly until the money runs out. Our money has run out.[69]

July would be a cruel month. The money had, of course, run out—which did not necessarily guarantee against the emission of more money. Such depended on a divided government's resolve.

FNPR, predictably, faulted the decision before it went into effect on July 1 as violative of the RTK regulations and the principles of social partnership. The government had moved on energy prices "without prior consultation with the unions and the adoption of preemptive social protection measures."[70] By July 6, FNPR was demanding that the government "ensure the state regulation of prices of energy resources" and calling for bilateral talks between the union and the government.[71] Although the government did not accede, a temporary compromise was arrived at in the cabinet on July 13, Chubais proposing a kind of gentlemen's agreement between coal producers and consumers to limit prices charged. Some coal regions reportedly sought to raise prices eight- to tenfold; metal fabricators complained that this would drive their own prices 20–30 percent above world levels.[72] Such compromises could not hold off the long-feared move against the high-cost, high-subsidy mines of the Komi Republic.

In Vorkuta in mid-July, plans were announced to close seven mines, three before the year was out; as a start, the layoff of 300 miners of the 1,500 in the Yun-Yaga mine was declared, with 3,000 more layoffs expected soon in the mines scheduled for closing. The thirteen Vorkuta mines struck in protest for one hour on July 19, demanding an end to redundancies until the government had a coherent plan to deal with the special problems of the region. This was not, simply, a labor protest: Managers, pensioners, all dependent on the coal industry in this Arctic area were involved with no evidence of any deep division between the independent NPG and the FNPR-affiliated NPRUP. Miners in Vorkuta were reportedly demanding "privatizing of mines and other enterprises of the coal industry in the interests of their workers' collectives." How this would help, however, when coal prices in the area had "soared by a factor of 7–8," leaving customers very unlikely to buy (and indicating as well that the gentlemen's agreement was not working), was not evident.[73]

Finance Minister Fedorov, in an interview published on July 20, had somewhat confusedly laid out the government's policy on mine closings, promising "sufficient benefits … to insure that the coal industry has a normal life" and denying that brutal surgery was planned.

> We cannot simply close mines—there are settlements around them, and they contain people. It takes money to move people to places with more of a future. But even if 50 percent of mines can live a normal life on their own income, we will still have to support the rest. That is our policy. It is aimed at increasing coal exports; we do not need so much inside the country, and there are customers abroad.[74]

Fedorov's remarks seemed to bear little resemblance to the situation on the ground. A July 24 report had Vorkuta mines totally halting deliveries to metallurgical enterprises—among them the previously mentioned Cherepovets plant—because of unpaid debts. Such a strategy might be fruitless, but it was occasioned by the government's reported failure to deliver any more than half the promised 135 billion ruble June subsidy to the mines and "not a kopek" as of that date of the 240 billion promised for the month of July.[75]

In the midst of what seemed as much confusion in the government as in the coalfields, Chernomyrdin, on July 30, decreed continuing large-scale subsidies for the coal industry. Funds of unspecified magnitude would cushion the shutdown of loss-making pits, the modernization of the survivable ones, and social protection for the displaced.[76] Keeping all the mines open was impossibly expensive, but the cost, political and social, of closing a large number of them probably looked even more expensive to the government. Compromises, however, would also prove expensive.

The RTK: Government Versus FNPR, Again

With the benefit of hindsight about what happened the following October, FNPR-government summer bickering in 1993 assumes a peculiar quality: verbal sparring on familiar ground over familiar issues but with no evidence that either party—especially FNPR, with its ritual threats of all-Russia strike actions—suspected that it was drifting toward a major crisis that would draw blood rather than merely bruises.

The RTK again figured as the locus of expression for recurrent dissatisfactions while (just as in the previous year) proving inadequate as a mechanism for their resolution. In the language of one critical appraisal published on July 1, "Agreements were adopted in spring. … They are not being carried out [including those] in the sphere of price regulation and labor remuneration. But what can be more important for the working man?"[77] RTK deliberations in mid-1993 looked no higher a priority for the government than they had been a year before. "Summer holidays and urgent business trips" were cutting the numbers in attendance at meetings; even coordinator Shumeiko was absent from a sparsely attended July 23 meeting, which could thus conduct none of the business before it.[78]

The familiarity and intractability of many of the problems before the RTK no doubt contributed to reluctance to attend on the part of government representatives to whom so many demands were addressed. Indeed, to a degree, the terms of reference, if not the competence, of the trilateral had increased as its membership had changed. At a June meeting Lira Rozenova, chair of the government's State Committee on Price Policy—her presence on the RTK was one of the evidences of a more social emphasis in the composition of the government side in 1993—agonized over the emergence of a "scissors" crisis in agriculture (with a large FNPR branch union), as prices for industrial products sold to the rural population had risen twice as fast as those for farm products. Earlier resources allocated to the farm sector had "disappeared as though in a bottomless barrel," and government subsidies to agriculture were not enough to fend off crisis.[79]

A special RTK meeting on July 19 grappled with linking wages, pensions, and social benefits to the "subsistence minimum" (the lag between minimum wages and the subsistence minimum was, by some calculations, 60 percent or more) and with wage arrears for government-dependent budget personnel. A Finance Ministry representative promised that the government would finance those wages "on priority" but, "crying poor" on behalf of a hand-to-mouth government, also specified that they would be "financed only within income limits and with regard for assets received," warning that "most expenditures will be underfinanced by 25–30 percent. As of today, financing of budget-supported institutions is '40 percent of the established figure.' Current indebtedness is covered at the end of the week after regular budget receipts."[80] Budget workers might thus well have wondered how much their prioritization would help.

FNPR stirred the pot in August; *Rabochaia Tribuna* quoted Klochkov, who warned that "trade unions would rise in opposition to the current policy of the government," and cited a number of warning strikes and protest plans in mines, plants, lumbering enterprises, and among doctors and teachers.[81] Even *Trud,* the former AUCCTU organ, now decidedly independent and no ally of FNPR, noted the general perception that the government made promises to workers and then did not keep them and sounded a monitory note about the alarming rise in the social temperature of Russia: "While the power struggle is under way on the political Olympus, the country is beginning to live in a state of anarchy."[82]

Rossiiskaia Gazeta, the parliament's organ, drew a picture of impending waves of wildcat actions and an FNPR faced with the necessity of placing itself at the head of the protests and channeling them. If FNPR "let slip the initiative," there loomed a "mire of chaos"; circumstances were "forcing" FNPR "to abandon the tactics of negotiations, which have produced no results."

> The authorities remain silent. The government assures us that the most difficult part is already behind us and that it is doing what it considers necessary. It is in fact ignoring its social partners, which both the unions and the employers are. And the latter simply cannot escape the image of suppliant which has adhered to them. And it is no accident that V. Shumeiko, coordinator of the commission, has not been to the meetings for a long time—this is of no interest to him, he knows what his opponents count for.[83]

Whatever FNPR might or might not count for, it was not prepared to play shrinking violet; it instead cranked up the volume and struck some ominous notes. It issued an appeal for a direct meeting to Yeltsin, Khasbulatov, and Chernomyrdin, citing a "situation … which … may become unmanageable in the very near future" and asking them to meet with the union on "13–14 August, and listen without intermediaries to a brief report on the true state of affairs in the labor collectives, industries, and regions."[84]

Virtually simultaneously with the meeting appeal, however, FNPR was preparing yet another elaborate plan for phased collective actions in September and October: from September 1 to 8, a series of meetings, picketings, short warning strikes and the (near-ritual) announcement of states of "prestrike readiness"; from September 6 to 15, a series of national "sectoral conferences" to analyze results of sectoral negotiations with employers "and to announce an all-sectors all-Russia strike starting 2–5 October 1993." According to the plan, an intersectoral union conference and planning for "unity of action of budget-financed and production sphere[s]" would take place on September 10 and on September 19, an "all-Russia meeting of trade union representatives" with the government and Yeltsin being "invited."[85]

The reference to unity between production workers and those in the budget sector had a point. Solovev of the FNPR council made it explicit: The government's capitulationist policies toward those who had generally given it solid political support had led to the contrast between the high wages of Kuzbass and Komi miners and the low pay of the budget personnel, who were under the government's thumb and relatively defenseless.

> After all, their wages, despite numerous decrees, were practically frozen by the Gaidar liberalization of last year. Three one-time increases in the wage rates after 3–5 monthly inflationary collapses, and one in the current year, have not improved the material position of the budget workers, but rather have deteriorated it, since they only partially replaced the losses from previous inflation and at the same time gave a sharp upward impetus to the price index.

A "radical flaw" in government policy was that "liberalization of prices on goods and services was not accompanied by liberalization of prices on the primary commodity—the work force." Thus, the government was urged to adopt another "platform," which "must consist only of stabilization and expansion of production, of the creation of new jobs, and not of limiting the amounts of the worker's wages."[86]

Perhaps Yeltsin's government feared that FNPR threats this time might have more backing than previously. In mid-August it issued an "appeal" (*obrashchenie*) to the "trade union organizations and labor collectives of Russia." Reciting both the objectives with which the government had started out in January 1992 and the problems that had arisen since, the document asserted that the government had dealt constantly with labor unions within the RTK context and in direct dialogue with those outside it. Now, the government was seriously concerned about "confrontation" stances by the unions that were members of the RTK (that is, FNPR and its allies); instead of participating in "constructive dialogue" within the context of social partnership, these unions were proposing various mass actions. In the current economic situation, where "the preservation of stable operations in industry and transport" was called for, such actions hardly promoted socioeconomic stability; "they can only be explained by the political interests of certain trade-union leaders." The government appealed to "all workers, in whose names" those leaders were making their threats, to reject such action.[87]

FNPR responded in tones of outrage; *Rabochaia Tribuna* reported it as a "storm of indignation." In its official response, FNPR accused the government of flagrant violation of the 1993 general agreement, the RTK of working ineffectively, and Shumeiko of ignoring his job as coordinator. FNPR asserted that it too was for social harmony, opposed to political games; it offered the government "open, public," partnerly negotiations while warning that if things continued as they were, "an intensification of the strike movement, the concentration of economic demands and their growth into political demands, and a maturation of an all-Russia strike are inevitable."[88]

In a separate response to the government appeal, the head of the FNPR union of defense-industry workers asserted (as a member of the labor side of the RTK) that FNPR had reached agreements with the employers, thus by implication isolating a government that was playing the "rather dishonorable role of insolvent debtor," and rejected the implication that union actions "were aimed against the government and at splitting up our whole society." FNPR had formed no bloc, associated itself with no political party; its "sole task" was "to protect the people of labor from the consequences of the economic crisis and the ill-advised actions of the government."[89]

But of course the FNPR's actions were political. FNPR leaders warned on September 3 that government persistence in its policies would "inevitably lead to a major social explosion in the country."[90] Klochkov outlined on September 10 a series of mass strikes (agriculture and timbering on September 15; defense industry on September 17, medical personnel on October 5; and workers in machine-building, culture, and education on October 15) involving "several million"—an explicit, if inaccurate, projection. Around the same time, as reported on September 17, Klochkov and Chernomyrdin met to set up a prospective session between the premier and leaders of branch unions in FNPR. This suggested something of a reprise of the move in fall 1992 from the trilateral commission to bilateral government-FNPR negotiations (although given FNPR dominance of the labor side on the 1993 RTK, it might now have seemed superfluous). In an article, Klochkov projected a dark picture of government insensitivity and duplicity.

> The government ... course ... has led to the curtailing of production, the transformation of the country into a raw materials–producing adjunct of the world market, and the impoverishment of the bulk of the population. In this context the violations of the General Agreement ... and the flagrant disregarding of the principle of social partnership are understandable and even logical. The executive is not entering into serious negotiations or seeking rational compromises and acceptable solutions. It makes promises but does not intend honoring them. The [RTK] is being used as a cover to conceal that policy.[91]

Should the government have taken FNPR's saber rattling seriously? There was no dearth of opinions. In the government's own newspaper, one commentator suggested that whereas FNPR had never been good at delivering on its recurrent threats of all-Russia action, in the face of genuine grassroots dissatisfaction, the union might now be seeking to take a leading and coordinating role in order to reconcentrate financial resources in the national leadership's hands that in recent times had been retained by regional affiliates.[92] At the same time, the Sotsprof head, Khramov, indicted the government that earlier in the year had cut Sotsprof and other independents out of the RTK and had indulged FNPR and hinted that it was taking FNPR too seriously, or not seriously enough. "Does it really not understand that it blundered in the full sense by not routing the bosses of the [FNPR]—the last nomenklatura structure with offices everywhere—a year ago and not taking away its billions in trade union money, which today are going to finance antigovernment actions?"[93]

By mid-September, *Trud* sounded convinced that real disorder did impend: If the government did not take seriously the FNPR offensive, "it cannot be ruled out that this will grow into a general all-Russia strike as early as November." But the newspaper was expressing a recently more critical view of the Yeltsin government's tactics in the RTK more than any support for FNPR. It noted the promises made in April by the government about indexing the pay of budget-sphere workers, promises seemingly made willingly.

> Lulled by the ease with which concessions were granted, the trade unions did not immediately notice that the government had no intention of fulfilling its promises and decisions. Consider the above-mentioned indexation of pay for budget-sphere workers. All summer they kept talking about this problem in the [RTK], but not even by September had they reached agreement on complete repayment of the debt with respect to budget-sphere workers' salaries. The government still owes billions of rubles to workers in this sphere.[94]

Rossiiskaia Gazeta, no friend of Yeltsin's government, had in late August drawn a critical portrait of an FNPR leadership whose declarations had minimal resonance at local levels. A meeting of an FNPR coordinating committee for collective actions revealed confusion and unwillingness to commit to strike action as outlined in the schedule of September-October actions. The head of the defense workers' branch union, reciting the numerous grievances of the branch, still dismissed strikes as out of the question, as did heads from Moscow and St. Petersburg. An FNPR deputy chair, V. Kuzmenok, presiding over the meeting, responded to a question on the provenance of the action plan: He did not know who had authored it, and indeed—this on August 26—"had hardly even seen the plan before that day." Thus, commented the paper, "the 'naval commanders' of the trade unions had effectively run the FNPR aground."[95]

There were some strikes in September; workers after all had reasons aplenty to be unhappy. Miners' strikes early in the month were of inconsistent pattern. In some coalfields they underlined differences between the NPRUP and the NPG; in others frustration drove both unions together. On September 17, a scheduled RTK meeting that Finance Minister Fedorov was supposed to chair was canceled when he did not appear. Miffed about the finance minister's absence from a meeting where enterprise debts, wages, pensions, and benefits were to be discussed, Klochkov commented that the nonpayments in question had "reached 13 trillion rubles. This is comparable to the state's annual budget"; he thus underlined, consciously or not, the impossibility of any real settlement on FNPR's terms.[96]

But nothing that followed resembled the phased, coordinated strike plans FNPR had announced. The presidential-parliamentary conflict grew more bitter; the battle of the budgets continued. On September 16, Yeltsin in a sense telegraphed some of his intent to break the deadlock, announcing in a visit to an elite Interior Ministry guards regiment quartered near Moscow that Gaidar would be returning to the government as a first deputy prime minister. However compromised the government's pro-market policy had been in practice, no personnel appointment could have more clearly indicated Yeltsin's conclusion that compromise with the parliament was impossible. The stage was set for events that would have been hard to contemplate only a short time before.

Endgame: September–October 1993

Yeltsin's move came September 21 with a decree (of dubious legality) suspending the parliament and announcing elections for a new bicameral parliament for December 11–12. Thus he sought to relegate Khasbulatov, Rutskoi, and the others to the status of ex-parliamentarians. The parliament then counterattacked, deposing Yeltsin and naming Rutskoi acting president in a move that also stretched its prerogatives. All this took place against the backdrop of the much-amended Russian constitution—dating from 1978 and never meant as more than decoration—which had given major power to the legislature.

Parliamentary speaker Khasbulatov called upon the armed forces not to obey Yeltsin. By September 28, the defiant parliament had been sealed off in the White House; regional bosses throughout Russia generally waffled, calling for simultaneous early presidential and parliamentary elections. Events moved toward the bloodshed of October 3–4.

FNPR reaction to the Yeltsin decree had been swift. Within hours, an official statement of its council's executive committee aligned the union with the constitutional court's position; it called the president's move a "flagrant violation" and a "state coup" leading toward a "personal power regime." It appealed to "membership organizations, labor collectives, and workers and employees to use all available means, including strike action, to express a resolute protest against anticonstitutional actions whatever their origin" and called for simultaneous presidential and parliamentary elections.[97]

The FNPR council executive committee had thus called for strikes but tried to sound somewhat evenhanded (the "whatever their origin" phrase) while insisting that the presidential elections be held at the same time as the parliamentary elections Yeltsin was demanding. A statement by Klochkov showed no such moderation. Yeltsin had "now subordinated everything and everyone to himself"; what was projected for December "would not be free elections" but instead a "staged performance, a political game." Ominously, in the light of what would follow, Klochkov went on.

> [FNPR] has called upon Moscow Region's trade union organizations to stop work, to go out into the square by the Supreme Soviet building, and to defend constitutional order in Russia. There can be no time wasted, especially in Moscow Region. It is vital to close down plants to board the suburban trains, and to go to Moscow, because maybe not today, but soon, we will simply be silenced.[98]

The air traffic controllers' union, FPAD, supported Yeltsin's move. Somewhat cryptically, the NPG threatened to support the campaign for early elections if the "president, government, and Supreme Soviet" did not fulfill their obligations;[99] this statement may have reflected the normally pro-Yeltsin union's mounting concerns over the fate of the coal industry's subsidy politics and the diminished focus on high affairs of state.

The RTK had a session scheduled for September 23; its agenda—presumably set by Shumeiko—was to deal with measures to *implement* Yeltsin's decree. FNPR stayed away. Shumeiko invited the NPG, Misnik's mining-metallurgy union, and the union of cooperative workers to sit at the table. He then revealed that the previous day he had signed a decree banning "financial organs" in the factories from automatic collection of trade union dues—striking finally at the checkoff that replenished FNPR's coffers.[100]

FNPR was beleaguered. On September 28, the new independent daily *Segodnia* headlined a story "Leaders of FNPR Prepared to Go Underground—The Federation is trying to save [its] property and will prepare an all-Russian strike." It portrayed an FNPR leadership hunkered down in its Moscow headquarters on September 27, fearing that "democrats" might occupy the building at any time. Telephones—at least the long-distance lines—had been cut after the FNPR response to Yeltsin's decree; Klochkov was reportedly communicating with regional FNPR officials via teletype. Plans were afoot to safeguard union funds and property against sequestration, and a second set of fallback union leaders had been selected should the current leadership be neutralized; a move out of Moscow was also prepared. Meanwhile, since the VKP—the now inter-state successor to the old AUCCTU with affiliate organizations in ten of the former republics—was at the time holding its own scheduled congress in Moscow, FNPR scheduled an emergency meeting of its regional and branch leaders already in town for that congress, to consider the possibility of an all-Russian strike.[101]

That meeting was held on September 28; according to one source, Yeltsin's government was at the same time preparing an outright ban on the FNPR. FNPR determined to maintain a state of prestrike readiness but did call for a strike; such would have signaled total confrontation whether or not the strike was successful. During the meeting, word came to the participants of another Yeltsin decree, issued that day, removing social insurance funds from trade union jurisdiction; the decree, like the checkoff ban, was an attack on the FNPR resource base. As usual, things seemed rather confused. Klochkov, for all his previous rhetoric, now said that local union bodies were not ready for a mass strike and that antici-pating events might jeopardize the whole organization—a moderation some leaders questioned. The FNPR delegates decided on an emergency congress of the FNPR for October 28, a month hence.[102]

The state's attack on the social insurance funds, although it mainly affected FNPR unions, applied across the board, and therefore poten-tially affected all that had managed to establish such funds. This was a murky area with little indication of whether the government was chan-neling some resources into non-FNPR unions' coffers or whether FNPR might in fact be sharing some of its intake from the government with unions that had become, in 1993, its allies. A wire service reported, on September 30, a joint protest by FNPR and some unnamed unions, claiming that the government's move would reduce spending "on the medical, prophylactical, and health-building needs of workers and their children."[103]

This protest did not go unchallenged. Just as in early 1993 the appeal of FNPR and some other unions against any government takeover of social insurance funds had not been joined by any of FNPR's antagonists, now the Confederation of Free Trade Unions of Russia (KSPR—a small independent labor group) asked the government to consider dissolving the FNPR (a fear Klochkov presumably had in mind when he counseled against the danger of "anticipating events"), taking its property, and placing it "under public control." The KSP accused the FNPR of "purely political activity" aimed at creating conflict between working people and the government.[104]

Meanwhile, Sotsprof warned against any "general political strikes" and counseled its member organizations to prepare for legislative (but not presidential) elections, thus lining up with Yeltsin's position.[105] The miner-based workers' committee in Vorkuta backed Yeltsin, and mines belonging to the Vorkutaugol and Intaugol associations continued working, ignoring strike calls.[106]

The final moves in the "big" political game—street violence in the neighborhood of the White House where the parliamentary diehards were hunkered down, the violent and nearly successful assault by antigovernment forces on the Ostankino TV complex, and the shelling of the White House at the order of a Yeltsin whose securing of decisive military support was, in retrospect, a near thing—are as well known as most of the labor politics byplay is obscure. They need not detain us here. Violent confrontation had occurred. The government won—or better, its opponents lost. Its moves pressed the limits of peaceful revolution, but so had those of its parliamentary and extraparliamentary opposition. Still, this was not the sort of government to exterminate its opposition; nothing ruled out the possibility of political confrontation renewing itself, as indeed it would.

In the aftermath, it seemed that FNPR's confrontational abilities, modest as these may have been, were used up. *Rabochaia Tribuna* now fell under Yeltsin's press ban, and it was Volskii rather than Klochkov who announced that he would go to Chernomyrdin to see about getting the ban lifted.[107]

On October 11 (according to one source—as early as October 8, according to another) Klochkov resigned as FNPR chair. After the earlier strike call, the FNPR plenum had on September 23 reportedly "passed a 'softer' statement which in fact reversed the original strike call." Klochkov had continued to argue for a zero-option solution to the confrontation, involving the suspension of Yeltsin's decree and the annulment of all the decrees the Congress of People's Deputies had passed in its "siege" state since. Klochkov had finally been converted to moderation, but it was, according to one source, a late conversion, since he had "only pledged his support for the president's actions the morning of 4 October when tanks were already pounding the parliament building." Reportedly, Deputy Premier Shumeiko, also coordinator of the RTK, had demanded Klochkov's resignation. The FNPR council accepted it, naming the longtime number-two man, Vasili Romanov, as acting chair. He would soon yield this post to Mikhail Shmakov, head of the Moscow Federation of Trade Unions (MFP). On October 12, the FNPR leadership expressed a desire to be "free of all political affiliations."[108]

Rabochaia Tribuna was restored October 8; in that day's issue, it published the text of an official October 4 statement from the FNPR council's executive committee.

> The events which occurred 3–4 October 1993 in Moscow shook the country. For the first time in the acute political confrontation blood was shed.
>
> The [FNPR] considers criminal the actions of the armed, extremist groupings in Moscow which provoked the bloody clashes which led to the loss of life.
>
> The [FNPR] Council Executive Committee appeals to member organizations and the workforce at this difficult time to remain calm and not succumb to extremist appeals.
>
> Order and legality in the capital must be restored. Only under these conditions are free elections possible. The problem of power must be resolved via the people's say.[109]

Those unwilling to let FNPR off the hook for whatever share of the blame might attach to it were voluble in their denunciations of the course it had followed. *Izvestiia* gave space to Boris Misnik, head of the mining-metallurgy union. Klochkov had changed his tune, Misnik noted, only "after the announcement of the surrender" of those in the White House but had "managed to sign on in the ranks of the victors, nonetheless." Misnik accused Klochkov of a "considerable contribution to the destabilization of the situation in Moscow and Russia which led ultimately to the bloody tragedy." Citing a *Trud* report of September 23, he quoted Klochkov's words of September 22 at the VKP congress: "We have called on the union organizations of Moscow and Moscow Oblast to express their protest as far as the organization of strikes. We need to stop the enterprises, take to the streets, and defend the White House." FNPR leaders, Misnik argued, "most likely recognized deep down that these calls did not amount to much" and that no mass stoppages and demonstrations would follow, but others at the center of the action had been less realistic. "Rutskoi and Khasbulatov obviously believed in an all-Russia strike and the nonexistent millions of [FNPR] members ready to support the White House. Bewitched by its slogans and pamphlets, they moved their militants to Ostankino and city hall, counting on the support of the 'trade union masses' led by I. Klochkov."[110] The *Izvestiia* editors added their own comment to Misnik's article, leaving no doubt where they stood. Klochkov's announcement of his resignation "for the purpose of preserving the unity of the trade union center" signifed, to them, an intent to preserve the organization that, "together with the soviets, served as a screen for communist omnipotence and was a stronghold of the totalitarian regime."[111]

Trud, according to its recent pattern, was critical of both sides. The government was not guiltless:

> Beyond any doubt, the executive authority bears a great amount of guilt with regard to the increase in social tension. The fear syndrome prior to strikes has become so developed in this group that, for example, the ministers, almost without a murmur, have plugged up the "branch holes" using deficit budgetary financial resources. They promised billions in subsidies and various unrealizable benefits and in this manner they provoked the trade unions into the next round of protest actions.

"Without justifying" Klochkov's fall offensive threats and the call to go into the streets to defend the White House, the paper argued, "the unfulfilled promises of the government promoted the transformation of the economic emphasis in the demands of the FNPR into a political emphasis."[112]

Another commentator—Professor Marat Baglai, a researcher on worker movements and trade unions—evaluated both those who thought the large FNPR organization could and should be made to go away and the union's tactics and program. He believed that FNPR had failed to appreciate the diversity of the labor force, mistaking the sector that might think in its terms and follow it for the much larger whole. Facing the "fundamental issue in the life of our society: Should reforms be continued, or should we go back?" it had come out "in favor of the latter" the day after Yeltsin's decree. It had, though, apparently believed that labor would follow it. "What is the source of the unexplainable self-assurance that, in response to appeals by the [FNPR] and its council, labor collectives will begin to shut down production and to hold strikes for political considerations? Have there not been enough fiascoes with all those 'all-Russian' strikes and collective actions?" Baglai suggested that work at the enterprise and regional level over labor issues was more likely to advance the hard business of solving social contradictions than a "fruitless struggle with a government that has no money and is trying to change the economic system for the better." True, the government was given to signing "agreements that it does not meet and plainly cannot meet," which did not make matters easy for FNPR in the game of social partnership. But the government's objectives were more coherent than FNPR's inconsistent program.

> The [FNPR] is sort of "in favor" of the market, but against free market relations; "in favor" of conversion, but against shutting down the "defense sector," which the people do not need; "in favor" of efficiency, but against the bankruptcy of unprofitable enterprises; "in favor" of carrying out privatization, but against the transfer of enterprises to private

control; "in favor" of financial stabilization, but against a reduction in state expenditures; and so on. No matter how many times the attention of the leaders has been drawn to the need to develop a serious and realistic program if they do not like that of the government, the endeavor has not gotten off the ground.[113]

Baglai tried to make the point that not all workers were similarly situated in labor market terms. Some were doing much better than others. All Russians—workers included—were not in the same foundering boat. But to some FNPR people, these elements of differentiation were problems to be denounced rather than realities to be reckoned with. An Omsk region official vented frustrations over a lack of solidarity between those who had more and less matter for grievance and complained as well about center-region divisions that eroded FNPR's unity and its purse. Although most trade union oblast committees were chaired by "former Soviet and party workers," these, for some reason, resisted sending much back to central FNPR headquarters—Moscow, used to receiving "as much as 35 percent" of regional dues, was getting only 3 percent.[114]

One could sympathize with the conflicting perspectives emerging in the wake of the September-October debacle. Those thoroughly sick of the FNPR could surely be excused for hoping that in a period where tough decisions were the order of the day, the union's existence might be put to an end by decree, as had been the Congress of People's Deputies. Someone like the Omsk union official could be excused for confusion; after all, labor activists in functioning market economies had also faced the problems of solidarity between higher- and lower-paid wage earners and the problems of split forces versus nationwide labor federations (though it could hardly be said that the FNPR or the AUCCTU before it, as "rich" organizations, had done much that was effective in defense of their members).

The government had no money. The FNPR, in effect, rejected the market without saying so. It had neither signed on to the overall project of economic transformation nor represented labor as a whole on its side of the RTK table. Its members did not listen to it. The major independent unions had been excluded from the table in 1993. Employers as a category still lacked clear definition by interests distinct from government and labor. It was as hard to detect elements of a real corporatism in autumn 1993 as it had been a year earlier.

Aftermath: FNPR Looks Inward

The crisis over, FNPR survived to look toward its October 28 congress. The early word was that the union would change its name to the All-

Russian Confederation of Labor (Vserossiiskaia Konfederatsiia Truda, or VKT)—nominally distancing itself from the recent unfortunate events. Mikhail Shmakov of the MFP was now acting FNPR chair. He indicated a desire to shift from Soviet-style democratic centralism in central leadership toward a more decentralized, truly confederative, structure. With privatization beginning to pick up in tempo, he specified a new task, "to work out a mechanism for protecting the interests of workers employed by nongovernment businesses," and called for continuing strong union influence on the administration of the social insurance fund.[115]

A spate of interviews preceded the congress, Shmakov and other officials staking out positions on past and future concerns. Shmakov asserted that FNPR itself had "nothing to do [with] the blood that was shed in Moscow." By way of clarification he noted that FNPR itself had no "primary organizations"; these belonged to its branch union bodies. Somehow this confusion had helped produce a situation where FNPR "was getting the blame for everything." (This was a bit of tortured logic that seemed to deny Klochkov's earlier statements.)[116]

He warned, in another interview, of possible government abuse of its power over social insurance funds. The unions would watch the government in this matter, since the latter's takeover—mainly amounting, it seemed, to greater oversight—of the pension fund threatened unfortunate consequences. They would "see that government officials do not use the social insurance fund to patch up budgetary holes. If that does happen, clearly we are going to fight it." As to the rumors, rife since the September days, that the government might move to nationalize the FNPR's considerable properties, he noted that nationalization had brought consequences to Russia that now had led to the beginning of a "reverse process." "I think the country's leadership has sufficient wisdom to bear in mind the sad practice from the history of the state and not to repeat past mistakes."[117]

Others concentrated on distancing, at least by implication, their branch unions from whatever guilt attached to the FNPR central leadership. A sympathetic *Trud* commentator, reporting on a pre-October 28 plenum of the branch union for auto and agricultural machine-building workers (an industry immensely hard hit by the fall in orders for tractors from the agroindustrial complex), argued that unions that were in the FNPR had certainly been critical of the government and its policies but had "never called upon the workers to overturn the limits of a civilized struggle for their social interests." Those who claimed otherwise were either in error or "consciously trying to smear all trade union leaders wholesale in the workers' eyes." He quoted A. Surikov, head of the union: "No matter what our opponents say over and over again about a return to the past, we again emphasize that we will insist on the need for a balanced and step-by-step transition to a market and one using state regulation."[118]

The FNPR met October 28. When the one-day congress was over, it was still the FNPR; no new banner unfurled in the place of the now-tattered old one. Shmakov became the permanent leader via a show-of-hands vote among the 479 delegates present; for whatever reasons, the same delegates rejected the leadership's proposal for the name change.

As a whole the congress got mixed reviews. It had been called hurriedly, took place at the tail end of an extraordinary month, and was obviously no model of agenda setting and advance work.[119] Perhaps the most striking element of the short congress was the appearance of Vladimir Shumeiko, who had thrown down the gauntlet to the FNPR after its criticism of Yeltsin's September 21 decree. Shumeiko's speech was, in the circumstances, a rather peculiar one. He reminded the delegates of the particular nature of the old official unions, how they fit into the old Soviet structures, how the current disorientation was "understandable." Shumeiko, using the pronoun "we," spoke as a former union member; virtually everyone was.

> Throughout all the last few years of Soviet power, we have all, we members of the trade unions, treated them as some kind of philanthropic organization. Mikhail Shmakov's report stated it correctly: during these years, large funds were invested in sanatoriums and in rest homes, and all of us in the trade union obtained travel permits, and regarded the trade union as a kind of milk cow. We never considered it to be a real force in protecting the workers.

He called on FNPR to rethink its role and its tasks even though with the hard economic times, many still looked to the philanthropic side, to the old milk cow, for help. Poverty was, however, not the result of the reform, as "certain orators" proclaimed, but of "the lack of these reforms, which we have been talking about for the last six years." The inherited burdens of waste and mismanagement from the Soviet past were immense.

> Every fourth person in the Soviet Union worked in the defense sphere. Every fourth one! They made so much "hardware" that there is no place to put it. There is virtually no army. The army has turned into a watchman guarding all this "hardware," which no one needs. There is a surplus of tanks per capita, but there is not enough of what is needed. All this must be altered and structurally reorganized.

Resolution of such problems required "social partnership." Shumeiko made some comments about the RTK and its deficiencies, mainly on its faulty "geometry," then turned to the issues of trade union inclusion and unity. Not all trade unions sat at the RTK table; and thirty-three unions that were not FNPR affiliates had been invited to the congress he was addressing. "If … we ultimately succeed in approaching the creation of an All-Russian Association of Trade Unions, so that all the trade unions are joined into one single striking force, you will solve your internal problems." The unions should settle, themselves, the ownership of "sanatoriums, rest homes, nurseries and stadiums," on which settlement the "state will not in any case infringe." Organizational problems were the unions' to resolve as well, however they saw fit, but, Shumeiko said, "we would like … for it to be, I repeat, a unified and powerful trade union striking force, which represents real strength."[120]

What was Shumeiko asking for? FNPR leaders had traded in the rhetoric of unity but shown no real ability to lead their "millions" in any kind of action. Any unity linking bodies as disparate as FNPR, the NPG, the air traffic controllers, Misnik's apostate mining-metallurgy union, and a host of others looked unlikely. Was Shumeiko's an invitation to the old FNPR to recognize its weakness and in some sense capitulate via an umbrella extended, however improbably, over both unions that had backed the government and those that had not? Why would the government want a united, powerful striking force? Against what targets would it be deployed?

Other comments by Shumeiko seemed aimed at mollifying the organization, especially regarding the social insurance fund issue. The unions, FNPR obviously included, would not be "cut out"; Shumeiko referred to a Council of Ministers decree "just signed," specifying that the various government ministries involved in drafting a new legislative act on the Social Insurance Fund of the Russian Federation would work "with the participation of the all-Russian trade union associations." During the three months (an optimistic projection) the work was to take, administration of the fund was to be controlled by the Council of Ministers, but again with the participation of the unions. But the end was a warning, which might explain to a degree the earlier insistence on trade union unity: "If many of [the trade unions] are different, we will be looking for paths to partnership for a long time." Thus Shumeiko implied that a united body of trade unions should arrive at a reasonable position—one the government could accept.[121]

He called off local government moves against FNPR affiliates and properties within their jurisdictions, asking in a letter to regional heads of administration "that such illegal actions against the trade unions, their elected organs, publications and trade union property not be allowed," since "according to existing legislation, trade unions are independent self-managing organizations."[122] A. Surikov, the chair of the autoagricultural machinery union and now an FNPR deputy chairman, welcomed the move, stating, "[the] fact that today the government demands of its structures strict compliance with the law is encouraging."[123]

Despite what seemed at the time "unions on the defensive," the prospect of forthcoming elections to a new Russian legislature focused some attention and speculation at the end of October and beginning of November on the unions' possible course and leanings in those elections and which parties FNPR might support (or seek support from). One pro-government analysis (overoptimistic as it would turn out about a solid pro-reform result from the elections) saw FNPR as weak: No united trade-union front in support of any party would be forthcoming, since the Trade Unions and Democracy bloc, fostered by politicians grouped around the reformist party Russia's Choice had excluded FNPR while bringing under its umbrella most of the anti-FNPR independent unions. FNPR leaders seemed to lean toward common cause with the "industrial bosses." Thus it seemed likely that FNPR would be seen by its worker members as interested in advancing the fates of the bosses while at the same time abandoning, in its engagement in "partisan" politics (which held less and less attraction for rank-and-file citizens), the simple defense of the interests of hired labor. This analysis projected as well an erosion of the FNPR social base. Young people entering the labor force were not going into state industry. Workers were leaving state employment for "commercial structures" and were defecting from FNPR. It envisaged (not quite correctly) a very weak antireform vote.[124]

More realistic about both the protest-vote potential and where FNPR upper-echelon leaders stood was the head of the Communist Party of the Russian Federation (KPRF), Gennadi Zyuganov, who as a guest at the October 28 FNPR congress counseled its leaders against any move to create a new party of their own and made an offer:

> The platform of our party is very close to the position of [FNPR]. Therefore, it is much more effective, in my opinion, to unite our efforts. Incidentally, we are actively heading for a rapprochement. If the trade union leaders are not intimidated by the attitude of the current authorities toward our party, then this could evolve into a very strong alliance. And, in the final analysis, the workers will win.[125]

October, then, had marked the crisis of the inherited political system of 1990–1991. But the slate had not been wiped clean. FNPR, although demonstrably a weak organization, survived. The government was stronger but preoccupied with elections that would also be a referendum on Yeltsin's presidential constitution. Its decree on the social insurance fund was published on November 6. A welter of "shalls" specified much of what Shumeiko had mentioned earlier; how the questions of who controlled the money would be resolved and how the participation of the trade unions would relate to the process remained to be seen.[126] Previous experience counseled against expectations that these knotty problems would be effectively resolved.

After what was called an extended interval, the RTK met on November 9. The focus of the meeting was price policy. Lira Rozenova, head of the state's price policy committee, Roskomtsen, noted that twenty-two regions were subsidizing prices for foods and other "socially necessary" items—a gray area not really approved by the central government but not really forbidden. She proposed a regularization of the practice, explicitly allowing regions so inclined to continue with it to limit profits or link maximum price increases to the local inflation rates. Deputy Premier Yuri Yarov, a government representative on the commission who would later replace Shumeiko as coordinator, complained that this was the wrong way to go. Relatively cheap subsidized goods from one region would surely find their way to other regions where prices were not controlled; better than a policy of price (and hence producer) subsidies would be a targeting of direct aid to people of scant means. The commission voted, however, to send the Roskomtsen proposals with its approval on to the appropriate ministries and departments for their comment and revisions—but without any deadline for those revisions. The implication of one report was that this was the end of the matter.[127]

With respect to the non-FNPR unions, the government got perhaps less relief in the wake of October than it might have hoped for. The air traffic controllers (FPAD), usually a government ally (though often a nuisance as well) was calling in November for the dismissals of Labor Minister Melikian and the head of the government's air transport department, accusing them of collusion with three aviation-related unions in signing, early in the year, a branch trilateral agreement that sought to deprive FPAD of the possibility of negotiating its own deal.[128] Vorkuta and Kuzbass miners, fearing the uncertainties of pit closings, wage arrears, and other backwash from the unanticipated consequences of price decontrol, were threatening an all-Russia coal strike for December 1.[129] Seemingly reenergized were the enmities between the NPG's Sergeev and the FNPR union of coal industry workers (NPRUP). Sergeev criticized the latter union's leader, Vitaly Budko, for paying no attention to getting a government commitment to find jobs for miners who would be let go as pits closed and mocked the NPRUP's inclusion of everyone, "from the [mine's] general director to the clothing attendant who issues overalls to the miners."[130]

In early December, the labor side of the RTK went through another reshuffling. Seventy-two representatives of trade unions gathered in Moscow and by secret ballot elected twenty-eight representatives to fill the union side of the trilateral for the 1994 edition of the RTK. The first reports indicated that among the organizations to be represented were the Congress of Russian Trade Unions (KRP) and eight unions that were not FNPR members; how many seats the FNPR got was not specified. There was some implication that a greater measure of unity across the organizational lines might have finally, following Shumeiko's advice, been achieved. In any case, Irina Ledeneva, deputy chair to Boris Misnik in the mining-metallurgy union and presumably therefore no friend of the old FNPR, expressed confidence in the elected: They were "workhorses who will take upon themselves a load of problems and be worthy opponents to both the government and the business side."[131]

Pessimism or optimism about how this or that set of players might work in the RTK, however, was to a degree beside the point. Privatization was proceeding, now touching the large state enterprises. Over the horizon, if not yet in full view, was a fundamental shift; although many forces would likely retard the process, the state was getting out of its nearly 100 percent proprietorship of much of industry. How new owners would behave was still unclear, but distance was being put between the world of 1991–1993 and a new situation wherein open interest conflict between management and labor might be expected to develop.

5

Institutions and Conflict in the Russian Transition

THE MACROPOLITICS OF THE POST-OCTOBER period are well known. Russia went to the polls, as Yeltsin wanted, on December 12, 1993, after hastily organized campaigns by a range of parties from the Gaidar-led, strongly pro-reform Russia's Choice to the Liberal Democrats led by the bombastic Vladimir Zhirinovskii. Reformists divided their forces, however: Three other pro-market parties, billing themselves as more centrist than Russia's Choice, contended. At the other end of the spectrum, Zhirinovskii's party was joined by the relegalized Communist Party and the closely related Agrarian Party, all seeking to draw the protest votes of those feeling the pains of economic problems and a politically diminished present and nostalgia for the "great power" past.

The results showed that there was plenty of pain to capitalize upon. In the new State Duma, its 450 seats to be filled half from parties' national lists on the proportional representation principle, half through single-member constituencies, the largest share—70 seats—went to Russia's Choice. But close behind were the ostensibly fringe Liberal Democrats (LDP) with 64 seats. In the national list contest, the LDP garnered by far the largest share of the popular vote—22.79 percent versus Russia's Choice at 15.38 percent; Zhirinovskii's style proved extraordinarily effective with large numbers of voters. Things looked different in the constituency contests: 30 of Russia's Choice's 70 members were so elected versus only five of the LDP's 64.

In all, the four reform parties' share in the Duma amounted to 116; the figure for LDP, Communists, and Agrarians combined was 145. Other parties, only four of which had been large enough to run national lists, and more than 100 constituency members elected as independents made up the rest of the State Duma. The specter of a three-party antigovernment bloc versus a less-united four-party reformist bloc facing each other across a swamp of independents and others—a parliament no more effective than the old Congress of People's Deputies—had risen.

143

Such, however, has not quite been the case. Russia also voted in a new constitution with much more power clearly delegated to the president. Such, at least, went the reported results of the election referendum, although there were reasons to question the accuracy of the tally with respect to both the turnout necessary to pass the constitution and the party votes.[1] In any case, the arrangements were left undisturbed. In these circumstances, the factional struggles and infighting and the weaknesses of party discipline and even identity that led to changes in the spectrum virtually from the moment the Duma first met had less effect on policy. After a shaky start, the Duma showed a tendency within a generally critical orientation toward the executive to isolate the extreme reactionaries in its membership.[2] Gaidar, briefly back in government, was now out again, and Finance Minister Fedorov left as well; but in a number of critical areas government economic policy remained, on the whole, steady, following the lines established earlier.

Chernomyrdin had been prime minister for over a year. Despite early 1994 remarks about bidding farewell to market "romanticism" and such—which had helped drive Gaidar and Fedorov from government— he had learned, it seemed, a good deal about economic realities; he was a convert to a more or less tight money policy (although he would stray in implementation). A realist in politics as well, he had proven on the whole a more effective manager in difficult circumstances than many had expected. What had initially seemed the woodenness of a former apparatchik from the gas industry gradually seemed to translate itself, against the background of Yeltsin's mercurial style, to a sort of gravitas that the president, by 1995, lacked.

There were still problems aplenty, opportunities for making big mistakes in pursuing a gradual moderation of inflation and budget deficit. But there was some room for maneuver, more than might have been expected after the December 1993 elections. Voters had rejected the three moderate-reform centrist parties as well as the Civic Union industrial lobby, none of which made the 5 percent popular vote threshold for allocation of proportional representation seats. Arguably, this was because they *were* centrist and thus inappropriate vehicles for the protest in December's polling.[3] But policies the reform-centrists had advocated found a home of sorts in the government executive itself, however thin their partisans might have seemed to be on the floor of the State Duma.[4]

The new parliament could not paralyze the executive or create general crisis, as had the old in 1993. Still, the force of habit prevailed. Communists and Agrarians hunkered down in a better semblance of unity than the reform parties, whose policy and personal divisions had prevented unity in the December elections.

But if 1994 was a relatively quiet year, marked within the Duma by the splits and recombinations of blocs and factions, the coming of 1995 focused attention anew on elections, scheduled for the parliament in December under the provision that the first-time 1993 elections were for two-year, rather than the "normal" four-year, terms. Parties, blocs, and groups roused themselves to the challenge of getting organized anew.

In early March, the FNPR central executive announced a decision to create an electoral association—Russian Trade Unions—to field a national list to contend for the 225 proportional representation seats in the Duma. The battered FNPR had run no candidate list in 1993, and FNPR endorsement of candidates in the 225 single-member constituencies had carried very little weight. Regional and branch components of the FNPR, in the meantime, had lined up informally with a variety of parties: the large agroindustrial union, logically, with the Agrarians; many regional organizations, as well as the military-industry branch union, with Zyuganov's Communists (KPRF). To some degree, the notion of fielding a national list (at the top of which, it was contemplated early on, non-FNPR luminaries such as Chernomyrdin, Duma speaker Ivan Rybkin, and Sergei Glaziev, chair of the Duma's economic policy committee, might be invited to stand) was aimed at bringing those regional and branch FNPR power brokers back under a single umbrella.[5]

Still, this seemed a doubtful prospect. More likely was an alliance with another party or parties; but here again the diffuse nature of FNPR affiliations and the weak linkage of its claimed 60 million members to the organization and its electoral counsels made for a confusing situation. Partial clarification seemed on the way in May 1995—"partial" is surely the operative word in assessing party-organizational events and developments in Russia—when FNPR, along with the new Russian United Industrial Party (Rossiiskaia Obedinennaia Promyshlennaia Partiia, or ROPP) and the Union of Realists, announced the formation of a "single electoral bloc"[6] whose objectives included "socially oriented economic reforms," "the rebirth of national industry," and a "system of social partnership to ensure extensive rights for people of labor and the entire population."[7] This was a familiar litany for both FNPR and much of the industrial lobby. It was not surprising that the ROPP partner, then, established only in early April itself, numbered among its founders Volskii of the RSPP and similar figures,[8] although Yuri Skokov's commodity producers' organization, with which FNPR's Moscow central executive had an ambiguous relationship (see further on), was not in evidence.

That such alliance making (however strong or weak was the glue to hold the parts together) resembled the earlier RASP alliance of 1992 was not lost on FNPR's antagonists, who probably were anticipating this move. On the heels of an April 12 FNPR protest, seven non-FNPR unions with Sergeev's NPG among them formed the new Confederation of Labor of Russia (Konfederatsiia Truda Rossii, or KTR). Sergeev, in announcing the new body, said that it aimed to pursue the painful problem of wage arrears with employers at the enterprise level rather than in demands to the government, as had been FNPR practice. The new confederation was silent on any building of electoral blocs of its own—not necessarily because, as one commentator put it, "no more than 200,000 wage workers back [it] at this stage"[9] (probably, in strict numbers, an underestimate) but more because, in the light of the Kuzbass debacle of 1993 when authentic unions could not deliver their members' votes to reformists, there was little reason to think that 1995 would be different.

As spring moved into summer, the waters were muddied further by high-level moves with Yeltsin's blessing to organize two superparties, center-right and center-left in orientation, to draw support away from the extremes in the December elections. Premier Chernomyrdin presided over the rapid organization of the center-right "Russia Is Our Home" (Nash Dom-Rossia, or NDR), criticized by many as a quintessentially establishment party of all currently in the government and determined to remain there. Duma speaker Rybkin, affiliated with the Agrarians, took upon himself the slower process of forming a center-left party, tentatively labeled "Concord." In late April, he talked about the likely inclusion of the three allies—FNPR, ROPP, and the Realists—under its roof,[10] but this seemed premature. Three weeks later, Shmakov, in response to a question as to whether FNPR would collaborate with a Rybkin-led bloc, said that it was "difficult to work with something that does not yet exist"[11] only to be quoted three weeks later as saying that an FNPR-led union movement might form the backbone of a center-left bloc under Rybkin.[12] All in all, it was a cloudy picture. With Russia moving toward elections whose very rules and formulas (including the 225–225 balance between proportional representation and constituency seats in the Duma, the balance of Moscow as opposed to regional candidates on national lists, and so forth) were still a matter of political wrangling, it seemed unlikely that those clouds would be dispelled quickly.

Privatization: Shifting the Ground

By mid-1995, a process that had been going on in earnest since the end of 1992 had reached major results. The process was privatization: the deetatization of Russia's command-economy Soviet inheritance. The result was that about two-thirds of the labor force was by late 1994 officially employed outside the state sector,[13] on which, as recently as two years before, they—as well as their parents and, largely, their grandparents—had been totally dependent. More than 100,000 state enterprises from shops to giant factories were now private in that the state held, at most, a minority interest. About 15,000 industrial plants containing approximately 60 percent of the industrial workforce had left the state sector. Between 80,000 and 90,000 retail shops and small service enterprises—about 70 percent of the Russian total—were now off the state's books. Anatoly Chubais, the privatization head and the only member of the economic cabinet to last the distance since the outset in 1992, had made clear his intent many times: to hang on to his ultimate objectives; to resist the resistors of privatization; to compromise when, but only when, politically necessary; and in the end to get enough property off the state's books to make the escape from the command economy irreversible. From the numbers, it looked as if he had succeeded.

Many small retail shops and other businesses had gone early and rather easily into the private sector through various sorts of leasing or buyout arrangements; these joined the growing number of small- to medium-sized enterprises that had originated as private operations over the past two to three years. The big factories and enterprises that had been the hallmark of the old economy were the objects of a more arduous process, one that began in earnest late in 1992. Thousands of plants had been slated for privatization. Most were offered a choice between two main procedural variants enabling their managements and workforces to acquire significant to controlling equity at very low prices; they had, by late 1994, done so. Added to this was voucherization—the issuance to every Russian, regardless of occupational status or workplace, of a privatization check to be used to bid for shares of enterprises going on the auction block, thus creating a vaguely hoped for nation of shareholders. The total face value of the vouchers issued represented more than one-third of the equity of the enterprises going on the block. By the time the voucherization program ended in late June 1994, nearly 140 million of the vouchers had been invested; Russia had 40 million shareholders and more than 500 mutual investment funds from the more or less honest to the fly-by-night.

Success in this area highlighted a series of other problems whose very emergence was testimony to the reality of change in Russia's economy. Capital was short, investment scarce; enterprises were finally facing the reality of something like the hard budget constraints that had hitherto been lacking. Privatization itself had thus far not generated injections of cash. The management and labor force acquisitions were free or bargain priced. The vouchers were claims, not cash, and put no new resources at the disposal of management. Outside of Chernomyrdin's favorite gas industry and a few other selected areas, the government was hardening its stance on credits. Industrial production continued to fall, and services proportionally made up a larger share of a (poorly measured) GDP than ever before, thus moderating the GNP effects of the fall in industry, if not the political-emotional impact on those nostalgic for the smokestack skyline of the old USSR.

Further, deeper change yet was in prospect. From mid-1994 on the government concentrated on a third phase—selling off a good deal of what remained in its hands, but this time via a cash privatization program through auctions with starting prices established in a revaluation that would peg asset values some ten to twelves times above those used in the labor force and voucher buyouts. At least 51 percent of the proceeds were to go to the enterprises rather than the state and thus would help provide the badly needed investment of which even potentially quite profitable plants had been starved. Cash privatization—controversial, conflictful, raising fears about selling off Russia's wealth to moneyed privateers, even foreign investors—would be a major issue in 1995.

All, to be sure, was not well. This Russian protocapitalism was rude and crude. It fell far short, in 1995, of the objective of "profit-seeking corporations, privately owned by outside shareholders and not dependent on government subsidies for their survival."[14] Yesterday's state enterprises, now joint-stock companies, were largely run by insiders. Outside shareholders, individual or investment funds, had less leverage and access than they would in a mature market economy. Insider bosses and owners did their best to get subsidies from the government. Reminiscent of what the late Ed Hewett called the "battle for exceptions"[15] during reforms in the old Soviet economy, plants fought for exceptions from new rules and standards they could not meet, and those with clout and connections got tax relief and concessions that the less well placed did not; this was still an economy far from the market's level playing field. All this explained, to some degree, the tepid response of foreign investors to the promise of the new Russian economy. This mixed outcome could be traced, to some degree, to several ironies. Gaidar and the reformers had perhaps in a neoliberal sense expected that after shock therapy cleared the ground, market institutions of the necessary sort would sprout simultaneously; but on Russian soil, given Soviet history and the people who populated that soil, they did not. A strong state, clear in its objectives, was needed, it can be argued, to clear the ground and build the new institutions. But given their own fears and the results of Russian-Soviet hyperstatism, a strong state was not what the reformers wanted. Nor was a strong state what Yeltsin and company actually had in 1992–1995 even had they seen the need for one to create a new market economy.[16] Hence, we have the mixed picture that is so striking both to "hard-line" pro-market advocates and to those more critical of market logic, whose major concerns and fears focus on the fate of the working class in Russia today and tomorrow.[17]

But for all the messiness, compromise, and corruption, the deetatization of much of the industrial core of the old economy created at least a potential base for the development of distinct interests of labor and employers. What loomed as a possibility was an alteration of the social-economic landscape in the direction of the sort of reality that corporatist mechanisms aimed to regulate, and hence new possibilities for the government as referee. If we look back to autumn 1991, this counted as a massive change. How had it been brought about?

"In the only way that was politically possible" is what Anatoly Chubais would probably have answered at mid-1994. He had not really wanted the mass voucherization, but it was a political necessity.[18] He had not really favored the insider-privilege partial buyouts either. But these were compromises with which he could live better than with the more radical, syndicalist, third-way thinking we saw in Chapter 3, which was readily exploitable by demagogues.

Early in 1992, STK representatives and some trade unions[19] had demanded that in privatization, workers should control the "form and schedule" and that the labor force should receive 25 percent of the equity totally free with voting rights and unrestricted as to its value; this last point was relevant to equity issues between workers in plants with apparently solid futures and those employed in the darkest sectors of sunset industry. Chubais demurred; labor collectives and managements would not get controlling blocks of stock free. Nor was he partial to the even more radical idea of the transfer of the whole of a factory to collective ownership as a "closed" joint-stock company. But in the end, privatization proceeded in a manner mixing insider privilege and broad giveaway; the primary objective was to allow the government to offload the burden of ownership.

The compromise with insider interests was manifest in what emerged as the two main variants. Under variant 1, enterprise workers and employees would receive 25 percent of the equity free as nonvoting (preferred) stock and the right to buy an additional 10 percent of equity as voting (common) stock at 30 percent discount off the low face value (established in a 1991 assessment to which the vouchers of mass privatization were keyed). Vouchers themselves could be used for any portion, up to 100 percent, of this additional equity. Management for its part could acquire 5 percent of equity in voting-stock form at the low 1991 prices.

Under variant 2, management and workers together could opt, on a two-thirds vote by the labor collective, to buy out 51 percent of equity as voting stock without any bidding by outsiders. Vouchers could be employed for up to half the price; the price was to be set at 1.7 times the value established in the 1991 evaluation and used in variant 1.[20]

Readers following the arithmetic will have concluded that these processes, carried to their conclusions, would leave the state with a 60 percent packet of shares after first-variant, a 49 percent one after second-variant privatization. Economist critics of the government's plan, and of Chubais, who were not syndicalist, worried that this would not be enough to extricate the state and leave managers and workers to assume responsibility and power on their own and had advocated full, rapid giveaways.[21]

Although not an answer to such objections, the voucher plan, which began in earnest in late 1992, did serve to extricate the state from a further share of equity in the enterprises scheduled for 1993 privatization. It vested each citizen, whether or not employed in a privatizing or privatizable workplace, with a share of the value all had created. Rough and inelegant to be sure (since workers with a free or discount claim to a piece of their enterprises by virtue of being there could use their vouchers to additional advantage, as noted earlier), it was nonetheless a response to a social justice issue that would not go away. Thus, in later 1992–early 1993 Russians received paper they could (1) sell for cash to any buyer at a mutually agreed price; (2) use, as workers, to buy a share of their own enterprises as in the variants just described; (3) use to bid directly for stock in enterprises scheduled in voucher auctions; or, more likely, (4) use to invest in a myriad of emerging mutual funds that would do the same.

Investment being still an alien concept, many would sell their vouchers (against Chubais's advice to wait and see with some confidence that these were instruments whose real value was much greater than a rapidly deflating 10,000 rubles in cash). Before the issuance began, a futures market developed in rights to receive someone else's voucher: Typical offering prices were in the 4,000–8,000 range, though prices above the voucher's notional 10,000 ruble face value were reported.[22] Stories abounded of what people, unsure of what vouchers meant, were doing with them. A teenager reportedly exchanged hers for a large box of (immensely popular) Snickers bars. In Siberia and the Far East, where many areas were among the first in the issuance process, traders were buying vouchers "for next to nothing"; "elderly women [were] reported to have agreed to exchange their vouchers for sugar."[23] In mid-October, vouchers were selling for "from 200 to several thousand" rubles; in the Altai region, some "exchange rates" were one voucher to one bottle of vodka. Someone in Orenburg proposed trading his cow for a voucher (or vice versa?).[24]

Stories like these, we should remember, are less than three years old. The past they reflect, by itself, is enough to render unrealistic in the extreme any expectations that an orderly market lubricated by law, habit, a changed psychology, and firm, functioning institutions—a "*civil* economy"[25]—could have existed by the mid-1990s. Russian privatization was flawed and controversial in many ways; under the circumstances, it could not be otherwise. That privatized enterprises did not immediately change their spots, that some directors might see no logical problem with a hat-in-hand approach to the state for subsidies, and that some were surely headed for bankruptcy (or worse, avoiding it when it provided the needed opportunity for reorganization) did not alter the fundamental fact of economic revolution in Russia, and with it the possibility that a state interested in refereeing employer-worker relations might be, finally, on the way to finding a class or category of owners-employers distinct from itself.

Workers, Wages, Militancy

During the approximately eighteen months that elapsed between the October crisis of 1993 and late spring 1995, patterns of union activity already familiar were for the most part repeated. But these now played against a background of contextual change. Privatization, flawed and ambiguous as we have seen it to be, was altering the stage on which labor politics was played. The government's attempts to come to grips with the coal industry's problems—the heritage of the unique planned-loss sector, the dependence of one-industry communities on continuing subsidies—would strain its relations with its erstwhile labor supporters. The continuing shift, however hard to trace in detail, of political initiative to an emergent category of bosses and owners carried its own implications for hired labor.

Militancy increased in the first half of 1994, somewhat reminiscent of 1992. Now the action was predominantly in the coal sector. In late January there were strike threats in the Vorkuta coal pits and the Komi oil fields, as well as warnings of production cuts by West Siberian oil workers. Mine construction workers occupied a pit in Vorkuta in protest from February 9 to 14.[26] The independent NPG and the FNPR-affiliated coal industry branch union, less often now at loggerheads, were evidently collaborating in the Komi region on a one-day protest strike on March 1, though in the Kuzbass their relations were less cordial. Despite the democratic labor history of the area and the support the Kuzbass miners had generally given the government, December had seen electoral support strong for Zhirinovskii in the region, and the old-style regional boss Aman Tuleev had been elected to the upper house of the legislature.[27] The one-day stoppage, according to the NPRUP branch union, was 75 percent effective; as it ended, oil and gas workers mounted a strike threat for March 15.[28]

Yeltsin issued an edict on March 10 on "citizens' labor rights," condemning the months-long pay delays driving the strikes and instructing state prosecutors to look into managerial responsibility in this area.[29] However, edicts could not produce immediate responses. On March 30, 500 miners were picketing the White House in protest over unpaid wages. Yeltsin and Economics Minister Shokhin promised that they would be paid; Deputy Premier Soskovets ordered that this be done. On April 12, the government—behind on subsidies it had promised the coal mines—ordered the State Bank to release 300 billion rubles immediately and a like sum each month thereafter.[30]

Once a darling, now an orphan, the defense industry was hurting as well. Lack of government orders put many workers on short time and furloughs—perhaps half of the industry's workforce by May 1. Many plants joined a June 9 protest action—a ten-minute cessation of work on the production of consumer goods, with whistles blowing—and the FNPR's military industry branch union called for the withdrawal of the union's signature to the spring Civic Accord.[31]

Midyear analyses viewed this record as much more turbulent than that of 1993. Employing no-doubt-approximate figures, different sources produced different estimates. The Labor Ministry in July reported that 100,000 workers had participated in strike actions from January through May—almost as many as in all of 1993.[32] *Rossiiskie Vesti* put the number of strikers in the first quarter of 1994 at 114,500—versus only 18,200 in the same period of the previous year.[33] An FNPR report put the number of strike actions in the first quarter at 10.3 times the number in January through March 1993.[34] *Pravda* gave a figure of 130,000 strike participants in the first half of the year, citing Labor Ministry figures[35]; all of these were very small numbers.

The latter half of the year seemed even quieter—or at least marked more by standard FNPR politicking. FNPR scheduled its all-Russia day of action for October 27, its grievances and demands directed, as before, at the government: minimum-wage increases, more antiinflation measures, and complaints over wage arrears. With regard to the latter, FNPR critics, notably Sotsprof, again made the point that the government should not be held totally responsible. Bosses were, at least outside the budget sector, more directly implicated in this abuse of workers.[36] Presidential chief of staff Sergei Filatov asked, citing the Civic Accord, that FNPR not go ahead with its day of protest, but Vladimir Shumeiko, former RTK coordinator and now chair of the Federation Council (the upper house of the legislature), issued a statement of support for FNPR's planned action.[37]

Both appeal and support statement meant less than they might have. Government—the president's office, the executive, the legislature—were (see further on) in rather regular contact with FNPR outside the moribund RTK, and neither was likely to surprise the other. In any case, October 27 was planned by FNPR as a day not of strikes but of demonstrations, meetings, marches, and speeches. And so it was.

The year changed, but as 1994 drifted into 1995, the problems did not. True, much of the economy was operating off the books, and many in the indubitably hard-pressed population continued to draw on resources beyond their stated wages. This made accurate estimates of welfare and poverty difficult in the extreme. But unemployment, though still in smallish numbers, was growing. Real wages for many were falling. The already tattered safety net faced further deterioration as Moscow tried to shift more burden to local governments, the latter already the target of similar attempts by enterprises no longer able or willing in many cases to maintain their ancillary functions in education, health, housing, and other areas.

Coal-industry problems had grown more vexing. The government's growing reluctance and delay tactics in the subsidy area were in a sense supported by World Bank advice about downsizing and closing pits, which led to cries of protest from both sides of the FNPR-NPG divide.[38] On February 8, a one-day warning strike across Russia's mine regions had broad support,[39] with NPG announcing it would support the FNPR branch union in its economic demands—wage arrears—if not the broader political ones.[40] Given that the fate of miners and mining communities was such a third-rail issue, it is understandable that the government's reluctance to touch it looked like a judgment that on the whole, continuing subsidies might be cheaper. But in a bitter early-April strike in the mines in the Far East Primorskii region, settled when the government anted up funds for miners' wages, Chubais accused local coal bosses of having misused earlier Moscow subsidies, putting into question whether Moscow funds, once disbursed, got to miners at all.[41]

The FNPR central executive, in mid-March, called upon the regional and branch affiliates for a turnout on April 12 to protest deteriorating living standards, meanwhile giving the government time for corrective actions; this call came, as *Izvestiia* observed (in a rare reference to the RTK "sideshow" and its processes), with the ink barely dry on the 1995 General Agreement.[42] April 12, 1995, went off, like the previous October 27, as a day of rallies, speeches, and protest marches with major disagreements between FNPR and other observers about the breadth of its support. Shmakov cited 2 million as having "taken to the streets and squares" but also asserted that a total of 10 million workers, counting those who had taken part in "workers' meetings," had participated. A suggestion by the interior minister that the number was closer to 450,000 was ridiculed by the antigovernment *Sovetskaia Rossiia*, which suggested that the minister was counting "militia nightsticks" rather than protesting workers.[43]

If all this seemed somewhat ritualized, if there was something here of familiar roles being played on both sides, the appearance was not altogether misleading. In 1994 and 1995, many factors worked to limit the impact of strikes and strike threats and to limit as well what the government could do to affect the situation. In the first place, with industrial production falling so rapidly from a combination of nonlabor-related causes (this was reflected in dismissals, furloughs, and short time for workers), the voluntary withholding of labor (strikes) had only marginal impact on economic indicators. Strikes were a consequence, in an indirect sense, of production decline and not a cause of it. The government had bigger economic issues to worry over.

Second, government had less of a handle than before on managers. In the confusing context of accelerating privatization, managers had opportunities for more control over workers. Limited in what it could do, the government sought to redirect rank-and-file anger away from itself and toward the bosses. Against those who sought to lay the whole blame at its door (*Rabochaia Tribuna* in January attributed the growing sum of unpaid wages to the Finance Ministry's "draconian measures on the regulation of [inter-enterprise] financial mutual relations" in an attack on the government's inflation-fighting strategy[44]), the government hit out at greedy and unfeeling bosses eager to maximize their own advantages. Factory managers largely set their own salaries whether in private, mixed, or state-sector plants, and these were reaching a hitherto-unheard-of twelve to fifteen times the pay of rank-and-file workers.

Labor Minister Melikian expressed himself sharply on the matter: "It does frequently happen that wages are not paid, while enterprises have foreign currency accounts or own shares of large banks. Sell them and pay your employees."[45] Managerial reluctance to pay workers was one thing. The unwillingness of managers to pay their debts to creditor plants even when they had the wherewithal could mean the creditor enterprise's workers going without. Melikian recalled a conversation with a metallurgical enterprise boss: "I knew who he was not paying. Miners had shipped coal, he had received it and was sitting tight. I shamed him, but he laughed: 'Stop picking on me with those moral principles of yours,' he said."[46]

But Melikian admitted that the government's roughly administered tight-money policies had their effect too. They led to "uncivilized" methods of suppressing inflation: "not paying grants, ... depriving the budget-financed sphere of funding, ... not paying for products ordered by the state, and so on."[47] Still, as time wore on and wage arrears mounted, the directors—who, after all, had given little comfort to the government in the past years—remained a target. In July 1994, Yeltsin called the situation "outrageous," especially in enterprises still in the state sector at that time, and asked, "Why aren't those executives being kicked out?"[48]

There were plenty of reasons. That directors grabbed what they could hardly required explanation in the world of Russia 1994. That state enforcement of decrees left something to be desired had to do, as well, with the material interests of many of the enforcers.

But beyond this, the government's project was not the building of a more egalitarian or secure society—except, perhaps, over the long term—but the establishment of a market economy, and progress in the two areas was bound to remain unequal in striking ways for a long time to come. Misindustrialized Russia was going through a period of primitive capital accumulation, an unpretty but necessary process. Melikian and Yeltsin himself might thus condemn the more egregious excesses, but major intervention was not part of the government program. Thus, people were asked to remember that less-evident but still steep inequalities had been part of the Soviet order. Words like Melikian's, balancing these elements, were cold comfort to those who felt victimized by the new economics. Admitting that the top decile of earners averaged about thirty times the pay of the lowest 10 percent ("according to this indicator, we have 'surpassed' the civilized countries and have come much closer to the Third World"), he went on to stress the absence of alternatives. "We cannot get away from an increase in the differentiation of incomes—especially during the period of the initial accumulation of capital. This is an inevitable and objective process, although I agree that it is proceeding too rapidly, which is intensifying social tension."[49]

The government was limited in capacities and aspirations. Commitments to international monetary authorities centered on limiting the state budget deficit; looking good involved limiting inflation. Both pushed the government to avoid pumping money into the system and to delay the money it did pay out—even to creditors, as Melikian admitted. Against the background of the economic activity going on even in chaotic Russian conditions, this was a poor government. Filling its budget coffers depended on tax collection, an activity at which it was not notably successful. Immense amounts of economic activity went unrecorded and untaxed. Through account shuffling and various modes of evasion, many enterprises looked poorer than they were and paid less in taxes than they might. Only in state enterprises—and not in all of these—did the state have some real collecting power; from these, the state attempted to exact revenues at tax rates set very high because of low rates of compliance. As (measured) industrial production continued to fall, so the tax base eroded. The Russian state, committed on the one hand to a tight budget and hence a limited deficit, found on the other that its revenues fell constantly short of even its own limited projections.

In spring 1994, Melikian announced a partial solution to the wage-payment problem. Aside from plants that made something, but could not sell it and had no money and those that made and sold but received no payment from the buyer, factories had money coming in. In these—at least the ones on which the state had some sort of grip—moneys coming into the factory account were "automatically disbursed" to cover taxes due, pension fund contributions, and payments to "main suppliers" (evidently of fuel). This practice, Melikian admitted, had itself led to avoidance patterns whereby management paid workers in kind—"teapots, saucepans, irons"—and let the workers then sell these for what they could get. Workers were hence "paid" while the factories avoided tax liability. Now, a compromise between the Labor and Finance Ministries would leave half of the funds due as federal taxes in the plant accounts with the stipulation that these be used to pay wages.[50] (The government, itself responsible for the large budget-financed workforce, could hardly forgo the other half to see industrial workers paid.[51])

How effective this move turned out to be, even within its own limits, was obvious by 1995. It was less than likely that governmental jawboning and attempts to shame managers into playing straight with the labor forces would work with the recalcitrant. Massive delays in wage payouts continued, as Deputy Premier Soskovets reported in early September: A total wage arrears figure in industry and agriculture that had been 800 billion rubles at the beginning of 1994 had grown to 4 trillion by August. Eight months later, in April 1995, FNPR would cite a figure of 5.6 trillion rubles in pay arrears nationwide.[52] Factories still hid stashes of hard currency while not honoring their debts; factories that pleaded inability to pay their debts were paying dividends to shareholders.[53] Effective bankruptcy procedures were moving closer, and some firms had been declared insolvent; the government now threatened to use this weapon against managements who cried poor while hiding funds and assets. But at the same time, it remained under ever present pressures for injections of credit into the seemingly bottomless sump of enterprise debt, and the more alarmist urged renationalization of plants where management was not doing its job.

In all of this, there was little to comfort the unions. Protests might be numerous, but their results were ambiguous. FNPR might demand, but the Moscow center did not necessarily control the branch and regional unions. Pending new legislation, the state was playing a large role in administering the social insurance fund. Though developments were, arguably, moving toward a differentiation of economic interests between workers and employers, neither of these forces had developed enough coherence to change, fundamentally, the situation in the RTK and make it into the main mechanism of corporatism. There was, perhaps, a certain amount of exhaustion of old patterns and postures of conflict between FNPR and the government and of the reserves of energy and emotion from which both sides drew the wherewithal to fight. In February 1994, eight base-industry trade unions demanded a meeting with Chernomyrdin, complaining of government economic policy but issuing no strike threat.[54] In April, FNPR head Shmakov had a meeting with Yeltsin. Reporting on their discussions, he stressed their meeting of the minds on issues of bankruptcy. If some of the president's advisers were pushing a bottom-line strategy of simply declaring bankrupt all the plants that could not pay their bills for raw materials, fuel, and transport, this could lead to half the workforce going into unemployment. They agreed, he said, that enterprises must be dealt with individually and that particular account (here, again, revealing the limits of economics as a guide to policy) must be taken of enterprises "often being shut down not because there is no demand for their output but because consumers do not have the means to purchase it." They remained divided, he continued, on the matter of the social insurance fund and on a draft labor code that gave fewer guarantees to unions and workers. But Shmakov had (after the meeting, which looked like a warm-up to the event) signed the Civic Accord with the government. It was, it seemed, a time for solidarity, since "today the problem of civic peace in society worries the country's entire population equally. The squabbles on the political Olympus are costing our state too dear."[55]

This was, certainly, a style different than Klochkov's. The ex-FNPR chairman was by now a legislator. As an independent, listing himself as head of an FNPR-related bank, Klochkov had been given a place on the anti-government Agrarian Union's national list, and now sat in the State Duma. If Klochkov had seemingly courted or blundered into crisis, Shmakov for all his combative past was stressing here not the fractures of class and economic lines but the commonality of problems. This was appropriate if only because FNPR was weaker; as he put it, the FNPR "cannot have political goals today" but had to concentrate on social and labor issues.[56]

It was, then, an interesting time. Trade unions, especially the FNPR, had barely found their feet in the post-Soviet period; yet the ground was still shifting. Privatization; unemployment; the looming threat of bankruptcies; the inability of the government, except by cranking up inflationary currency emissions, to satisfy demands for cash—all limited the space in which unions could maneuver. Weaker unions surely suited the government even without Gaidar and Fedorov. Although officials who, like Melikian, declared themselves in favor of strong trade unions were not necessarily lying, this was a long-term matter. In the time in question, making the moves toward a new economy on new, irreversible foundations was an end better served by a labor movement that was not too strong.

In the same vein, the RTK was evidently a quieter place in 1994. It had, again, been rechartered by a Yeltsin edict of March 21; Deputy Premier Yuri Yarov was its new coordinator, and the labor side had been reshuffled to its post-October 1993 configuration.[57] And for the third time, it had produced a general agreement, on April 8, with the state evidently making more promises than the unions.[58] There was little new in the documentary style. A skeptical *Rabochaia Tribuna* writer asked, "Given that [the agreement] overflows with phrases such as 'prepare proposals' and 'develop drafts,' when is its effect to be expected?"[59] The same reporter quoted Shmakov on an upbeat note, seeing the "very fact" of the signing as positive, "a step … that makes confrontation less likely, and safeguards peace in our house." The FNPR leader was happy that many union proposals had been incorporated into the agreement, citing as an example the following text (which, upon examination, bears again the stamp of the sort of government undertaking hard to fulfill and unlikely, in the end, to be met fully).

> A set of measures shall be taken to provide coordinated regulation, including by the state, and control over prices (rates) for energy resources, individual socially significant foodstuffs (regulated at the regional level), principal types of medicinal preparations and drugs, the services of passenger and freight transportation, communications, municipal and other services to the population, and products (goods, services) of monopoly enterprises.[60]

Shmakov voiced familiar grievances in 1994. In May, he criticized the government's unilateral preparation of decrees on various matters that were left unpublished but then cited in speeches by government officials. Both the General Agreement and the Civic Accord "envisage[d] preliminary discussions and coordination with trade unions regarding any legislation that affects social and economic issues." The government was thus violating the "basic principles of social partnership," but then the RTK had been "standing idle recently."[61] The notion that the poor attendance habits of government officials in previous versions of the RTK were characteristic as well of the post-October 1993 and 1994 versions found support from nonunion sources as well.[62]

If, then, Shmakov somewhat defensively reminded the government that the FNPR signature he had affixed to the Civic Accord was not a no-strike pledge,[63] this was not likely to upset the government overmuch. FNPR was weak internally, and Shmakov acted as if he understood this better than Klochkov, at least judging by his public rhetoric, ever had. There were troubles with regional union leaders who, looking for political clout, were associating themselves with former cabinet minister Yuri Skokov's Federation of Commodity Producers of Russia (Federatsiia Tovaroproizvoditelei Rossii, or FTR) against Shmakov's central-FNPR "apolitical-nonpartisan" orientation. The failure of Civic Union to score heavily in the December 1993 election had caused some of these to question the utility of the old alliance of FNPR with the Russian Union of Industrialists and Entrepreneurs (RSPP), the Volskii-led organization that with the union had founded RASP in 1992. As one commentator put it, when at a conference with regional organizations Shmakov reposed hope mainly in the regions; characterizing the central organization's difficulties with the government with the words "nobody reckons with the poor and weak," he must in fact have had in mind not only government attitudes toward the Moscow FNPR headquarters but the attitudes of the regional affiliates themselves.[64]

Over 1994–1995, then, it probably grew easier than in the past for the government to meet with FNPR leaders; less was at stake, and little could be lost across the table. In August, Shmakov and others from FNPR met with Sergei Filatov, Yeltsin's chief of staff, and some other government officials to complain about wage arrears, employment policies and provision for unemployment, the tax burdens on enterprises, and the whole functioning of social partnership. Sergei Khramov, head of the uninvited Sotsprof, confessed himself "sick of all this," accusing the president of finding it simpler "to deal with the old trade union nomenklatura than with us." Government commissions on the arrears and tax problems, it was agreed, would include FNPR representatives, and the government undertook to keep Finance and Economics Ministry bureaucrats at their desks through the summer to produce a draft budget by November—which would allow the drawing up of a general agreement for 1995 before that year began, thus for the first time implementing one of the elements of the original RTK design.[65] (Of course, those commitments were only partially met—the 1995 agreement took longer.)

A pattern of meetings and consultations looser than any corporatist design and with more than a hint of ritual emerged. Thus, in the wake of the October 1994 "action day," in early December, Deputy Premiers Soskovets and Chubais headed a government delegation in a meeting with Shmakov and others from FNPR. If no love feast, it did produce a union acknowledgment that the government was making major inroads into clearing the budget-sector wage arrears for which it bore direct responsibility.[66]

Another meeting in early March 1995 brought the FNPR leaders together with Chernomyrdin and Chubais for more private talks on wage arrears, interenterprise debt, and other matters: Arrears took center stage with "all the other" union demands being referred to the "currently operating" RTK.[67]

Although the government executive and FNPR were, then, no strangers to one another, the latter found more understanding in parliament. This was not remarkable, since so many FNPR objectives—the maintenance of production and employment, the raising of minimum-wage levels, the softening of whatever hardness could be found in budget constraints—were also popular issues for which a Duma majority could happily vote with no responsibility for finding the funds and in expectation, in any case, of a presidential veto. One such issue that surfaced from time to time was a retrospective indexation of state-savings bank deposits of 1991, whose value was wiped out by the inflation of 1992; this was a compensation move as popular, at first glance, as it was economically impossible.

To a certain degree, the commodity producers (FTR), headed by Yuri Skokov, was an intermediary in these FNPR-parliament contacts despite its ambiguous relationship with FNPR's Moscow headquarters. In a September 1994 statement, Duma economic policy committee chair Sergei Glaziev expressed agreement with FTR's industrial policy and acknowledged the high degree of his committee's coordination with that body: "The interests of the commodity producers and the workers coincide—overcoming the drop in production and the preservation of jobs are interrelated. Just as are economic growth and an increase in the well-being of the workers."[68]

Evidence thus grew that FTR and FNPR were growing tighter with one another at the top despite the Moscow headquarters' concerns about regional affiliates making their own deals with Skokov's organization. Previous to the October 1994 action day, one source cited a significant measure of coordination between the two bodies on demands to be made to the government. Volskii, whose Russian Union of Industrialists and Entrepreneurs (RSPP) was a member organization of the FTR, had also suggested to the government that Skokov be invited to an October session of the Civic Accord conciliation commission, though the FTR was not one of the signatories.[69]

Skokov, for his part, had called in September 1994 for the government to show more "partnership" toward producers[70] and envisaged a broad consultative process that would link the government, the FNPR—no other union was mentioned—and the FTR. *Kommersant-Daily* characterized this as a recipe for a "corporate state."[71]

Still, there were limits on the degree of coziness developing between the government and an FNPR that still exercised—albeit on a shorter leash with more government oversight—some of its traditional welfare functions and held on, given the legacies of history, to a huge membership. A draft law on trade unions had been working its way through the legislative process, receiving first-reading approval from the Duma on

November 16, 1994. Attacked by the reformist Russia's Choice (Gaidar) and Yabloko (Grigori Yavlinskii) factions, the law exempted from taxation trade union funds "received for the purpose of conducting ... charter-mandated activities." Given loose interpretations and a wild legal climate and the fact that unions were allowed to engage also in nonmandated commercial activities that were deemed taxable, this looked like a valuable and readily abusable tax shelter of impressive elasticity. Guaranteed as well was the "inviolability" of trade union property. In effect the draft law, according to its critics, was a gift to FNPR. It possessed a massive amount of property, courtesy of the Soviet past, and with it a potentially huge business base. Moreover, the draft seemed to guarantee the various rights, privileges, and tax relief to only *one* union organization in each plant. In the vast majority of cases, this would be an FNPR local.[72]

Understandably, the non- (and anti-) FNPR unions cried foul. On April 12, 1995—as noted earlier—NPG and Sotsprof, together with five other unions, had founded the Confederation of Labor of Russia. Two days later, the Duma, apparently on third reading, had again passed the draft trade union law. NPG and Sotsprof mobilized 100 pickets outside the upper-house Federation Council on May 4 in protest, accusing those behind the law of trying to reestablish the old FNPR monopoly.[73] Late in the month, Yeltsin—despite the fact that relations between the government and the non-FNPR unions were frayed somewhat—vetoed the law.[74] FNPR, if no longer the government's enemy since the chastening experiences of late 1993 and thereafter, was not its indispensable ally. It and the independent unions were left largely in their old opposing stances. There matters stood.

Labor politics, then, seemed mired in the complicated economic transition, and interpretations of trends differed. In April 1994, Melikian still found it possible to stress the union-employer collaboration pattern as typical for the economy: Admitting that "we sometimes try to make use of a ready-made mechanism such as it exists in the West," he implicitly faulted RTK corporatism, since in Russia "the employers and the trade unions are on one side, and the government is on the other."[75] Not long after, former deputy labor minister Kudiukin, however, saw signs of erosion of labor-management solidarity at the enterprise level—the sort of thing that had made, in spring 1994, for collaboration between the two coal unions and that might presage, finally, the emergence of class conflicts of the sort Melikian could not yet see. When directors awarded themselves fat pay envelopes while failing to pay their workers,

the old song about the common interests of all enterprise employees in the struggle against a bad government is no longer reassuring. The ver-

tical-corporate conflict is becoming a class conflict (labor against capital, employee against employer), although it is still on a local scale. The
gap between the "traditional" and the new trade unions is beginning to
be surmounted here and there on this basis.[76]

It was a matter of the glass being at the same time half full and half
empty. Whether the resentments, tensions, and fears that certainly existed could be translated into any kind of real class politics remained,
given the incompleteness of the transition, a somewhat premature question. What one could count on, it seemed, was more pain, more burdens.
The government, with the generalized long-term objective of a market
economy, lacked short-term capacity to guide various aspects of the
process, to relate them to the long term. Unemployment, Melikian had
said in late 1993, would be mainly a regional problem, concentrated in
some of the eighty-nine territorial components of the Russian Federation, "market corners" hard to leave because of "the absence of a housing
market, and even … the infamous residence permits." In one-factory
towns—even those with no real future—government intervention would
be necessary;[77] but this meant that in the mining sector, for example, the
most hopeless areas would claim the bulk of "transitional" subsidies.[78]
This would take money. Not only was the government not good at collecting it from enterprises, but given the social tensions attendant on
ever-more-blatant material inequalities, any system of redistribution
through personal income taxation was still distant. "We do not know
how. Russian citizens are not accustomed to paying taxes or even to fig-
uring out their incomes."[79] With cash privatization and the commercial-
ization of the economy moving further forward in 1995, enterprises were
looking to off-load responsibilities for housing, education, medical care
and other benefits for employees. Would these elements of a tattered
safety net survive in the hands of the local government authorities to
whom they were to be transferred?

Corporatism and Democratic Transition Revisited

In Chapter 1, I discussed some perspectives on the broad political
processes that led to the decline and fall of the USSR and the objectives
and processes of political change the Yeltsin government subsequently
pursued in the Russian Federation.

To restate the position adopted earlier: The USSR Gorbachev inherited in 1985 was still in essence and structure a totalitarian rather than
simply an authoritarian polity. Weakened, stagnating, its population's
common life one of quotidian repression and shortage rather than terror, it still exemplified a syndrome of mutually dependent characteris-

tics that previous post-Stalin leaders had left in essence undisturbed. Seeking reform, Gorbachev disturbed them. Using the powers of office, he carried out major changes against the better judgment of much of the old state-party elite. Mistaking the Soviet totalitarian system for one that was reformable, he brought about its collapse.

Gorbachev's role in history, thus, will differ both from the Jaruzelski who pacted the beginnings of the Polish democratic transition and from the Honneckers, Zhivkovs, and Ceauşescus who fell by way of regime collapse—whether to Velvet Revolution or firing squad. He fell by way of a preservationists' coup. The preservationists' failure, in turn, spelled the end of a political-economic system and the multinational state it had held together.

Yeltsin faced political and economic tasks of immense magnitude. Peaceful revolution seemed a good characterization of his project: an amalgam of elements of revolution and democratic transition. There was no market economy up and running and no bourgeois propertied interests to leave largely in place, as have the state brokers of transition in Southern Europe and Latin America. It was part of the project to build the base of such an economy, demolishing along the way those major elements of the old command-administrative economy that still littered the ground. Democracy was still novel, institutionally weak, with little context in which to be embedded. Building it was still, thus, something of a top-down matter with all the risks that implied. Doing so without recourse—at least until October 1993—to violence to promote the revolutionary political and economic objectives was a hopeful commitment but a complication as well.

Within this context, evident and anticipated problems in labor politics were to be handled in a corporatist framework of the societal variety via the trilateral commission, the RTK. The difficulties with the brand of corporatism adopted have been addressed; they centered on the non-correspondence between the design of the RTK's trilateral social partnership and the actual geometry of the Russian economy in 1992–1993, which lacked the structure of distinct group economic interests. Trilateralism, the RTK, the aspirations of the government to play the role of neutral third party—all were more expressions of hope than a response to what actually existed.

The corporatist choice was one Russia was constrained to make; a hands-off, laissez-faire Madisonianism was hardly an available alternative given Russia's history and the state's role as owner-proprietor in the economy it had inherited from the USSR. With respect to the latter, what made a corporatist design (even a societal one where the state hoped in a sense to "grow" its partners) inevitable also left the government uncomfortably connected to the employer side.

All this is, by now, familiar ground. Before leaving the recent past to look at prospects for the future, one more consideration of the linkages among posttotalitarian political change, market reform, and corporatism, taking account of some additional perspectives, may be useful.

Earlier, I noted Schmitter's argument that a move from the harsher state corporatism to the more benign societal variety was difficult. The two varieties grew from different sources, conditions, histories; the characteristics that might facilitate such a transformation seemed also to be exactly the sort that made a state-corporatist outcome unlikely in the first place.

How much harder, then, was the move from the legacy of Soviet totalitarianism, even of the weakened sort Gorbachev inherited, to the seemingly societal corporatism Yeltsin hankered after? Or did that very weakening of the totalitarian legacy include the development of corporatist elements in the Soviet system in its twilight (thus suggesting that peaceful revolution might involve a transition from one corporatism to another)?

So, in a rather explicit sense, had Valerie Bunce and John Echols argued in a 1980 essay.[80] Examining some of the other labels of the time, notably general and institutional pluralism and "groupism," they used Schmitter's 1974 definitions to argue that Soviet politics in the later Brezhnev regime was best understood as corporatist. In retrospect, the stability and adaptive capacity they ascribed to the Soviet system look misplaced indeed; their use of corporatism was an instance of stretching a concept beyond its utility. But such could be said of so much else of late-Brezhnev period analysis that we need not linger on this in any detail save with respect to one point. As for whether the USSR exemplified societal or state corporatism, they agreed that the USSR could hardly be of the former variety, hardly one of those "liberal corporatist systems [that] permit a far wider range of civil liberties and political rights than does the Soviet Union." But citing the welfare statism of the USSR,. the "guarantees of jobs, minimum incomes, and certain services" as well as egalitarian trends in income distribution, they argued that the Soviet system did not "fully fit the *state* corporatist model either."[81]

Fair enough. But Schmitter's societal-state distinctions do not really turn on these sorts of welfare outputs of the system, however real (or at the time Bunce and Echols wrote, overestimated) they might have been but rather on structures, on the original and continuing relationships of the state to the other corporate units and actors. It is hard to see how the old USSR exemplified any kind of corporatism. If this be the case, it cannot be that useful elements of corporatism in any real sense were included in the weakened totalitarianism that Gorbachev inherited in 1985 or, thus, in Yeltsin's 1991–1992 legacy from the final Soviet collapse.

The new Russia's corporatism had thus to be built from the top down. Inherited units like the FNPR, descendant of an AUCCTU tightly linked to state power ("there is no question in the Soviet Union of the trade union federation [AUCCTU] or any other major association breaking off from the system"[82]), had neither the history nor the organization to truly further the process from the ground up.

What such an analysis missed is suggested by Baohui Zhang's interesting exploration, fifteen years later, of the conditions under which retreating political elites can successfully "pact" transitions to democracy and of why, with the exception of Poland, such conditions were lacking in the East European and the USSR's political collapses.[83] For Zhang, successful pacting requires that elites possess the ability to "exclude the mass from direct participation in the transition process" to afford room for negotiation and compromise and that they—especially opposition elites—have the ability to "enforce those pacts on the popular sectors." This, then, is a view of what a certain process requires of elites. What makes it likely that they will have these abilities? It is a matter of institutions as much as elite motivations or "contingent choice."

> These ... conditions require the existence of strong societal institutions that provide the means of both social representation and control. On the one hand, elites from these institutions can represent the society in negotiations for democratization. On the other hand, because of their control abilities, these institutions can help elites exclude the mass from direct participation in the process and then later help enforce the pacts on the mass.
>
> These ... should ideally have a *semiofficial* and *semisocietal* status. If they are completely official institutions, then they are merely extensions of the authoritarian regime and cannot represent the society. If they are entirely societal, then they would not be tolerated by the regime in the first place and so would not be available to represent the society when democratization comes. Also, pure societal institutions offer little control capabilities. Their elites cannot effectively exclude the mass from the transition process and enforce the pacts on the mass.[84]

As Zhang sees it, it is precisely corporatist authoritarian regimes that have or can evolve such institutions. Not all will; not all that reach some approximation of democracy will manage the pacting route. Spain and Brazil, in his view, did; Portuguese and Argentine authoritarianism collapsed rather than pacted out because of lost wars and economic collapse. Such institutions were absent, however, in what he sees as the essentially totalitarian institutional structures of the People's Republic of China (PRC) (where in Tienanmen Square the 1989 democracy movement was crushed) and the old USSR, which did not survive the democratic challenge.

One need not agree in toto with Zhang's explication of the fall of the USSR (which to me overestimates the political solubility of the nationalities and secession problems) to appreciate his most important structural and institutional points. Central was the deficit of semiofficial, semisocietal institutions the opposition could employ in dealing with the regime. Gorbachev retained an institutional base and might himself have been able to pact for the government side. But who would sit across the table? Totalitarian institutional legacies had deprived opposition elites of the institutions they needed for pacting. Instead, oppositions in late, "post-terror" communist regimes faced situations in which "autonomous societal institutions were still not tolerated."[85] Opposition then took on the form of social movement rather than organization. Movements are creatures of a different sort; they are general in their demands, tend toward radicalization and demagogy in style, and support leaders who, rather than fully controlling them, must orient their politics to the movement in order not to lag behind. ("I am their leader; therefore I must follow them.")

In the USSR's accelerating slide toward the end, there was no opposition organized enough to make a deal with Gorbachev, no "institutions to stand upon" for opposition leaders who might have been ready for compromise. Yeltsin might have been one of these leaders until August and the coup: There was support for a new and weaker union of a confederative variety, albeit minus the Baltics; the creation of fifteen new countries was not really on anyone's political agenda in July 1991. Perhaps no pacting effort could have worked if one accepts Karklins's logic on attempted reform as the bullet that killed a totalitarian regime. But then, the point is that such a regime lacked the institutions through which opposing sides could pact. The deep opposition—the forces behind the failed coup—had they succeeded, would have produced "a complete reversal of [Gorbachev's] democratizing course."[86] But they failed and, in doing so, left Gorbachev and a center so radically weakened that these no longer had pacting power either.

A perhaps-salvageable Soviet state died because its institutions, so far removed from anything that might be labeled pluralism, fell far short of the institutional apparatus of authoritarian corporatism as well. Thus, the attempt chronicled in this work, the building of a corporatism to deal with the pains of economic and political transition in the toughest of times, was the difficult work not of adaptation, of amelioration, of reform, but of creation.

Given the nature of the problem, the RTK, thus, could hardly function well as a mechanism of corporatist coordination; what a disorganized sideshow it seems when held up against the criteria Schmitter laid out.

> Formally designated interest associations ... are officially recognized by the state not merely as interest intermediaries but as co-responsible "partners" in governance and societal guidance. Ostensibly private and autonomous associations are not just consulted and their pressures weighed. Rather, they are negotiated with on a regular, predictable basis. Their consent becomes essential for policies to be adopted; their collaboration becomes essential for policies to be implemented.[87]

There was, after all, a great distance to be traversed between the old Soviet institutional order and the world of conflicting interests the RTK anticipated and was designed to regulate. The chaotic state of late perestroika, the post-August collapse of the USSR, had not allowed for a thorough negotiated dismantling of the old institutional structures. The once-dominant Communist Party had, by 1990, been sidelined to a significant degree, but this was not the case with many economic institutions or with the FNPR. However poorly many such institutions and organizations might function, they existed. Relatively new bodies such as the USSR Scientific-Industrial Union, later the RSPP, or old institutions such as FNPR might even add an element of surface plausibility to the corporatist recipe. (How, after all, does one dispense with an organization of over 60 million that is called a labor union, that claims it is a labor union, and that is now critical of its own past of subordination to the state?)

"Some institutions are around because they have been around for a long time. Change is costly," as Przeworski put it.[88] The forces that give such staying power to institutions need not all be consensual; strong enough defenders of the status quo can make change too costly to pursue. Even in market economies, "economic institutions are often determined for reasons unrelated to economic efficiency";[89] this is very much so for the case of the USSR, whose politically driven, antimarket economic institutions were inefficient, wasteful, ultimately corrupted, and stumbling but still functioning upon Gorbachev's accession to power. In retrospect, those who would accuse Gaidar and other shock therapists of knowingly understating the chaos and pain that would come in 1992 might link their understatements to quite-plausible hard-line reformist perceptions that the critical task was destruction of precisely these institutions. For Gorbachev, however, the tasks of structural reform were more complicated: Perestroika meant restructuring, not destruction, and thus required different processes. In the way of restructuring were what have been called the transaction costs of changing institutional arrangements long in effect: risks of breakdown, of settling on a "wrong" solution, of indispensable participants in a restructuring process anticipating losses from the outcome. "Even when institutional arrangements are not optimally suited to a given environment, they may nevertheless endure because prospective gains from change are more than outweighed by the costs of effecting them."[90]

One might limit the transaction costs of institutional change by preagreeing on the methods whereby institutions might be changed, but Soviet institutions were by definition correct, embalmed in ideology, in need of nothing but "perfecting" (*sovershenstvovanie*). Thus, they had absorbed, rejected, and ultimately defeated earlier pre-Gorbachev attempts at more modest reform. Nested in a strong but brittle political order that collapsed in late 1991, they too collapsed, but not totally. FNPR survived. The Ministry of Industry rose in the place of the old panoply of branch ministries, but some of its departments had areas of responsibility that bore a striking resemblance to the old branch-ministry layout. A whole subinstitutional world of personalized networks and connections (especially in the regions) remained. Much thus survived the old USSR to become part of the new Russian Federation's legacy.

Post-Soviet reform, then, commenced in 1992 on a field that had not been cleared of much of the old debris. Its social costs were bound to be high, and these would be run up in a political "democracy" that was very new—posing with particular sharpness the problem of potential political opposition to those costs versus the economic necessity of their being borne. Were democracy and market reform compatible in Russia? How close might Russia come to that scenario wherein "democracy may be undermined or reforms abandoned, or both"?[91] The answer, obviously, would depend not only on the intensity of the pain but on whether opposition to the reform course could be effectively organized at the political level and on whether the population's pains were translatable into political resistance.

With respect to the latter, Russia at the outset of 1992 was not the same as Poland two years earlier. There, the political liberation from Soviet domination in 1989 and the public identification of the new government with Solidarity, with Walesa, and with a set of symbols of independence and authenticity regained meant that the population was clearly ready to cut the government some slack in what it had to do economically. This did not mean that the population really understood the market but, in Mira Marody's words, that it was ready to hold its breath, offer "simple endurance," and wait until it was announced that the market transition had been achieved.

> The acceptance of surrendering to the consequences of market mechanisms introduced by the government is in this situation more a moral choice than compliance with necessities having a socially obvious char-

acter. It is … a form of "escaping into a collective lot," a reaction to a threat perceived (consciously or not) as external, looking for psychological support in the spirit of community and the sense of social solidarity. This is the result of a confidence that delegates to the authorities full responsibility for the process of reforms and at the same time absolves everyone of the necessity of making personal decisions about his/her future.[92]

Hers is no sugar-coated view of Poland. But there, the acceptance did last long enough for the critical, transformative economic moves to be made. There, "confidence" was subject to depreciation, making for a succession of Polish governments and allowing the ex-communist democratic left to return later to power on a platform of alleviating economic pains. But even the left's economic policy has not challenged market principles at their base.

Such was not so clearly the case in Russia. Russian "independence"—from a USSR many thought synonymous with Russia, from a Ukraine and Belarus many felt were part of Russia—created no similar feeling of something regained. Yeltsin's post-August popularity was personal, not something that extended to the legislature of 1990 or the cabinet he would pick. No alternative political movement, no Solidarity, took power in Russia at the close of 1991, and the situation in which government and people, employers and workers, found themselves thus had much less of national consensus about it.

The corporatist strategy as manifest in the RTK was designed to share out responsibility (and blame) for the measures that would cause pain, to channel conflict, and to negotiate disagreements. Beyond the simple (of course, it was anything but) conflict-channeling goal, the main risk to the government's program that had to be averted was not a restoration of the Soviet-type order, full-blown, but rather adjustments that would in fact gut the march toward the market in favor of a heavily statist economy. The adjustments in question, to be pursued both through upper-level politicking in the parliament and executive and in the lower-level RTK were essentially the program of a major segment of the industrial lobby, the policy ground on which, in 1992, the RSPP and FNPR announced their agreement. The objective—thrown into sharp relief against the background of lost superpower status and Russia's uncertain place in the world—was not the preservation of socialism and not capitalism but the preservation of Russia's industrial economy itself, the halting of a slide toward the third world. A statist economic order that defended an industrial Russia at the periphery of the world market and that was driven by much the same factors that earlier in the century had driven "peripheral, delayed-dependent capitalism" toward state corporatism (among them "awareness of relative underdevelopment," "resentment against inferior international status," and "desire for enhanced national economic and political autarky"[93]) was a possible outcome if the industrialists' program was actuated.

No wonder then that the RTK became a cockpit of conflict about big issues, about ends (however vaguely expressed) and about means of reaching market economic objectives. Those objectives were not totally accepted. To those who did accept them, the government's ability to reach them via the pursuit of certain policies was not automatically evident. The FNPR had not, as noted earlier, adopted an alternative project—neither third-way syndicalism nor any other. But its pseudoneutrality on questions of economic system did not prevent it from attempting to play populist politics against market reform.

Social pacts between government and labor in new democracies face a whole set of formidable obstacles, as Przeworski argues; many of the weaknesses he addresses, drawn from the Latin American–southern European transition context, are amplified in Russia's 1991–1995 experience. His characterization of the difficulties a market-reforming government faces sounds much like a description of Russia and, if read as polemic or criticism, like the accusations FNPR directed at the Yeltsin government's economic policy and its performance as social partner in the RTK.

> Governments begin to vacillate between *decretismo* and *pactismo* in search of a peaceful resolution of conflicts. Since the idea of resolving conflicts by agreement is alluring, they turn to making bargains when opposition against reform mounts; they turn back to the technocratic style when the compromises involved in pacts imperil reforms. They promise consultation and shock the eventual partners with decrees; they pass decrees and hope for consensus. As a result, governments appear to lack a clear conception of reforms and the resolve to pursue them. The state begins to be perceived as the principal source of economic instability.[94]

Corporatism, then, had an exceedingly mixed record in the 1992–1993 period. In the aftermath of the October crisis, the December 1993 elections, and the new constitutional arrangements, its profile was lowered further and remained low in 1994–1995. Like many other organizations and structures created in the death throes of the USSR and the heady early days of 1992, the RTK was at once hopeful and premature. Predestined, likely, to become the sideshow that it was (and perhaps because this is what it remained), it did, at least, no harm.

Whether there is a place for corporatism and the RTK or some similar mechanism in the Russian future depends, first, on specific developments in critical areas of property relations, privatization, and the organizational resources and capacities of employers and labor; second, on broader developments in the "high" politics of presidential-parliamentary relations; and, finally, on the volatile politics of Russia's identity and place in the world. All of these are to some extent tied to the issue of whether and to what degree Russia will come in the future to be a civil society—itself a major question. It is to these matters, in conclusion, that I turn.

Russian Futures: The Labor Arena

Two cardinal points seem apparent three years and more into Russia's new politics: First, labor as a whole is weak and second, this fact is understood by labor and its governmental and employer-owner partners. To the degree that one views labor politics as a management versus worker game, managers have emerged for now as the winners. But they will, for some time, remain a diverse lot depending on what it is they are managing and how they got there. Ex-state managers of large and medium enterprises now possess significant ownership interests, gained in various collusive arrangements with cash-heavy silent partners and local officialdom. But they have also inherited, for a time, the heavy social overhead typical of many state plants. "Greenfield" entrepreneurs, who started new private enterprises, are also owners with hired labor under them. But they are not typically in large industry and have had neither the incentive nor the need to overstock their workforce or to add schools, housing, and other benefits to their productive base. They face nothing—or very little—similar to the potential controversies and constraints ex-state managers do. (The "directors' corps" in coal mining, and some other exceptional sectors, are, of course, differently situated, tied both to the state and to organized, more militant workforces.)

Nothing suggests that ex-state manager-owners are likely to be sentimentalists about their enterprises' inherited obligations toward workers or that they will be consistently paternalistic. A good deal of strain can be anticipated as employers do what they can to transfer the welfare and safety-net functions to local governments and the central government seeks to moderate potentially huge obligations in this area given its own recent history of less than effective revenue gathering. (For the first nine months of 1994, Moscow's reported tax and other receipts reached only 37.3 percent of the anticipated level.[95])

But this is not necessarily the stuff of social explosions. Unemployment is rising, but even when we allow for inaccurate measurements, it remains lower than might have been anticipated. It is true that some paternalism remains; managers who in many years of Soviet-system practice sacked no one now find unfamiliar rights in this area not inviting enough to exercise. But there are more compelling reasons than inaccurate data or paternalism for lower-than-expected unemployment rates. Wage costs are low; the wage bill is not necessarily a huge component of the factory's expenses. If workers will stay at low wages, there is no urgency about shedding them. Even these modest wages are, as we have seen, often not paid on time. Sometimes, the employing plant itself is insolvent; but often enough, bosses simply use their funds to bolster managerial "savings" rather than deal with debt. If workers endure this and stay aboard, they do not enter the ranks of the unemployed. State-paid unemployment benefits are in any case very modest and are weak motivation for workers to cut ties to the plant that may still provide something they cannot get otherwise. Many managers of former state enterprises face labor forces with a rather high "abuse threshold" without market reasons to dismiss them. Because of subventions from the state employment service, some managers can marginally increase compensation for short-time workers without using their own resources. Because some workers in some privatized factories, however ill paid, are also shareholders under one of the privatization variants, they can be used to block outside takeover attempts. So long as these conditions persist, the problem of unemployment will have its own peculiarities in Russia.[96]

But has the phenomenon of workers as shareholders conferred some kind of power, hitherto unaccounted for, on those workers? It seems quite unlikely. Would workers settle for the low pay, the arrears, if they had clout? There is at present in Russia little resemblance to workers' control scenarios wherein the tendency is for workers to vote themselves higher pay but to attend less to their simultaneous status as owners with interests in long-term growth, investment, capital improvements, and so on. With respect to privatization, the real dynamics of manager-worker participation are still somewhat shrouded; probably only retrospective research, when the dust has settled, will yield a rounded picture. But on the whole, the indications, again, are that the process has been privatization for the managers (and their allies). The variant 1 process with its block of equity transferred free as nonvoting stock to the workers (as distinct from management) was not as popular as variant 2, wherein an unspecified combination of workers and management could acquire 51 percent of equity. The declining value of the rubles in which equity was priced under variant 2 surely encouraged the adoption of this method, which in theory seemed more expensive in that it required more cash. Who had cash? Not, likely, the workers. Fifty-one percent buyouts, one assumes, have been predominantly managerial buyouts.

Voucherization—real enough (as were the enterprise privatizations) in terms of taking ownership out of the state's hands—probably was marginal in relation to labor's acquiring equity and influence at the plant level. Some vouchers were sold for cash. Some have been invested in the various funds, making shareholders (or victims of scams of various sorts), in a small way, of citizens who took this route. Some no doubt were pledged by workers against some of their home factory's equity, in addition to what may have been received free. Prior to privatization, some cash-short workers sold their vouchers to their own relatively cash-rich managers. Since privatization, is it not as likely that workers with some equity have been bought out by managers with cash to offer?

The point is that ownership is getting concentrated in new hands; much of what was in state ownership in 1992, if not really under its control, is no longer there. With this shift, too, the end of the management-worker alliance against the state on so many issues with which the RTK was faced looms on the horizon. As the alliance decays, it is possible that "militant labor unions could well arise to defend the workers' interests, while the managers develop stronger business associations and lobby groups,"[97] but outside some exceptional sectors, these developments, especially the former, will not come automatically.

Much, then, depends on the employers. The state, whatever its inclinations, does not have the resources to construct a strong safety net as yet, to sustain the under- and unemployed while they await new job opportunities. Securing those resources depends, among other things, on property and tax laws, assurances of their fair enforcement, and the creation of a business climate that will moderate tax-evasion tendencies among domestic employers as well as attract foreign investment.

The market is new to the capitalists, as it is to hired labor. The newness of capitalist opportunity, the fascination with accumulation of wealth (as well as with the most conspicuous of consumption for some), the lack of a settled etiquette and ethics of business, all will make Russian capitalism "raw" for some time, even leaving aside mafia-type enterprise and predation. Not too much can be expected soon. An *Economist* observation (in the Polish context) fits, even better, the economics and ethics of Russia. "Capitalism begins with isolated escapes from shared misery. Only slowly do capitalists become strong enough to pull their fellows out of the cauldron—or charitable enough to douse the flames."[98]

Russian capitalism is peculiar. On one side are some giant players, lobbies, and groups with access to the government of a sort that makes a joke of any concept of conflict of interest; on the other side are the relatively powerless masses. It is poised, as EBRD head Jacques de Larosiere put it in mid-1995, between two alternative lines of development, one leading to a "transparent, rule-based market economy," the other to "a distorted market economy centered on a limited group of powerful lobbies vying for a slice of the stagnant economic pie."[99] Though a measured optimism is not impossible, one might assume that he saw the situation at the time of the statement as closer to the latter than the former.

What, then, is there for labor to do? Basically, it will have to concern itself with making the best deal within the context set by a new, neither very kind nor gentle, capitalism. Wages and employment, not broad policy or labor's role as social partner, as codeterminer of policy, are likely to be the stuff of union concerns. Dealing as they are from weakness, unions for the most part—whether of the FNPR variety or the independents—will be on the defensive. As privatized enterprises adjust, split up, or downsize, their union locals will be weakened. New enterprises are not fertile fields for organizing. Their owners and managers are unlikely to be welcoming, and their workforces in any case are likely to be better paid than the average. Gradually, but at an accelerating pace, the artificial total unionization of the labor force, legacy of the Soviet-model economy and the AUCCTU, should erode. Union membership will become less typical and the Russian workforce more similar in this respect to others. There is not much stomach for striking: If low-paid workers for the most part sit still for long delays in the payment of their wages, if employers find carrying a cheap labor force easy even when reported production is dropping, work stoppages are hardly a promising weapon. Propensities toward militancy, withholding of effort, and hard bargaining persist in certain sectors noted earlier and might develop in the public sector among the poorly paid budget personnel whose employer is government itself. Much of the budget sector cannot be privatized; the state cannot sever its ties to its workforce. But the state in this respect bargains hard, runs up its own wage and salary arrears, and faces little organized pressure.

In a sense, some of what the anarcho-syndicalist line of thought summarized earlier saw as a danger has come to be a reality, and it is difficult to see how it could have turned out otherwise. "Democrats" are not especially sensitive to worker economic concerns, and given that the "democrat" label covers a lot of ground in Russia, they have been heavily represented, along with others whom the label would not fit, in important positions in the government. There is much at stake in political maneuvering at the top; material security and enrichment for the players and their families serves as insurance against political losses. Several years ago, none of these had any real opportunity to enrich themselves; today's unfamiliar opportunities may be fleeting. This militates against any strong conflict-of-interest ethics, against the emergence of commonly accepted rules to channel political conflicts (as in the events leading to the crisis of September–October 1993), and against much concern about the workers.

Many of the democrats in the government, and indeed many of the new entrepreneurs without a history of state-sector management, are of the intelligentsia—the educated, diploma-bearing stratum that did not in the past enjoy the material advantages over the workers typical of market systems. Though the point can be overemphasized, as opposed to traditional authoritarianisms where workers bore the major class burden and regimes tilted in the direction of favoring the bourgeoisie, under old Soviet-model socialism only the upper nomenklatura really enjoyed elevated living standards. To a degree this facilitated the intelligentsia's articulating the broader society's interest in democratization,[100] but the postcommunist period has offered new opportunities for the intelligentsia—actually, the enterprising segment of it—to narrow the gap between its accustomed standard of living and Western comfort while simultaneously widening the distance between it and rank-and-file citizens.

On the whole, and understandably so, members of the intelligentsia seem not very sensitive or conscience-stricken about the new unequal outcomes that leave them on the right side of an economic divide. The "rightness" of the market, the lack of any third-way alternative, can help rationalize their advantages and justify their exploitation of new opportunities. A certain retrospective resentment of the old social contract, the provisioning of workers at a level similar to the intelligentsia, can make for a harsh realism. (As one of Shokhin's aides put it to me in early 1994, advancing the market economy might require "a Pinochet" or at least "a leader democratically elected to do undemocratic things.") However we as observers judge the convictions and views of the new leaders (there was never reason to assume that they would prove saintly in self-abnegation), all this is not, over the short-to-medium term, good news for the workers.

If we allow that the government is largely in the hands of such, how is it likely to act on its side of the employers-workers-government triangle? Predictably, what the government will aim at will be more in the line of long-term, growth-promoting policies with "eventual" benefits for all, since various factors move it in this direction. Beyond the attitudes, as just sketched, of many political actors, which tend to put immediate worker interests on the back burner, the government, uniquely, must deal with the IMF, the World Bank, and other international organizations. Financial stabilization, limits on government spending, and budget deficits all figure larger on the agendas of the international financial organizations than do labor concerns. Though the government at any given time may temporize, combining austerity rhetoric with credits and ruble emission (and often operate too closely to that limited number of powerful lobbies for the taste of international lenders), it is eventually pushed back in the toughness direction by the results—as in the tight 1995 budget Chernomyrdin laid out in October 1994 after the ruble crisis and attendant alarms of the fall. Though the danger of backsliding always exists, the government has had sufficient experience with "simple" solutions to some problems that it should now be inclined to concede to the realities. Chernomyrdin's rapidly abandoned notion of price control through profit control was an early one. Another was a decree that caused considerable flap in September 1994. The decree sought to cope with the debt problem by limiting upper-level wage increases in indebted enterprises. It targeted "only" wages fifteen times or more the legal minimum. But in fact many workers would have been affected because the average wage in September had risen close to that multiple of the minimum. This matter, again, ended in embarrassment; the decree was never issued.[101]

Weak labor, stronger employer-owners, and a government compelled to keep its eye on the big picture should make for a labor politics, whatever its rhetorical flourish, with little populist content. Where progress may be possible, where all three sides might agree—with support from international lending organizations and indeed foreign investors—is on targeting social benefits and knitting together a stronger safety net for truly needy individuals and households (rather than for whole labor forces in declining enterprises, sectors, and branches). Such consensus would, finally, transfer from enterprises and employers responsibility (beyond that to the tax collector) for such supports and place their administration in government hands. But even this— given the likely stance of the more traditionalist elements in FNPR and a reluctance government may feel if not express—will be hard to achieve.

The intractability of so many of these problems is, as well, an indication that Russia is still well short of being a civil society whether one conceives of this as a fortunate political-social outcome involving a long list of attributes including economic structures, elections, judicial-legal systems independent of politics, robust but "transparent" state institutions, and a healthy panoply of voluntary associations[102] or whether one sees the matter more simply in the manner of Adam Smith as private property plus the rule of law. Russia is moving away from the universal state ownership of the past, but it has not yet arrived at a solid, accepted private-property system. Having divested itself of much, the state is still in a sort of limbo, retaining much that it should, probably, shed. The onetime state directors who now own substantial equity behave, frequently, as if this change in no way reduces state responsibilities for subsidies in the old fashion. Nor, as owners with responsibilities to pay suppliers and to pay their own workers the agreed wage on time, are they particularly punctilious in the discharge of these duties. If property confers a necessary independence from the state, it also involves obligations; the rule of law amounts to a guarantee that rights and obligations will be enforceable and enforced. It is clear that Russia is still far from this desirable state.

Russian Futures: The Politics of Presidency and Parliament

In a time of new, shallow-rooted institutions, national-level politics is necessarily personalized—a fact relevant not only to outsize personalities like those of Yeltsin and Zhirinovskii but also to the grayer Chernomyrdins. Performance, perceived or real, confers authority; little can be derived from officeholding by itself when the offices and constitution are too new to clothe the incumbents in more than a very thin mantle of authority. The authority of presidents thus "will rest dangerously on their ability to deliver policy successes, a difficult thing to do in a weak government."[103]

Authority is also tied up with avoiding policy failures, or what the public sees as such, and this, too, limits what presidents or presidential hopefuls are likely to dare. In a very optimistic reading of the situation in *Foreign Affairs* in autumn 1994, Anders Aslund saw Chernomyrdin already "identified with the attempts at stabilization and their costs." With Gaidar and Fedorov long gone from the government, they could not be blamed for pains and costs. Having already "gone so far," Chernomyrdin's "rational political choice [was] to go all the way and defeat inflation."[104]

One thinks that Chernomyrdin might have found this debatable. Talking a monetarist policy, he had nonetheless bought a certain measure of peace by acting differently: Government borrowing was growing from spring on, its effects masked by the time lag between money injection and retail inflation. Arguably, this gradualism, which must have recommended itself politically to a prime minister with presidential aspirations, contributed to the ruble crisis of October 11, 1994.[105]

Russia's constitution and its high-level politics are presidential and are likely to remain so for some time. Is presidentialism the format within which the peaceful revolution can proceed, democracy and the market can be consolidated, and the problems of labor politics can adequately be addressed? Wariness is surely warranted here. The perils of presidential as opposed to parliamentary government for new democracies were detailed by Alfred Stepan and Cindy Skach. Although their findings were based on an impressive sample of states that were mainly postcolonial, they saw implications for emergent postcommunist states.[106] They argued that parliamentarism tends toward a mutual and benign dependence between the executive and lawmakers and that presidentialism tends toward a riskier independence,

> encouraging the emergence of minority governments, discouraging the formation of durable coalitions, maximizing legislative impasses, motivating executives to flout the constitution, and stimulating political society to call periodically for military coups. … Presidents and legislatures are directly elected and have their own fixed mandates. This mutual independence creates the possibility of a political impasse between the chief executive and the legislative body for which there is no constitutionally available impasse-breaking device.[107]

Without trying to force this general description on particular facts, I find it hard indeed to resist noting the parallels with the pre-October 1993 relations between the Russian president and parliament: Yeltsin with a mandate from 1991; the nonparty Supreme Soviet with its mandate from 1990 RSFSR elections; no stable parliamentary coalitions; and the uncertain umbrella of a much-amended constitution never designed for the purposes of a democratic polity, held dispensable by the executive, and opportunistically exploited by legislators.

Stepan and Skach extend their discussion to the matter of the temptations that constitutional presidentialism lays before chief executives: Their separate and fixed mandates, counterposed to the frequent absence of a legislative majority, can push them to making end runs around parliament and toward rule by decree. Typically, it is hard to impeach presidents who overstep the bounds; presidential constitutions make this an arduous matter. This links with O'Donnell's concept of a new pattern of "delegative (as opposed to representative) democracy,"[108] wherein presidents pose themselves above parties, treat parliament and judiciary and executive accountability to them as nuisance factors, and center politics in themselves and their staffs. All this relates to a tendency for presidentialism to produce presidents whose rhetoric features attacks on key actors such as parliament and parties and who aim to connect directly with society, marginalizing organized political groupings.

Again, it requires little stretching to find both pre-October (1993) and post-December reflections of this pattern in the Russian situation. The parliamentary rebellion was a sort of impeachment, but it did not work; Yeltsin as president was non- or above-party in relation to the old and new legislatures. It is the president and his staff who make politics, who take most initiatives (though here Chernomyrdin has become more and more of a player as well). The 1993-model Yeltsin was surely given to antiparliamentary rhetoric and direct appeals to Russian society, though in 1994 and 1995 there was less attention to a more orderly (if constitutionally constrained) Duma and fewer appeals direct to the people from a president who seemed, in many contexts, tired, disenchanted, and burdened by the office.

Whatever the general risks of presidentialism versus parliamentarism, analyses of the Stepan-Skach sort do not seem to take sufficiently into account the deficiencies that may qualify the role of a parliament (or a judiciary) in the particular national context of a new democracy. Even critics of Yeltsin's hyperpresidential moves of September 1993 would acknowledge that the rump of the old Congress of People's Deputies and Supreme Soviet sitting then in the White House was, as a body, beyond fulfilling legislative functions and that its earlier degeneration flowed mainly from internal factors. Nor could the constitutional court of the time be separated as an institution from its current members or claim the high ground of an historically legitimated arbiter between the two other branches.

The recent past need not predetermine the present and the midterm future. The new parliament is not the old; the 1993 constitution is not necessarily the one of 2003. In the mid-1990s, parliamentary politicking, if not moderated by rules older than the members or by party discipline tied to coherent platforms, is still not quite the spectacle it once was; a parliament with fewer prerogatives cohabits in a more orderly way with the president. All such observations are of course relative, but the failed no-confidence votes in the Duma both in October 1994 and June-July 1995, although showing continued president-parliament tensions, were procedures by the rules, not improvisations that went beyond constitutionally defined boundaries.

Whether the trajectory of development will be one of further settling in or of recurrent crises cannot be predicted in any detail, but Russian politics will, likely, continue with a strong measure of presidentialism. Presidents, thus, will be important in labor politics whether visibly active or not. Important, then, is what they will be like—populists, managers, arbiters? No president can avoid a certain populism in style (to communicate an understanding of the electorate's problems and thus to secure their votes), but at issue here are matters of substance and the balancing of economic interests.

Labor's weakness reduces the effective pressures on chief executives to assume populist positions, but the broader problems of social justice and low living standards will pressure presidents toward acting in a populist direction. Fears of a social explosion as a result of government economic policy have probably abated (many times predicted, no such explosions have occurred), but no politician can completely dismiss them; nor should they. The December 1993 Zhirinovskii protest vote for a candidate who made an effort to connect at gut level with popular frustrations, including the economic, was in this sense a warning. But what can be offered by way of populist substance is limited by the government's difficulty in collecting revenues, a difficulty likely to persist.

It is likely, then, given the balance of power and clout, that a president will articulate the interests of prime movers—interest groups and institutions now emerging—that control new sorts of economic resources and that are both effective players by and authors of the rules of new Russian political games. Among these figured, in a mid-1994 analysis, "new owners of property, mainly factory managers, [who] have property, but no capital," and capital itself—"big private money in Russia," which was "acquiring new political power."[109] Among them did not figure trade unions or labor in its millions. The analysis may go too far in attributing to big private money the major stabilizing role in creating the "political calm" of spring 1994;[110] such assessments can obscure the degree to which these interests still depend on the state to protect them and thus are constrained by the state even as they in turn constrain that state to a degree. But the trends seem to run in the direction of a tight relationship between the two.

Thus, the present and future presidents of Russia seem more likely than not to be articulators of emergent financial and industrial interests. Presidents who stand for these things can appear to be uncaring, remote, and captives of special interests to broad segments of the public (as has Yeltsin). Growing inequality, the blatant distinctions between clear winners and losers in the new economy, will not be wiped away quickly. Neither domestic economic dynamics nor plausible levels of Western aid that may be forthcoming are likely to be adequate for a social safety net sufficiently strong to calm frustrations and fears.

What presidents, parliament, and people may face if they are unlucky are two major risks as the market makes headway in the Russian economy and distributes its short- to-medium-term benefits quite unequally. First, political forces articulating the grievances of large numbers of losers might coalesce to a greater degree than today (though much of what has been detailed here seems to argue against its happening, at least outside the realm of campaign rhetoric). Labor may grow stronger, less as an independent subject of politics than as an object that political operators must take more into account than currently. In the way of economic policy changes, a populist "fair deal" is announced, but wage rises, inflation, and tax hunger all put brakes on economic growth. The pie refuses to grow. More general paralysis and impoverishment follow, and Western aid and investment are withheld. A president who rides this wave will paint over with populist rhetoric the generally sad economic conditions of a weak and compromised market economy. Some of the most disgruntled may respond with enthusiasm to what would be the politicization of a leveling-down egalitarianism, but such is as unlikely to enhance their material welfare.

An alternative outcome involves a proactive stance by worried winners in the market: Before the discontented losers can really get organized, private-sector moneyed interests draw on their tight linkages with national and local political elites and make common cause with other elements of the "party of order" to construct something resembling a more typical authoritarianism.[111] The chief executive in this case would be, depending on a mix hard to specify before the fact, either a creature of these interests, or—if the state preserved its own autonomy from the interests it was committing itself to protect—the presider over something like Schmitter's statist corporatism, disciplining both capitalists and labor but favoring the former in the service of what would resemble a peripheral, delayed-dependent capitalist order of the sort that statist corporatism attempts to save. Some might argue that this is a fair characterization of the state of affairs in Russia today. But this would, I think, go too far: There would be little room in such an outcome for the contentious, if hardly objective, free press of today; for elections, however flawed by irregularities and voter disinterest; and for a number of the other elements of autonomy Russians lacked under the Soviet regime but have now—however little they may seem to value them.

Whether presidentialism makes Russia more vulnerable to these risks than a parliamentary system depends, in the end, on the assessment one is ready to make of how well a parliamentary alternative might function in the foreseeable future should the political architecture be altered in that direction. My hunch is that we will see only moderate parliamentary responsibility and performance. Since the beginning of 1994, the parliament has been relatively quiet because it has been constrained, constitutionally and otherwise, and not because it represents a new level of civil achievement.

Again, these problems—too much presidentialism and the unlikelihood that a solid parliamentarism can develop for some time—reflect the weak development of important elements of the civil society package. Unlike in Poland and Hungary, there was little development in the old USSR in late Brezhnev to early Gorbachev times of anything approximating a second society, an organized autonomous sphere of activity beyond state control. True, areas of activity became harder for the state to control by the old means that were all it had; more behaviors escaped its direct supervision.[112] But these behaviors largely belonged in the realm of what Grzegorz Ekiert has categorized as domestic rather than political society, a "domain of purposeful action restricted to the private sphere and organized in terms of material needs and self-interests."[113]

This was not, then, a challenge to the regime, though it might be seen as a symptom of its eroding power.

With perestroika and glasnost came the efflorescence of all kinds of voluntary organizations—"informals" (*neformaly*)—espousing everything from environmentalism to a return to Russia's pre-Christian gods. Some were political; most were not. This surge of late-1980s voluntarism has not served as the basis for the development of any dense network of political parties and interest-based associations that in civil society can affect policymaking or "provide an incentive for increased political participation and raise feelings of political competence."[114] There is no stable party system in Russia; the notion of competing center-right and center-left superparties that are organized from the top down implies less a system than a substitute for one. There are no real linkages between party rank and file, of which there are few, and party leaders and there are no coherent platforms that might link them. All this has inhibited the disciplined organization, expression, and clarification of business and labor interests both in the presidential-executive sphere and in parliament. Public interest in politics, which is sustained and mobilized in other nations by a variety of associations that include but are not limited to political parties and which is a hallmark of civil society, is notable mainly by its absence. Expressions of disgust and disinterest in politics are reflected by low voting turnouts. The societal corporatism—one but not the only mode of coordinating interests in a civil society—at which Russia aimed in late 1991 required the sorts of associations and organizations that can carry out politics in a trilateral context according to commonly accepted rules, that can speak for constituencies, and that can comply with agreements openly arrived at; these characteristics, too, have been notable mainly for their absence.

Russian Futures: The Politics of National Identity

Compared to questions of national fate, the identity of peoples, and a nation-state's power and stature on the world stage, labor politics, as examined here, is thin stuff. National rather than class principles have been the movers of this century's turbulent politics. New states—and such is the Russian Federation—will have an easier time establishing stable, civil political procedures within which class conflicts can be resolved to the degree that questions of geographic boundaries, ethnic irredenta, and the fit between the ethnolinguistic nation and the territorial state are off the table. Unresolved, these issues are freighted with emotions, fears, and aspirations of a potentially explosive sort and can consume political energies that might otherwise be available to deal with more secular, less sacred, issues.

Labor, though a broad matter, is in the realm of the secular. Resolving labor issues depends on the dynamics of labor-employer-state relations, corporatist or not, and also on the shape of and power relations within the high-level politics of presidency and parliament. But the greater politics of the ultimate questions—What is Russia? Where is it going?—will also play a major role in resolving or failing to resolve many of the problems in the labor arena.

Though in the end the linkage of foreign and domestic affairs is profoundly important, the tendency to focus on "big" foreign affairs rather than on domestic affairs has rather straightforward consequences. The point is that failure to find lower-cost ways to resolve issues such as Chechnya or a preoccupation with foreign affairs, for example, asserting a shaky claim to global superpower status or intervening forcefully in Russia's "near abroad" with its 20-million-plus ethnic Russians, must divert attention and energy from the secular and intractable problems of economic and labor policy. The problems of defining what Russia is and will be are real enough. State-builders willing to work within today's borders and anxious to get on with a variety of internal problems are far better equipped than those nostalgic for "empire" of some sort to deal with the big secular issues, among them that of the inclusion of labor in the national body.

A simpler, neoimperial orientation will perhaps appeal more to workers because it emphasizes blood, language, and ethnic links as the key to inclusion. It transcends new, uncomfortable, unfamiliar divisions over economic interest and private ownership and seeks to enlist all in a national crusade that denies the fact of or the pain of losing superpower status. But in that way lies a massive risk, however compelling the vision may be, to political and economic progress and to a livable future for some 150 million people, bosses and bossed, owners and hired labor. Sacred missions are dangerous business. Working toward settling the secular questions—a matter of decades—is the safer, if often the less exciting, prospect. The mechanisms and properties of civil society, "an integral part of the system of rule"[115] in democracies, allow citizens to demand in orderly ways that the state direct a large measure of attention to those secular questions and focus less on sacred missions. Unfortunately, again, those mechanisms and properties are still new and weak, where they exist at all, and it is one of the characteristics of Russian history that the state's leaders have often been drawn to such sacred missions to the detriment of the people.

Epilogue: 1996_____

AS IT HAD DONE TWO YEARS EARLIER, Russia went to the polls in December 1995 to elect a new State Duma. Again, the results gave little comfort to those who would have wished for a solid endorsement of the market and the democratic-reform parties. But no one expected much in that direction. Yeltsin was unpopular. The government's tight money policy, aimed at holding the line on subsidies, the deficit, and inflation, was "working"—but at the cost of mounting wage arrears, which remained the major theme of labor protest (see further on), and growing unemployment.

Russia Votes

Only four parties—of forty-three on the ballot—cleared the 5 percent popular-vote threshold to qualify for a share of half the Duma's 450 seats allocated by proportional representation. The Communists (KPRF) led with 22.3 percent of the popular vote, followed by Zhirinovskii's LDP with 11.2 and Prime Minister Chernomyrdin's center-right bloc "Russia Is Our Home" (Nash Dom–Rossiia, or NDR) at 10.13 percent. The reform party Yabloko, headed by Grigorii Yavlinskii, brought up the rear with 6.9 percent.

Russia had voted its pains and frustrations—of which there were undeniably plenty—and its disaffection with Yeltsin, who though not a member was in a sense responsible for the creation of the NDR. The constitution adopted in 1993 limited the Duma's powers now as it had in 1993—but as a curtain raiser for the important presidential elections scheduled for June 1996, the 1995 elections were an indicator of rough sledding to come. They were a warning that the Communist leader Gennadi Zyuganov had positioned himself as a serious contender for the presidency. This was cause for concern. His KPRF was no duplicate of Poland's former Communist Party, whose leader, Aleksander Kwasniewski, had earlier in the year beaten Lech Walesa for the Polish presidency. Nor were the situations of the countries similar. There was good reason to think that in Poland, a politics with populist appeal would not affect essentially pro-market policies; in Russia, major issues of policy were, definitely, *not* ruled off the table.

A surprisingly large 65 percent, approximately, of Russia's eligible voters had turned out. Russians had voted their emotions, frustrations, pocketbooks (however thin), and pains—more, it seemed, than their hopes—and they had spread these broadly. The four parties that succeeded in getting any seats at all on the proportional representation vote together garnered only a whisker more than half of the 67.88 million valid votes cast. Only these, and the parties that finished in the next six places—fifth through tenth—drew more voters than the "none of the above" alternative, which 1.92 million Russians checked; "n.o.t.a." thus outpolled thirty-three of the parties that had presented their personalities and platforms—the latter word to be interpreted loosely—to the electorate.

Continuing Tensions

Autumn 1955 saw numerous protests. Between September and November, military industry workers in Saratov and miners in Vorkuta, Sakhalin, and Mezhdurechensk demonstrated over wage arrears. Teachers, similarly, complained about low, and unpaid, wages in a nationwide day of protest in late September—reportedly, half a million teachers took part, about 15 percent of all educational personnel—to protest a monthly pay packet averaging about $70.[1] This was, as things went, a large protest. Generally, though grievances might cut deep, the size and duration of protests remained moderate.

Shmakov of the FNPR announced a slogan of "Wages, Employment, Legality" for the upcoming elections—moderate also compared to earlier FNPR bombast. FNPR scheduled a Day of Action for December 1 but indicated that it would not call strikes before the elections—and indeed, the turnout on the day was small. The biggest demonstrations were reported in Krasnodar, where 30,000 demonstrated, and in Bryansk, where 13,000 gathered; no public demonstrations were reported in Moscow or St. Petersburg.[2] Earlier in September, in announcing the Day of Action, the FNPR head had complained of wage arrears totaling 8 trillion rubles, mainly attributable to the government failing to pay for what it had ordered from enterprises. Asked by a newspaper whether this sort of offensive had by now not become old hat, Shmakov replied that it made perfect sense—*some* government action on arrears generally had followed each FNPR protest. To the suggestion that, as the government had argued, the union should go directly after factory management for arrears, Shmakov responded by asking why there were laws, why, indeed, there was a government if it could not be called upon to make sure wages were paid.[3]

It was clear that the government *was* part of the problem, that not just unscrupulous bosses were to blame. Labor Minister Melikian had noted in August that, although the government eventually settled up its own arrears for budget personnel after running them up, the ripple effects of these delays were great. He admitted, as he put it, that "we went too far."[4]

The RTK was still in existence, but still, obviously, marginal. Even Misnik of the PGMR, who had signed the first (1992) general agreement and, as one of the few "survivors" from the original membership, had also signed the 1995 version, called that body "decorative" as he announced that PGMR would support the Yabloko reformers in the election.[5]

FNPR finally allied itself with Volskii's RSPP and the Russian United Industrial Party on September 5 in the Trade Unions and Industrialists of Russia–Union of Labor (Profsoiuzy i Promyshlenniki Rossii–Soiuz Truda) bloc. Volskii signaled in November to the Communists, then rising in the polls, that the new bloc could cooperate with the KPRF in the new Duma: A Communist spokesman replied that the unions-industrialists bloc had to get elected first.[6] This was not an ill-considered reply: Many regional FNPR bodies, such as the one in the Tambov "red belt," were already indicating support for the Communists and the closely related Agrarian Party rather than for the bloc of which FNPR was a part.[7] In the Russian Far East, the FNPR's Primorskii regional organization was offering support to the Communists, the Agrarians, and the Congress of Russian Communities as well, ignoring central headquarters: Volskii, in what turned out to be at least a partially correct prediction, said that his bloc's constituents seemed apathetic and unlikely to vote and expressed doubts that the FNPR-RSPP-ROPP combination would cross the 5 percent barrier.[8]

Labor in the Election: Personalities and Parties

Many of the dramatis personae encountered earlier contested the December 1995 parliamentary elections. Aleksandr Shokhin, who had begun 1992 as minister of labor and then moved to broader economic responsibilities in the cabinet and a deputy premiership, ran on the NDR—the so-called party of power—national list in the Moscow oblast. Igor Klochkov, elected to the Duma on the Agrarian list in the 1993 elections after his resignation under pressure from the leadership of the FNPR in the wake of the 1993 Moscow crisis, stood again on that basis in 1995, on the national list's Moscow oblast section, but also ran in a single-member constituency. V. I. Romanov, who had been the FNPR's deputy chair in the Klochkov years, ran on the national list of the Congress of Russian Communities (Kongress Russkikh Obshchin–KRO), a strongly "statist" party appealing to concerns about the welfare of ethnic

Russians in former republics outside Russia and effectively the creation of Yuri Skokov of the commodity producers' organization.

Pavel Kudiukin, the social democratic activist who had served as Shokhin's deputy at the Labor Ministry and was now based in a research institute, ran for the Bloc of Social-Democrats on the Moscow city segment of its national list and simultaneously in a constituency in Moscow. Among the labor leaders and activists who had been consistently anti-FNPR, Aleksandr Sergeev, who headed the independent coal miners' union (NPG), ran on the national list of what came to be called the Bloc of Ivan Rybkin—earlier, the supposed center-left superparty balancing Chernomyrdin's NDR—probably because of the increasing difficulty NPG had with government policy on payments and subsidies to mines and the Rybkin bloc's "softness" in this regard. Vyacheslav Sharipov, who headed the core NPG organization in the Kuzbass, ran on the Workers' Self-Government Party list. Sotsprof chair Sergei Khramov and cochair Vasili Mokhov ran on the list of For the Homeland (Za Rodinu), Khramov also contesting a constituency seat.

Yavlinskii's Yabloko—the only reform party to make the 5 percent threshold in the proportional representation race—finally had on its national list Boris Misnik, the head of the mining and metallurgy union (PGMR), which had "defected" from the FNPR back in what now seemed the distant time of fall 1992.

With only the Communists, the Liberal Democrats, NDR, and Yabloko managing the threshold for proportional representation seats, where had FNPR and its allies gone? The earlier discussions with Rybkin about a center-left "umbrella" organization having come to nothing, what had emerged, as noted previously, was the Trade Unions and Industrialists of Russia–Union of Labor organization. The top three spots on its national list were occupied respectively by V. I. Shcherbakov of the Russian United Industrial Party (ROPP), FNPR chair Shmakov, and Arkady Volskii as president of the now-somewhat-shopworn Russian Union of Industrialists and Entrepreneurs (RSPP). Yuri Gekht—noted earlier as the head of the hard-line Industrial Union and a man who had heralded the 1991 August coup—ran as the party's candidate in a Moscow oblast constituency, but Alexander Vladislavlev, vice president of Volskii's RSPP, ran in the number two spot on the national list of Forward, Russia—a list headed by the strongly pro-market former minister of finance Boris Fedorov.

Despite an FNPR membership still claimed to be around the 50 million mark, the exercise was futile: The unions and industrialists' bloc received only 1.55 percent of the popular vote, on the basis of slightly over 1 million voters checking the appropriate box. Even at that, however, it got a larger share of the party vote than twenty-eight of the other parties.

It was outpolled by Gaidar's Russia's Democratic Choice, as well as (surprisingly) by the hard-line "paleocommunist" Communists–Working Russia–for the Soviet Union" (Kommunisty–Trudovaia Rossiia–za Sovetskii Soiuz) bloc, on whose national list the street fighter and demagogue Viktor Anpilov appeared. None of the three crossed the threshold; all finished behind "none of the above."

Final Thoughts

Though the situation looks quite cloudy in early 1996—in the wake of both the 1995 Duma elections, in which large numbers of Russian voters expressed a protest against economic pains, and the executive shakeups in Moscow, which suggested a trimming of sails, and with the campaigns for the June 1996 presidential elections looming—it is not, taking the long view, one of impenetrable gloom.

Two points—one political, one economic, neither one quite independent of the other—are worth emphasizing. First, Russia's politics, however chaotic and flawed, are more democratic than ever before. That the democracy is far from self-sustaining stability is, if we take the long view, a smaller matter than the fact that, versus a thousand years of history tilted in the opposite direction, it *does* stand. The Duma of 1994–1995 was elected. Votes, coolly or emotionally cast, carefully considered or thrown away, put its members in their seats. The successor Duma that sat down to start its work in January 1996 was similarly elected: From Zyuganov to former Foreign Minister Kozyrev, its members are members because they got the votes. By itself, this may not seem like much; but measured against seventy-plus years of a Soviet order wherein there *was* no real legislature, to say nothing of public involvement of any sort in deciding who the law- or rule-makers would be, it is a great deal.

Those who would dismiss this as marginal, since so much power is concentrated in the presidency, should, nonetheless, take note: Yeltsin, Russia's first popularly elected leader in history, will to all indications finish the five-year term to which Russia's voters elected him in 1991. Whether he runs for a second term is his choice—a choice that would not exist had the events of October 1993 turned out differently. Spring 1996 will, to all indications, see Russia's first sustained presidential election campaign. By midsummer, Russia will again have elected a president. Be it Yeltsin, Zyuganov, even Zhirinovskii or someone else, whoever occupies the seat of power will have undergone a first-round, and likely runoff, balloting wherein Russia's consent has been sought and secured. Voters can be misled, foolish, simply "wrong"—as historical retrospect will sometimes prove them to have been. But who would, a decade ago, have thought that Russia would be going to the polls at all or that would-be leaders would have to depend on electoral consent to reach a position from which to reward their friends and also, one hopes, to make policy at least generally aimed at the public good? Russia's new democracy will take some time to "clean up its act"—too long a time for many—but it is democracy's act that is still occupying Russia's stage. One hesitates to use the term "irreversible"; but with the passage of time, the likelihood of returning to a regime that neither depends on popular consent nor affords people choice in any but the most inconsequential areas of their lives grows less.

In the economic sphere, however "uncivil" the market, however wild the still-nascent capitalism, however clouded the title to equity in various enterprises, the core fact is that the "state" no longer owns the economy—not even half of it. Chubais's departure was not a good sign in economic-policy terms, although his exit, like Kozyrev's, necessarily has a certain amount to do with electoral positioning, but the core fact is that he *did* the job of privatization. The job description never implied anything about the personal morals or business ethics of those who would, in the first instance, benefit from its execution. Given what the alternative was—manifest in the collapse of the misconceived "planned economy"—the notion that what has happened is theft and thus to be condemned is perhaps best put in perspective by a Moscow writer: "Capital is indifferent to morals. As soon as the money is taken from the cash box and goes to work for production, it loses whatever criminal stink it may have. Yes, you say, but what about historical retribution? They stole the money, and now they are millionaires. But historical retribution has no relationship to law. The experience of socialism in Russia has proved that either we think about retribution, about expropriation of the ex-proprietors, or we work toward a productive market economy and private property. Either/or—not both."[9]

This is not, perhaps, a very satisfying answer. There is much in Russia's "wild" markets that is not productive; there are many undeserving ex-politicos who have become owners. But capitalism is not, as many have noted, an "-ism" in the sense of an ideologically designed and decreed -ism like socialism. It is something, given certain levels of economic and legal development, that happens if a number of things go "right." But in its early industrial stages—in England two centuries ago, in much of the world since—it is both unfamiliar and unpretty and distributes its new benefits in a distinctly skewed direction. So it is in Russia, which had essentially no legal preparation for it and whose industrial civilization was built, top-down, by Stalin on an anticapitalist basis. Russia's flaws stand out all the more glaringly because at the end of the twentieth century, the world boasts many examples of more mature, civilized capitalist orders to which they may be contrasted. Given Russia's recent past, the political posturing over privatization's shortcomings, over the needs of industries for subsidies and tariff protection, over rejecting the *diktats* of the IMF, over foreign capital—posturing in which both Yeltsin and his opponents are involved—is cause for some concern, but not for surprise. These are the issues of a new, unruly capitalism, in a Russia engaged in the world market as it has not been for many decades.

If, then, it is accurate—and I think it is—to say that there is no going back to socialism, we need also understand that there is no going back to January 1992 to do things "differently" and better. There is no going back to give Russia a different parliament from the Congress of People's Deputies and Supreme Soviet it inherited from the 1990 elections, or a political-institutional arrangement in which the RTK and a corporatist approach might have worked better. There is no going back to January 1992 to alter Gaidar's shock-therapeutic approach, to modify what was then as much a sense of desperate urgency as it was misplaced neoliberal optimism about market institutions arising spontaneously; no way to give Russia those property laws and concepts, lacking so far in the transition, that might have altered the geometry of economic relations toward a better fit with societal corporatism.

None of this means that the only direction in which future events can move is forward. But realistic reflection on how far Russia had to go—not just from March 1985 but also from January 1992—should remind us of how remarkably far it has come. If retrogression is not ruled out, it is also not foreordained. If progress, albeit with fits and starts, is not guaranteed, it is, in the large scheme of things, not beyond reasonable expectation.

Notes

Acronyms Used in Notes

CDSP	*Current Digest of the Post-Soviet Press* or *Current Digest of the Soviet Press*
FBIS	*Foreign Broadcast Information Service–Soviet Union* or *Foreign Broadcast Information Service–Central Eurasia*
FBISR	*Foreign Broadcast Information Service Report–Central Eurasia*
NG	*Nezavisimaia Gazeta*
NPSP	*Na puti k sotsialnomu partnerstvu*
RFE/RL R	*Radio Free Europe/Radio Liberty Report*
RFE/RL RR	*Radio Free Europe/Radio Liberty Research Report*
RG	*Rossiiskaia Gazeta*
RLNB	RFE/RL New Briefs
Rossiia: Partii	*Rossiia: Partii, Assotsiatsii, Soiuzy, Kluby*
RV	*Rossiiskie Vesti*

Chapter 1

1. The democratic transition literature is very large. A good introduction to the issues, and the "state of the field" just on the edge of the Gorbachev era and all it brought in Eastern Europe and the USSR is Guillermo O'Donnell and Philippe C. Schmitter, *Transitions from Authoritarian Rule: Tentative Conclusions About Uncertain Democracies* (Baltimore: Johns Hopkins University Press, 1986).

2. Ken Jowitt, *New World Disorder: The Leninist Extinction* (Berkeley: University of California Press, 1992), p. 285.

3. Adam Przeworski, *Democracy and the Market: Political and Economic Reforms in Eastern Europe and Latin America* (Cambridge: Cambridge University Press, 1991), p. xii.

4. See Carl J. Friedrich and Zbigniew K. Brzezinski, *Totalitarian Dictatorship and Autocracy* (Cambridge: Harvard University Press, 1956; 2nd ed., 1966).

5. Ellen Comisso, "Where Have We Been and Where Are We Going? Analyzing Post-Socialist Politics in the 1990s," in William Crotty, ed., *Political Science: Looking to the Future*, vol. 2, *Comparative Politics, Policy, and International Relations* (Evanston: Northwestern University Press, 1991), pp. 88–89.

6. See Ken Jowitt, "Soviet Neotraditionalism: The Political Corruption of a Leninist Regime," *Soviet Studies* 35, 3 (July 1983), pp. 275–297.

7. In the aftermath of the Soviet collapse, the whole notion of the social contract—better taken, in my view, as a metaphor rather than as theory—has

come under a certain amount of criticism; not all of it, I think, is deserved. (Since a certain amount of responsibility for developing the idea has been attributed to me, I am not entirely unprejudiced, although I must say that I did not see myself as developing a theory.) Two illuminating and fairly lengthy treatments of the ramifications of the social contract, one from the Gorbachev era and one "after the fall," are, respectively, Peter A. Hauslohner, "Gorbachev's Social Contract," *Soviet Economy* 3, 1 (1987), pp. 54–89; and Linda J. Cook, *The Soviet Social Contract and Why It Failed: Welfare Policy and Workers' Politics from Brezhnev to Yeltsin* (Cambridge: Harvard University Press, 1993). For a conceptual critique, see Anna Meyendorff, "Analyzing the Social Contract: Towards a New Methodology," in *Analyzing the Gorbachev Era: Working Papers of the Students of the Berkeley-Stanford Program in Soviet Studies* (Berkeley: Berkeley-Stanford Program in Soviet Studies, 1989), pp. 69–85.

8. This argument, then, follows closely that laid out in Rasma Karklins, "Explaining Regime Change in the Soviet Union," *Europe-Asia Studies* 46, 1 (1994), pp. 29–45.

9. Quotes are from ibid., pp. 40, 35, 36, respectively.

10. Ibid., pp. 42, 30.

11. Przeworski, *Democracy and the Market*, pp. 58, 60.

12. Quotes from Karklins, "Explaining Regime Change," pp. 37–38, 31.

13. Marcia A. Weigle and Jim Butterfield, "Civil Society in Reforming Communist Regimes: The Logic of Emergence," *Comparative Politics* 25, 1 (October 1992), p. 15.

14. Quoted and translated from the archive TsKhSD (Tsentr Khraneniia Sovremennoi Dokumentatsii), f. 89, p. 42, d. 31, pp. 8–9 (Moscow), by Gordon M. Hahn, "Gorbachev vs. the CPSU CC Apparat: The Bureaucratic Politics of Reforming the Party Apparat, 1988–1991," (Ph.D. dissertation, Department of Political Science, Boston University, 1994). I am indebted to Gordon Hahn for numerous insights he gained in the course of energetic and painstaking research in party archives.

15. Karklins, "Explaining Regime Change," p. 31.

16. Not all may find the argument so telling, but those who do not assume a heavy burden of counterdemonstration. Some contemporary intellectual frameworks seem bound to lead them in the wrong directions. Writing in the same time frame as Karklins, another scholar asserts that "the label 'totalitarian' had an isolating effect, rendering the Soviet system somehow incomparable. ... The USSR was thus seen as an isolated system, rather than an extreme on a continuum." That perhaps it was such a system is not addressed as an issue; but the writer goes on to argue the utility of drawing on deconstructionism, on using Foucault and Derrida to illuminate how "a mystifying idea of dual opposites ... an artificial construct," had served a desire of "Americans and West Europeans ... to keep the Soviet experience separate from their own, using Russia's historical 'backwardness' as a distancing mechanism." But in "critical theory, a left-of-center approach would compare both societies, not separate them," thus presumably making good the defect in Soviet studies: "The Soviet Union was not used as a case for possibly illustrating what is wrong with 'our own society.'" What all this illustrates is somewhat beyond me. The fact that it appears in a major journal

would seem to indicate that failures of understanding will not be limited to the past failure of classic Sovietology to foresee the system's end. See Andrea Chandler, "The Interaction of Post-Sovietology and Comparative Politics: Seizing the Moment," *Communist and Post-Communist Studies* 27, 1 (1994), pp. 8–9.

17. Charles H. Fairbanks Jr., "After the Moscow Coup," in Larry Diamond and Mark F. Plattner, eds., *The Global Resurgence of Democracy* (Baltimore and London: Johns Hopkins University Press, 1992), p. 273.

18. Timothy J. Colton, "Politics," in Colton and Robert Legvold, eds., *After the Soviet Union: From Empire to Nations* (New York: Norton, 1992), p. 21.

19. The discussion follows Michael McFaul, "Russian Centrism and Revolutionary Transitions," *Post-Soviet Affairs* 9, 3 (1993), pp. 196–222.

20. Quotes are from ibid., pp. 197, 199.

21. O'Donnell and Schmitter, *Transitions from Authoritarian Rule*, p. 69, quoted by McFaul, "Russian Centrism," p. 200.

22. McFaul, "Russian Centrism," pp. 200–201.

23. Ibid., p. 201.

24. See Giuseppe DiPalma, "Why Democracy Can Work in Eastern Europe," in Diamond and Plattner, eds., *The Global Resurgence of Democracy*, pp. 265–266. In that 1990–1991 context, DiPalma reflects principally on Poland, Hungary, what was then Czechoslovakia, and the German Democratic Republic (GDR): "Once democracy has been chosen, its preservation demands the creation of a market; the creation of a market then becomes virtually inevitable. ... It is precisely the close and unprecedented connection between a political and a socioeconomic transformation that, instead of jeopardizing both, may help the latter ride piggyback on the former." Looking at the matter from the perspective of 1994–1995, the outcome goes some way toward justifying DiPalma's optimism. Poland and Hungary have made it over many critical hurdles; the GDR collapsed against, and into the arms of, the Federal Republic of Germany (FRG)—though the latter for a time was increasingly horrified at the potential costs of absorbing the best economic performer of the old Soviet bloc. Czechoslovakia underwent its "velvet divorce." The Czech Republic is a very strong performer, economically and politically; Slovakia remains a more ambiguous case. These success stories, however, rest on different and altogether more promising historical roots than does Russia.

25. Philippe C. Schmitter, "Still the Century of Corporatism?" *Review of Politics* 36, 1 (1974), pp. 93–94.

26. Ibid., p. 96.

27. See Randall L. Calvert, "The Rational Choice Theory of Social Institutions: Cooperation, Coordination, and Communication," unpublished manuscript, November 1992, pp. 5–6.

28. Przeworski, *Democracy and the Market*, pp. 11–12.

29. Schmitter, "Still the Century of Corporatism?" pp. 99ff.

30. The discussion follows ibid., pp. 102–104.

31. Schmitter (ibid., p. 102) bases the distinction on the work of the interwar Romanian corporatist theorist Mihail Manoilesco (*Le siecle du corporatisme*, 1936), who employed, respectively, the terms *corporatisme pur* and *corporatisme subordonne*.

32. Quotes from ibid., pp. 107, 108.

33. Ibid., p. 106.

34. Quotes from ibid., pp. 118, 119.

35. Ibid., p. 123.

36. Ibid., p. 126.

37. Ibid., p. 127.

38. On the matter of inegalitarian societies not readily characterizable as class-based, see Robert A. Feldmesser, "Social Classes and Political Structure," in Cyril E. Black, ed., *The Transformation of Russian Society* (Cambridge: Harvard University Press, 1960), pp. 238–240; and Walter D. Connor, *Socialism, Politics and Equality: Hierarchy and Change in Eastern Europe and the USSR* (New York: Columbia University Press, 1979), pp. 52–62. See also Stanislaw Ossowski's discussion of "nonegalitarian classlessness" in his classic *Class Structure in the Social Consciousness* (New York: Free Press, 1963).

39. This discussion is strongly influenced by ideas in Kenneth A. Schepsle, "Studying Institutions: Some Lessons from the Rational Choice Approach," *Journal of Theoretical Politics* 1, 2 (1989), pp. 133–135; see also Mark Granovetter, "Economic Action and Social Structure: The Problem of Embeddedness," *American Journal of Sociology* 91, 3 (1985), pp. 481–510.

40. Comisso, "Where Have We Been?" pp. 105–107.

41. Przeworski, *Democracy and the Market*, pp. 180, 182.

42. The story, as I tell it, concentrates on the "play" between government, employers, and labor and on the problems of corporatism. Though it is a complex story in itself, it necessarily cannot cover in detail any one of the "players." Quite literally as this book was going into the production process, a new book—Simon Clark, Peter Fairbrother, and Vadim Borisov, *The Workers' Movement in Russia* (Aldershot, UK: Edward Elgar, 1995)—came to hand, providing immensely detailed information on a number of the independent, non-FNPR unions. Written from a labor-left perspective, it is an extraordinarily rich and informative source on very tangled political and organizational processes, personal rivalries in the independent labor movement, and so on. Although it has not been possible to include its arguments and insights in this text, numerous references are made in the notes that follow.

Chapter 2

1. Interfax (English), 1000 GMT, July 25, 1991; *Foreign Broadcast Information Service—Soviet Union* (hereafter *FBIS*), July 26, 1991, p. 61.

2. Radio Mayak (Moscow), 0900 GMT, October 9, 1991; FBIS, October 9, 1991, p. 55.

3. *Trud,* October 30, 1991; *Rabochaia Tribuna* (hereafter, *RT*) October 30, 1991.

4. Interfax (English), 1700 GMT, October 31, 1991.

5. L. A. Gordon, "Russia on the Road to New Industrial Relations: From Unipartite Commands to Tripartite Partnership via Bipartite Conflicts and Bargaining," *Problems of Economic Transition* 35, 6 (October 1992), p. 10, n. 3, citing *Izvestiia,* June 10, 1991, and October 27, 1991.

6. See Elizabeth Teague, "Soviet Employers' Organization Celebrates First Birthday," *Report on the USSR*, June 28, 1991, p. 18, citing *Izvestiia*, June 17, 1991.

7. See A. Uliukaev, "Dvizhenie," *Kommunist*, no. 10, 1991, pp. 43, 46.

8. *Rossiiskaia Gazeta*, (hereafter *RG*), November 19, 1991, p. 2.

9. *Trud*, December 27, 1991, pp. 1, 2.

10. *Trud*, December 31, 1991, p. 1.

11. Olga Kirichenko, "Rossiiskaia trekhstoronnaia kommissiia po regulirovaniiu sotsialno-trudovykh otnoshenii v 1992–1993 godakh," unpublished manuscript, Moscow, 1993, pp. 5–7.

12. *Trud*, December 27, 1991, pp. 1, 2.

13. Ibid.

14. *RT*, February 19, 1992, p. 1.

15. *RT*, February 21, 1992, p. 2.

16. *RT*, February 25, 1992, p. 2.

17. L. A. Gordon and E. V. Klopov, "Trudovye otnosheniia: K trekhstoronnemu sotsialnomu partnerstv," *Politicheskie Issledovaniia*, nos. 1–2, 1992, pp. 168, 171, 174.

18. V. V. Komarovskii, "Vozmozhnosti i prepiatstviia na puti stanovleniia systemy sotsialnogo partnerstva v Rossii," in Institut Problem Zanaiatosti RAN i Mintruda RF, Tsentr Issledovanii Sotsialno-trudovykh Otnoshenii, *Trudovye otnosheniia v khode modernizatsii ekonomiki* (Moscow, 1992), pp. 157, 164.

19. L. A. Gordon, *Ocherki rabochego dvizheniia v poslesotsialisticheskoi Rossii* (Moscow: IMEMO/Russko-Amerikanskii Fond Profsoiuznykh Issledovanii i Obuchenia, 1993), p. 73.

20. Iu. Volkov, "The Transition to a Mixed Economy and the Prospects for the Labor and Trade-Union Movement," in Bertram Silverman, Robert Vogt, and Murray Yanowitch, eds., *Labor and Democracy in the Transition to a Market System* (Armonk, NY: M. E. Sharpe, 1992), pp. 56–58.

21. Ibid.

22. See L. Gordon and A. Temkina, "Krizis rabochego dvizheniia v postsotsialisticheskoi Rossii: Istoki i poiski vykhoda," in Institut ... Otnoshenii, *Trudovye otnosheniia*, pp. 152–153.

23. Ibid.

24. *Ekonomika i Zhizn*, no. 17, (April) 1992, p. 20.

25. See Elizabeth Teague, "Russian Government Seeks 'Social Partnership,'" *Radio Free Europe/Radio Liberty Research Report* (hereafter *RFE/RL RR*), June 19, 1992, pp. 18–19.

26. See Institut Massovykh Politicheskikh Dvizhenii, *Rossiia: Partii, Assotsiatsii, Soiuzy, Kluby* (hereafter *Rossiia: Partii*) (Moscow: RAU-Press, 1991), vol. 1, pt. 2, p. 323.

27. Though relations between these aviation-related unions would be strained at times, on the RTK they generally were united in an independent, or anti-FNPR, stance.

28. In fact, the RSPP's NPS predecessor had been engaged to a degree in earlier corporatist designs; NPS had been among the organizations specifically mentioned by the USSR government in June 1991 when it signaled its intent of entering discussions with the unions and employer organizations about the 1992

plan. Given what would come later in relations between the RSPP and the FNPR, there was irony in the way the NPS had been born. At its founding congress in 1990, Volskii had projected NPS as a counter to the growing activity of labor—represented by the VKP and new independent worker organizations—and as the representative of employers who should, as the USSR moved to a market economy, assume a place in the triangular structure of government, labor, and employers that is characteristic of many advanced industrial societies. See Teague, "Soviet Employers' Organization," pp. 17–18.

29. See Article 6, section 17, of the statute ("Polozhenie o Rossiiskoi trekhstoronnoi komissii po regulirovaniiu sotsialno-trudovykh otnoshenii"), in *Na puti k sotsialnomu partnerstvu* (hereafter *NPSP*) (Moscow: Konstitutsion-nyi Vestnik, n.d.), p. 226.

30. Otto Newman, *The Challenge of Corporatism* (London: Macmillan, 1981), p. ix.

31. Ibid., pp. 91, 92.

32. Christopher S. Allen and Jeremiah M. Riemer, "The Industrial Policy Controversy in West Germany: Organized Adjustment and the Emergence of Meso-Corporatism," in Richard E. Foglesong and Joel D. Wolfe, eds., *The Politics of Economic Adjustment: Pluralism, Corporatism, and Privatization* (New York: Greenwood Press, 1989), p. 46.

33. Ibid.

34. See, for example, Ilja Scholten, "Corporatism and the Neo-Liberal Backlash in the Netherlands," pp. 120–152, and Janine Goetschy, "The Neo-Corporatist Issue in France," in Ilja Scholten, ed., *Political Stability and Neo-Corporatism: Corporatist Integration and Societal Cleavages in Western Europe* (London and Beverly Hills: Sage, 1987), pp. 177–194.

35. See Allen and Riemer, "Industrial Policy," p. 47.

36. Kathleen Thelen, "Neoliberalism and the Battle over Working-Time Reduction in West Germany," in Foglesong and Wolfe, eds., *Politics of Economic Adjustments,* p. 66, citing Wolfgang Streeck, "Neo-corporatist Industrial Relations and the Economic Crisis in West Germany," in John H. Goldthorpe, ed., *Order and Conflict in Contemporary Capitalism* (New York: Oxford University Press, 1984), p. 298.

37. *Trud,* January 4, 1992, p. 1.

38. *Trud,* January 1, 1992, p. 1.

39. *Izvestiia,* January 11, 1992; *Current Digest of the Post-Soviet Press* (hereafter *CDSP*), February 12, 1992, p. 22.

40. Ibid.

41. *Kommersant,* January 27–February 3, 1992, p. 20.

42. See Teague, "Russian Government Seeks Social Partnership," pp. 18–19.

43. *Trud,* February 8, 1992, p. 1.

44. Moscow Radio One, 1600 GMT, March 11, 1992; *FBIS,* March 13, 1992, p. 25.

45. TV Ostankino, Moscow, First Program, 1200 GMT, March 18, 1992; *FBIS,* March 20, 1992, pp. 55–56.

46. *RT,* February 13, 1992, p. 1.

47. *Trud,* February 25, 1992, pp. 1, 2.

48. Interfax, Moscow, 1914 GMT, February 17, 1992; *FBIS*, February 19, 1992, p. 44.

49. Ibid., p. 2.

50. TASS (English), 1255 GMT, March 6, 1992; *FBIS*, March 9, 1992, p. 31.

51. *Nezavisimaia Gazeta* (hereafter *NG*), March 7, 1992, p. 2; *FBIS*, March 9, 1992, pp. 31–32.

52. TASS (Russian), 1022 GMT, March 9, 1992; *FBIS*, March 10, 1992, p. 31.

53. Radio Rossii, 1000 GMT, March 10, 1992; *FBIS*, March 10, 1992, p. 31.

54. Moscow Radio One, 1600 GMT, March 11, 1992; *FBIS*, March 13, 1992, p. 25.

55. Postfactum (English), 1346 GMT, March 14, 1992; *FBIS*, March 17, 1992, pp. 57–58.

56. *NG*, March 12, 1992, p. 2; *FBIS*, March 13, 1992, pp. 35–36.

57. Russian TV, Moscow, 1823 GMT, March 18, 1992; *FBIS*, March 25, 1992, pp. 44—45.

58. See *Kommersant*, March 9–16, 1992, p. 2; see also Teague, "Russian Government Seeks Social Partnerships," p. 22.

59. Later in the year, the NPG would express regrets that it had gone along with the FNPR coal union in the latter's demands for across-the-board increases for all coal-industry workers and employees (not only the coal-face workers who were NPG's base) in Vorkuta and later in the Kuzbass.

60. *RT*, March 7, 1992, p. 3.

61. *Trud*, March 14, 1992, p. 2.

62. *Trud*, March 26, 1992, p. 1. I have seen no authoritative reference as to which FNPR unions did sign; given general indications, the likelihood would run in the direction of Malinovskii's airline pilots' union and Misnik's union.

63. *NG*, March 31, 1992, p. 2.

64. *RT*, April 3, 1992, p. 3.

65. Ibid.

66. See *FBIS*, March 14, 1992, pp. 36–37.

67. See *RT*, April 17, 1992, p. 2.

68. For the text, see *Ekonomika i Zhizn*. For comment on its provisions, see Elizabeth Teague, "Pluralism Versus Corporatism: Government, Labor and Business in the Russian Federation," in Carol R. Saivetz and Anthony Jones, eds., *In Search of Pluralism: Soviet and Post-Soviet Politics* (Boulder: Westview Press, 1994), p. 116; Linda J. Cook, "Russia's Labor Relations: Consolidation or Disintegration?" in Douglas W. Blum, ed., *Russia's Future* (Boulder: Westview Press, 1994), pp. 72–73.

69. Interfax (English), 1943 GMT, May 8, 1992; *FBIS*, May 11, 1992, p. 37.

70. Interfax (English), 1341 GMT, May 30, 1992; *FBIS*, June 1, 1992, p. 31.

71. Interfax (English), 1309 GMT, June 3, 1992; *FBIS*, June 9, 1992, p. 44.

72. *Izvestiia*, June 6, 1992, pp. 1, 3; *FBIS*, June 9, 1992, pp. 44–49.

73. Ibid., p. 45.

74. Ibid., p. 47.

75. *Trud*, May 30, 1992, p. 1.

76. Interfax (English), 1409 GMT, June 11, 1992; *FBIS*, June 12, 1992, p. 43.

77. *Trud*, April 22, 1992, p. 2.

78. Ibid.

79. *RT,* June 16, 1992, p. 1.

80. *Trud,* June 20, 1992, p. 1.

81. *RG,* June 16, 1992, p. 1; *FBIS,* June 24, 1992, p. 45.

82. Interfax (English), 1846 GMT, June 19, 1992; *FBIS,* June 24, 1992, pp. 45–46.

83. Interfax (English), 1539 GMT, July 8, 1992; *FBIS,* July 9, 1992, p. 44.

84. *Trud,* July 9, 1992, p. 1.

85. *RT,* July 10, 1992, p. 1.

86. See the review of RASP's founding by Elizabeth Teague, "Russia's Industrial Lobby Takes the Offensive," *RFE/RL RR,* August 14, 1992, pp. 1–6.

87. See the "Polozhenie" in *NPSP,* p. 226.

88. See Philip Hanson and Elizabeth Teague, "The Industrialists and Russian Economic Reform," *RFE/RL RR,* May 8, 1992, p. 7.

89. This line of analysis is presented by Alexander Rahr, "Liberal-Centrist Coalition Takes Over in Russia," *RFE/RL RR,* July 17, 1992, pp. 22–25.

90. For an assessment shortly after its foundation, see Elizabeth Teague and Vera Tolz, "The Civic Union: The Birth of a New Opposition in Russia?" *RFE/RL RR,* July 24, 1992, pp. 1–11.

91. See ibid., p. 3.

92. See Interfax (English), 2009 GMT, July 21, 1992; *FBIS,* July 23, 1992, p. 33.

93. *RT,* September 4, 1992, pp. 1–2.

94. See Teague, "Russia's Industrial Lobby," p. 3.

95. Ostankino TV, Moscow, First Program, 1700 GMT, September 4, 1992; *FBIS,* September 8, 1992, p. 27.

96. See Teague, "Russia's Industrial Lobby," pp. 2–3.

97. ITAR-TASS (English), 1109 GMT, November 23, 1992; *FBIS,* November 23, 1992, p. 39.

98. *Rossiiskie Vesti* (hereafter *RV*), October 22, 1992, p. 1; *FBIS,* October 23, 1992, p. 32.

99. Interfax (English), 1046 GMT, October 22, 1992; *FBIS,* October 23, 1992, p. 32.

100. ITAR-TASS (Russian), 1555 GMT, October 22, 1992; *FBIS,* October 23, 1992, p. 32.

101. Interfax (English), 1046 GMT, October 22, 1992; *FBIS,* October 23, 1992, p. 32.

102. Interfax (English), 1506 GMT, October 26, 1992; *FBIS,* October 26, 1992, pp. 34–35.

103. Interfax (English), 1909 GMT, October 27, 1992; *FBIS,* October 28, 1992, p. 38.

104. See *RFE/RL RR,* May 22, 1992, pp. 37–38.

105. Ostankino TV, Moscow, 1800 GMT, October 26, 1992; *FBIS,* October 28, 1992, p. 37.

106. ITAR-TASS (English), 1100 GMT, November 2, 1992; *FBIS,* November 2, 1992, pp. 44–45.

107. ITAR-TASS (Russian), 1328 GMT, November 2, 1992; *FBIS,* November 2, 1992, p. 45.

108. *NG,* November 4, 1992, p. 2; *FBIS,* November 5, 1992, p. 40.

109. *RFE/RL RR,* November 20, 1992, p. 45, citing Interfax, November 7, 1992.

110. ITAR-TASS (English), 1203 GMT, November 30, 1992; *FBIS,* December 1, 1992, p. 17.

111. *Trud,* November 19, 1992, p. 1.

112. *RT,* December 8, 1992, p. 2.

113. *RT,* December 18, 1992, p. 2.

114. *RT,* December 25, 1992, p. 1.

115. This discussion follows some, but by no means all, of the points raised by George Breslauer, "The Roots of Polarization: A Comment," *Post-Soviet Affairs* 12, 4 (1993), pp. 223–230.

116. The phrases are Stephen M. Meyer's; see his "The Military," in Timothy Colton and Robert Legvold, eds., *After the Soviet Union: From Empire to Nations* (New York: Norton, 1992), pp. 113–146, esp. 135–140.

117. Pavel Kudiukin, "Reforma trudovogo prava i trudovykh otnoshenii v Rossii: Problemy i perspektivy," unpublished manuscript, Moscow, 1993, p. 12.

118. See Philippe C. Schmitter, "Still the Century of Corporatism?" *Review of Politics* 36, 1 (1974), p. 97.

119. Adam Przeworski, *Democracy and the Market: Political and Economic Reforms in Eastern Europe and Latin America* (Cambridge: Cambridge University Press, 1991), p. 180.

120. Ibid., p. 181, quoting Stephan Haggard and Robert Kaufman, "The Politics of Stabilization and Structural Adjustment," in Jeffrey D. Sachs, ed., *Developing Country Debt and the World Economy* (Chicago: University of Chicago Press, 1989), p. 269.

121. Ibid., p. 181.

122. See, on this point, Andrei Riabov, "Integrativnaia ideologiia i modernizatsiia sovremennoi Rossii," *Svobodnaia Mysl,* no. 15, 1992, pp. 58–69.

Chapter 3

1. Quotes from I. G. Shablinskii, "Kuda dvizhetsia nashe rabochee dvizhenie?" *Rabochii klass i sovremennyi mir,* no. 4, 1990, pp. 124–131 (trans. in *Soviet Sociology,* 30, 4 (July-August, 1991), pp. 53–70.

2. On the new worker, see Tatiana Zaslavskaia's essay "The Novosibirsk Report," *Survey,* no. 120 (1984), pp. 80–108, and her later *The Second Socialist Revolution: An Alternative Soviet Strategy* (Bloomington and Indianapolis: Indiana University Press, 1990); on the quiet revolution, see Blair Ruble, "The Soviet Union's Quiet Revolution," in George W. Breslauer, ed., *Can Gorbachev's Reforms Succeed?* (Berkeley: Berkeley-Stanford Program in Soviet Studies, 1990), pp. 77–94.

3. L. Gordon and E. Klopov, "Rabochee dvizhenie: Politicheskii potentsial," *Kommunist,* no. 10, 1991, pp. 29–30, 36.

4. L. Gordon and E. Klopov, "The Workers' Movement in a Possible Postsocialist Perspective," *Sociological Research* 31, 1 (January-February 1992), pp. 30–55.

5. Ibid., pp. 47ff.

6. TASS (English), 1426 GMT, January 9, 1992; *Foreign Broadcast Information Service–Central Eurasia* (hereafter *FBIS*), January 10, 1992, p. 23.

7. Moscow Radio (English), 1300 GMT, January 9, 1992; *FBIS*, January 10, 1992, p. 24.

8. See *Komsomolskaia Pravda,* January 14, 1992, p. 1; *FBIS*, January 14, 1992, p. 22.

9. TASS (Russian), 2028 GMT, January 13, 1992; *FBIS*, January 17, 1992, p. 58.

10. TASS (Russian), 1634 GMT, January 15, 1992; *FBIS*, January 17, 1992, p. 59.

11. Radio Rossii, 1000 GMT, January 20, 1992; *FBIS*, January 21, 1992, p. 69.

12. TASS International (Russian), 1340 GMT, January 22, 1992; and Interfax (English), 1920 GMT, January 22, 1992; both in *FBIS*, January 23, 1992, p. 30.

13. Ostankino TV, 1800 GMT, January 24, 1992; *FBIS*, January 27, 1992, p. 34.

14. *Commersant,* May 4, 1992, p. 7.

15. Russian TV, 1600 GMT, March 30, 1992; *FBIS*, March 31, 1992, p. 46.

16. Radio Mayak, 0330 GMT, February 8, 1992; *FBIS*, February 11, 1992, p. 61.

17. Radio Rossii, 0900 GMT, January 15, 1992; *FBIS*, January 16, 1992, p. 40.

18. TASS International (Russian), 1136 GMT, January 16, 1992; *FBIS*, January 16, 1992, p. 39.

19. TASS (English), 2119 GMT, January 17, 1992; and Interfax (English), 2141 GMT, January 17, 1992; both in *FBIS*, January 21, 1992, p. 55.

20. Interfax (English), 1819 GMT, January 21, 1992; *FBIS*, January 22, 1992, p. 36.

21. See *Radio Free Europe/Radio Liberty Research Report* (hereafter *RFE/RL RR*), March 6, 1992, p. 49, citing ITAR-TASS, February 20, 1992.

22. See *Pravda,* January 25, 1992, p. 2; *FBIS*, January 27, 1992, p. 33; Interfax (English), 1819 GMT, January 21, 1992; and *FBIS*, January 22, 1992, p. 36.

23. *Pravda,* January 25, 1992; *FBIS*, January 27, 1992, p. 33.

24. *RFE/RL RR*, February 14, 1992, p. 59, citing Radio Rossii, January 29, 1992.

25. *MN Business,* no. 12, 1992, p. 5.

26. Interfax (English), 1645 GMT, February 21, 1992; *FBIS*, February 24, 1992, p. 56.

27. Moscow Radio One, 1600 GMT, March 1, 1992; *FBIS*, March 2, 1992, pp. 49–50.

28. For a discussion of these strikes and their significance in what turned out to be late perestroika, see Walter D. Connor, *The Accidental Proletariat: Workers, Politics, and Crisis in Gorbachev's Russia* (Princeton: Princeton University Press, 1991), pp. 271–302; also Peter Rutland, "Labor Unrest and Movements in 1989 and 1990," *Soviet Economy* 6, 3 (1990), pp. 345–384.

29. See Sarah Ashwin, "The 1991 Miners' Strike: New Departures in the Independent Workers' Movement," *Report on the USSR,* August 16, 1991, pp. 1–7.

30. Radio Mayak, 0700 GMT, March 3, 1992; *FBIS*, March 4, 1992, p. 58.

31. TASS (English), 1330 GMT, March 5, 1992; *FBIS*, March 6, 1992, p. 25.

32. Radio Mayak, 1300 GMT, March 5, 1992; *FBIS*, March 6, 1992, pp. 24–25.

33. TASS (English), 1255 GMT, March 6, 1992; *FBIS*, March 9, 1992, p. 31.

34. One report (*Izvestiia*, March 7, 1992, p. 2) implied that miners had asked for a sixfold raise. But Simon Clarke, Peter Fairbrother, and Vladim Borisov (*The Workers' Movement in Russia* [Aldershot, UK: Edward Elgar, 1995]), in an account (pp. 152–156) of the Kuzbass crisis broadly similar to my own, also cite testimony by the head of the FNPR coal-industry union that although he and Gaidar had agreed on a twofold pay increase, the document they both signed—evidently without examining it—contained a misprint that specified a threefold raise! (p. 199, n. 46).

35. *Nezavisimaia Gazeta* (hereafter *NG*), March 7, 1992, p. 2; *FBIS*, March 9, 1992, pp. 31–32.

36. TASS (Russian), 0245 GMT, March 9, 1992; *FBIS*, March 9, 1992, p. 32.

37. Radio Mayak, 0800 GMT, March 9, 1992; *FBIS*, March 9, 1992, p. 32.

38. For a review of such conflicts between presidential and local power in the regions, see Richard Sakwa, *Russian Politics and Society* (London and New York: Routledge, 1993), pp. 178–200.

39. Postfactum (English), 1939 GMT, March 6, 1992; *FBIS*, March 9, 1992, p. 32.

40. *Izvestiia*, March 7, 1992, p. 2.

41. Radio Rossii, 1000 GMT, March 10, 1992; *FBIS*, March 10, 1992, p. 31.

42. Ostankino TV, 1800 GMT, March 11, 1992; *FBIS*, March 13, 1992, p. 25.

43. Moscow Radio One, 1600 GMT, March 11, 1992; *FBIS*, March 13, 1992, p. 25.

44. Ibid.

45. *Rossiiskaia Gazeta* (hereafter *RG*), March 12, 1992, p. 1.

46. Postfactum (English), 1346 GMT, March 14, 1992; *FBIS*, March 17, 1992, pp. 57–58.

47. Ostankino TV, 2100 GMT, March 14, 1992; *FBIS*, March 17, 1992, p. 58.

48. *NG*, March 12, 1992, p. 2; *FBIS*, March 13, 1992, pp. 35–36.

49. Ibid.

50. Ostankino TV, 1200 GMT, March 18, 1992; *FBIS*, March 20, 1992, p. 55.

51. Russian TV, 1823 GMT, March 18, 1992; *FBIS*, March 25, 1992, pp. 44–45.

52. See V. I. Kabalina, A. K. Nazimova, and L. A. Gordon, "Obekty i soderzhanie sotsialno-trudovykh otnoshenii: Kharakter trudovykh konfliktov," in *Na puti k sotsialnomu partnerstvu* (hereafter *NPSP*) (Moscow: Konstitutsion-nyi Vestnik, n.d.), p. 110.

53. ITAR-TASS (English), 1154 GMT, April 6, 1992; *FBIS*, April 8, 1992, p. 15.

54. ITAR-TASS (English), 0914 GMT, April 8, 1992; *FBIS*, April 9, 1992, p. 45.

55. Radio Mayak, 0330 GMT, April 7, 1992; *FBIS*, April 9, 1992, p. 45.

56. See the various TV and news service reports in *FBIS*, February 18, 1992, pp. 51–53.

57. TASS International (Russian), 1936 GMT, March 20, 1992; *FBIS*, March 23, 1992, p. 21.

58. Moscow Radio One, 1800 GMT, March 1, 1992; *FBIS*, March 2, 1992, pp. 49–50.

59. TASS International (Russian), 0810 GMT, March 17, 1992; *FBIS*, March 17, 1992, p. 57.

60. ITAR-TASS (English), 1249 GMT, April 15, 1992; *FBIS*, March 16, 1992, p. 46.

61. ITAR-TASS (English), 0656 GMT, May 8, 1992; *FBIS*, May 14, 1992, p. 43.

62. See L. A. Gordon, V. Gimpelson, E. Klopov, and I. G. Shablinskii, "Novye subekty trudovykh otnoshenii," in *NPSP,* p. 50.

63. *Komsomolskaia Pravda*, April 7, 1992, p. 2; *FBIS*, April 14, 1992, pp. 34–35.

64. Ibid., p. 35.

65. The following discussion draws heavily on Stephen Crowley's manuscript "Hot Coal, Cold Steel: Russian and Ukrainian Workers from the End of the Soviet Union to the Post-Communist Transformations" (Ann Arbor: University of Michigan Press, forthcoming).

66. TV Ostankino, First Program, 1100 GMT, April 20, 1992; *FBIS*, April 21, 1992, p. 26.

67. Radio Rossii, 0700 GMT, April 24, 1992; *FBIS*, April 24, 1992, p. 34.

68. *Kuranty*, April 28, 1992, p. 1.

69. *Izvestiia*, April 29, 1992, p. 2.

70. ITAR-TASS (English), 1919 GMT, April 30, 1992; *FBIS*, May 1, 1992, pp. 23–24.

71. *Commersant*, May 11, 1992, p. 25.

72. Russian TV, 1900 GMT, May 7, 1992; *FBIS*, May 12, 1992, p. 45.

73. Interfax (English), 1922 GMT, May 12, 1992; *FBIS*, May 13, 1992, p. 39.

74. *Izvestiia*, May 14, 1992, p. 2; the text of the decree was published in *RG*, May 15, 1992, p. 2.

75. *NG*, May 6, 1992, p. 2.

76. *NG*, May 8, 1992, p. 2; *Current Digest of the Post-Soviet Press* (hereafter *CDSP*), June 3, 1992, p. 24.

77. Interfax (English), 1024 GMT, April 30, 1992; *FBIS*, May 1, 1992, p. 36.

78. Interfax (English), 1922 GMT, May 12, 1992; *FBIS*, May 13, 1992, p. 39; *RG*, May 1, 1992, p. 1; *FBIS*, May 5, 1992, p. 38.

79. See *RG*, May 15, 1992, p. 2; *Izvestiia*, May 16, 1992, p. 2; Interfax (English), 2000 GMT, May 14, 1992; *FBIS*, May 18, 1992, p. 32.

80. *Izvestiia*, May 16, 1992, p. 2.

81. Ibid.

82. Kabalina, Nazimova, and Gordon, "Obekty i soderzhanie," p. 108.

83. On the MFP in the early post-Soviet period, see Elizabeth Teague, "Pluralism Versus Corporatism: Government, Labor and Business in the Russian Federation," in Carol R. Saivetz and Anthony Jones, eds., *In Search of Pluralism: Soviet and Post-Soviet Politics* (Boulder: Westview Press, 1994), p. 123, n. 22.

84. L. A. Gordon, "Russia on the Road to New Industrial Relations: From Unipartite Commands to Tripartite Partnership via Bipartite Conflicts and Bargaining," *Problems of Economic Transition* 35, 6 (October 1992), p. 33.

85. The whole structure and layout of the air personnel unions is confusing, and near-baroque in its complexity, born of a late Soviet period division of the old industrywide official union into more occupationally based components. Malinovskii, as an assertive union leader, acted as head of the larger-by-far segment of a pilots' union that had earlier split; the smaller segment was headed by Anatoli Kochur and Sergei Semenov. Both segments, however, still united as a

single body for some common purposes, and it seems likely that when Malinovskii signed the 1992 General Agreement, he was acting for both bodies. On the various splits and combinations, see Clarke, Fairbrother, and Borisov, *The Workers' Movement,* pp. 313–316, 383–386.

86. Gordon et al., *NPSP,* p. 62; much of the discussion of labor organizations in this section is drawn from this source.

87. Among others, I worried, perhaps too much, in 1990–1991 about the clout of this organization; see Connor, *The Accidental Proletariat,* pp. 293–297.

88. On this and other opposition parties in the early part of Yeltsin's presidency, see the very valuable and detailed account by Gordon M. Hahn, "Opposition Politics in Russia," *Europe-Asia Studies* 46, 2 (1994), pp. 305–335.

89. See on the STK (also sometimes styled the Interregional, or *MSTK*), Gordon et al., *NPSP,* pp. 62, 65–66; also Institut Massovykh Politicheskikh Dvizhenii, *Rossiia: Partii, Assotsiatsii, Soiuzy, Kluby* (hereafter *Rossiia: Partii*) (Moscow: RAU-Press, 1991), vol. 1, pt. 2, p. 295.

90. See ibid., vol. 1, pt. 1, p. 56. The organizational rivalries and local labor politics of the Kuzbass, including the KT, are dealt with at greater length in Clarke, Fairbrother, and Borisov, *The Workers' Movement,* pp. 17–132.

91. Gordon et al., *NPSP,* p. 67.

92. *Kuranty,* May 5, 1992, p. 1; *FBIS,* May 6, 1992, p. 20.

93. Ibid.

94. Preceding quotes from Interfax (English), 2000 GMT, May 14, 1992; *FBIS,* May 18, 1992, p. 31.

95. ITAR-TASS (English), 1101 GMT, May 21, 1992; *FBIS,* May 22, 1992, p. 39.

96. *RG,* June 3, 1992, p. 1; *FBIS,* June 3, 1992, pp. 29–30.

97. Ibid., p. 30.

98. Russian TV, 1720 GMT, May 18, 1992; *FBIS,* May 20, 1992, pp. 33–34.

99. *Izvestiia,* June 6, 1992, p. 7; *FBIS,* June 11, 1992, pp. 14–15.

100. See Postfactum (English), 1800 GMT, July 1, 1992; also Russian TV, 1600 GMT, June 24, 1992; both in *FBIS,* July 2, 1992, pp. 53–54.

101. *Commersant,* August 25, 1992, p. 21.

102. *Sovetskaia Rossiia,* June 9, 1992, p. 2; *FBIS,* June 10, 1992, p. 38.

103. Ibid.

104. *Sovetskaia Rossiia,* July 14, 1992, p. 2.

105. See Elizabeth Teague, "Splits in the Ranks of Russia's 'Red Directors,'" *RFE/RL RR,* September 4, 1992, pp. 6–10.

106. *Commersant,* August 25, 1992, p. 21.

107. *Moscow News,* August 9–16, 1992, p. 5.

108. *Izvestiia,* August 18, 1992, p. 2; *FBIS,* August 20, 1992, pp. 33–34.

109. Ibid.

110. See *Rossiia: Partii,* vol. 1, pt. 1, pp. 56–57, on the founding of the KT.

111. Ostankino TV, 1700 GMT, September 4, 1992; *FBIS,* September 8, 1992, p. 27.

112. *Komsomolskaia Pravda,* April 7, 1992, p. 2; *FBIS,* April 14, 1992, p. 34.

113. *Izvestiia,* August 6, 1992, p. 2.

114. See note 112.

115. Interfax (English), 1610 GMT, August 10, 1992; *FBIS,* August 11, 1992, pp. 27–28.

116. *Izvestiia,* August 12, 1992, p. 1; *FBIS,* August 12, 1992, pp. 30–31.

117. ITAR-TASS (English), 1444 GMT, August 12, 1992; *FBIS,* August 13, 1992, p. 31.

118. See ITAR-TASS (English), 1532 GMT, August 12, 1992; *FBIS,* August 13, 1992, pp. 31–32; also *RG,* August 14, 1992, p. 1; *FBIS,* August 14, 1992, p. 16.

119. Radio Rossii, 1000 GMT, August 14, 1992; *FBIS,* August 14, 1992, p. 16.

120. Russian TV, 1000 GMT, and ITAR-TASS (Russian), 1032 GMT, August 15, 1992; both in *FBIS,* August 17, 1992, p. 12.

121. *NG,* August 18, 1992, p. 2.

122. ITAR-TASS (English), 1047 GMT, August 17, 1992; *FBIS,* August 18, 1992, p. 25.

123. Interfax (English), 1859 GMT, August 25, 1992; *FBIS,* August 26, 1992, p. 25.

124. *Izvestiia,* September 19, 1992, p. 2; *FBIS,* September 25, 1992, p. 17.

125. Interfax (English), 1459 GMT, October 29, 1992; *FBIS,* October 30, 1992, pp. 42–43.

126. Interfax (English), 1742 GMT, November 24, 1992; *FBIS,* November 25, 1992, pp. 47–48.

127. ITAR-TASS (English), 0812 GMT, December 1, 1992; *FBIS,* December 1, 1992, p. 17.

128. Russian TV, 2000 GMT, December 2, 1992; *FBIS,* December 3, 1992, pp. 12–13.

129. The description here of the FPAD actions from August to November is necessarily rather schematic. See the lengthy and very detailed discussion in Clarke, Fairbrother, and Borisov, *The Workers' Movement,* pp. 335–371.

130. *Commersant,* September 22, 1992, p. 17.

131. *Trud,* July 28, 1992, p. 2.

132. *NG,* October 17, 1992, p. 2; *FBIS,* October 20, 1992, pp. 16–18.

133. Ibid.

134. *RFE/RL RR,* August 28, 1992, p. 74, citing Interfax, August 14, 1992.

135. ITAR-TASS (Russian), 1202 GMT, October 24, 1992; *FBIS,* October 26, 1992, p. 34.

136. Radio Rossii, 0800 GMT, October 29, 1992; *FBIS,* October 29, 1992, p. 45.

137. *Izvestiia,* October 29, 1992, pp. 1–2; *FBIS,* November 2, 1992, pp. 49–50.

138. Ibid.

139. *RT,* November 6, 1992, p. 2.

140. *Izvestiia,* November 13, 1992, p. 2; *FBIS,* November 16, 1992, pp. 29–30.

141. *RT,* November 27, 1992, p. 2.

142. See Elizabeth Teague, "Russia's Industrial Lobby Takes the Offensive," *RFE/RL RR,* August 14, 1992, pp. 1–6.

143. *RT,* December 11, 1992, p. 2.

144. Ibid.

145. *RT,* December 15, 1992, p. 2.

146. For a detailed, and quite critical, exploration of Sotsprof's history and activities, see Clarke, Fairbrother, and Borisov, *The Workers' Movement,* pp. 209–312.

147. See Ellen Comisso, "The Costs of Democracy," *Contemporary Sociology* 21, 3 (May 1992), p. 320 (reviewing Adam Przeworski, *Democracy and the Market: Political Reforms in Eastern Europe and Latin America* [Cambridge: Cambridge University Press, 1991]).

148. See Gordon et al., *NPSP*, p. 69. On the PT and the SP, see also Hahn, "Opposition Politics in Russia," pp. 312–313, 318–319; in the immediate post-August coup period, the PT, with the left intellectual Boris Kagarlitsky among its major figures, protested against privatization on the Moscow streets along with the Russian Communist Workers' Party (linked to *Trudovaia Rossiia*) but after that showed little association with hard-line restorationist groups.

149. See Boris Rakitskii, "New Buyers and New Sellers in Russia's Labor Markets," *Sociological Research* 31, 5 (September-October 1992), pp. 45, 50–51.

150. See G. A. Rakitskaia, "Hired Labor or Self-Management," *Sociological Research* 31, 1 (January-February 1992), pp. 86–87.

151. Ibid., p. 81.

152. O. I. Shkaratan, "The Old and the New Masters of Russia," *Sociological Research* 31, 5 (September-October 1992), pp. 55–69.

153. Boris Rakitskii, "The Struggle for the Interests of Working People in the Transition from a Totalitarian to a Democratic (Market) Economy," *Sociological Research* 31, 1 (January-February 1992), p. 75.

154. Rakitskaia, "Hired Labor," p. 85.

155. See A. D. Shkira, "The Employment Problem During the Transition to a Market Economy," in Bertram Silverman, Robert Vogt, and Murray Yanowitch, eds., *Labor and Democracy in the Transition to a Market System* (Armonk, N.Y.: M. E. Sharpe, 1992), p. 133.

156. Rakitskaia, "Hired Labor," p. 83.

157. Rakitskii, "The Struggle," p. 78.

158. Rakitskii, "New Buyers," pp. 48–49.

159. Rakitskii, "The Struggle," pp. 75, 77–78.

160. Rakitskaia, "Hired Labor," p. 86.

161. Rakitskii, "New Buyers," p. 43.

162. Shkira, "The Employment Problem," pp. 134–135.

163. E. N. Rudyk, "The Western Experience of Industrial Democracy and Its Significance," in Silverman, Vogt, and Yanowitch, *Labor and Democracy,* pp. 98–100.

164. L. A. Gordon, *Ocherki rabochego dvizheniia v poslesotsialisticheskoi Rossii* (Moscow: IMEMO/Russko-Amerikanskii Fond Profsoiuznykh Issledovanii i Obuchenia, 1993), p. 74.

165. See Crowley, "Hot Coal, Cold Steel."

Chapter 4

1. For an early assessment of Chernomyrdin and what looked like questionable turns in economic policy, see Erik Whitlock, "New Russian Government to Continue Economic Reforms?" *Radio Free Europe/Radio Liberty Research Report* (hereafter *RFE/RL RR*) January 15, 1993, pp. 23–27.

2. Conversations around this time with several economists, including Vladimir Mau, an associate of Gaidar, left a very confusing impression and a fair degree of doubt as to what future lay before the RTK, if any.

3. *Rabochaia Tribuna* (hereafter *RT*), February 5, 1993, p. 1.

4. See Klochkov's remarks on this in *RT,* February 9, 1993, p. 1.

5. *RT,* February 5, 1993, p. 1.

6. On the rechartering of the RTK, see Interfax (English), 1732 GMT, February 8, 1993; *Foreign Broadcast Information Service–Soviet Union* (hereafter *FBIS*), February 9, 1993, p. 15.

7. See the report in *RT,* February 27, 1993, p. 3.

8. *RT,* February 26, 1993, p. 3.

9. *RT,* February 27, 1993, p. 3.

10. *RT,* February 26, 1993, p. 3.

11. *RT,* February 9, 1993, p. 2.

12. Much of what follows here is drawn from Olga Kirichenko, "Rossiiskaia trekhstoronnaia kommissiia po regulirovaniiu sotsialno-trudovykh otnoshenii v 1992–1993 godakh," unpublished manuscript, pp. 25–26, and from conversations with Pavel Kudiukin, Moscow, October 1993.

13. Kirichenko, "Rossiiskaia trekhstoronnaia kommissiia," pp. 25–26; conversations with Kudiukin, 1993.

14. *RT,* May 21, 1993, p. 2.

15. Conversations with Pavel Kudiukin, Moscow, October 1993.

16. *Trud,* January 20, 1993, p. 1.

17. According to another story in *Trud,* January 22, 1993, p. 1.

18. Ibid.

19. *Trud,* February 24, 1993, p. 2; *Foreign Broadcast Information Service Report–Central Eurasia* (hereafter *FBISR*), March 6, 1993, p. 68.

20. A possibility suggested to me by Leonid Gordon in Moscow, October 25, 1993.

21. See *Delo,* nos. 22–23 (September 1993), p. 1.

22. *Delo,* no. 24 (October 1993), p. 1.

23. As Kirichenko, "Rossiiskaia trekhstoronnaia," does.

24. *RT,* January 9, 1993, p. 1.

25. *RT,* January 14, 1993, p. 2.

26. *RT,* January 19, 1993, p. 1.

27. *RT,* May 12, 1993, pp. 1, 2.

28. *RT,* January 9, 1993, p. 1.

29. *RT,* May 21, 1993, p. 2.

30. See Walter D. Connor, *The Accidental Proletariat: Workers, Politics, and Crisis in Gorbachev's Russia* (Princeton: Princeton University Press, 1991), pp. 225–235.

31. On this organization, see Institut Massovykh Politicheskikh Dvizhenii, *Rossiia: Partii Assotsiatsii, Soiuzy, Kluby* (hereafter *Rossiia: Partii*) (Moscow: RAU-Press, 1991), vol. 1, pt. 2, pp. 294–295.

32. See Connor, *The Accidental Proletariat,* pp. 226–227; also *Rossiia: Partii,* p. 261.

33. On Klebanov in the 1990s see Simon Clarke, Peter Fairbrother, and Vladim Borisov, *The Workers' Movement in Russia* (Aldershot, UK: Edward Elgar, 1995), pp. 14–15, n. 2.

34. Ibid., pp. 384, 393.

35. Indeed, this was only a more blatant manifestation of the tendency to claim organizational strengths that far exceeded reality; something that would prove true of many blocs, parties, and associations.

36. *RT,* May 7, 1993, pp. 1, 6.

37. *RT,* February 27, 1993, p. 3.

38. *RT,* May 7, 1993, p. 6.

39. *Trud,* May 4, 1993, p. 2.

40. Interfax (English), 1700 GMT, February 10, 1993; *FBIS,* February 11, 1993, p. 19.

41. *Izvestiia,* January 13, 1993, p. 1; *Current Digest of the Post–Soviet Press* (hereafter *CDSP*), February 10, 1993, p. 26.

42. *Rossiiskie Vesti,* February 16, 1993, pp. 2–3; *FBIS,* February 17, 1993, p. 29.

43. ITAR-TASS (English), 1720 GMT, March 1, and 0614 GMT, March 2, 1993; also Russian TV, 2000 GMT, March 1, 1993; all in *FBIS,* March 2, 1993, p. 46.

44. Interfax (English), 1922 GMT, March 12, 1993; *FBIS,* March 12, 1993, p. 25; Radio Rossii, 1900 GMT, March 13, 1993; *FBIS,* March 15, 1993, p. 45.

45. ITAR-TASS (Russian), 1320 GMT, and Russian TV, 1700 GMT, March 15, 1993; *FBIS,* March 16, 1993, p. 20.

46. Radio Mayak, 1430 GMT, March 22, 1993; *FBIS,* March 22, 1993, p. 57; also *RT,* March 23, 1993, p. 1.

47. *RT,* March 27, 1993, p. 1.

48. Interfax (English), 1109 GMT, March 22, 1993; *FBIS,* March 22, 1993, p. 54.

49. Ostankino TV, 0900 GMT, March 24, 1993; *FBIS,* March 24, 1993, p. 49; Interfax (English), 1550 GMT, March 25, 1993; *FBIS,* March 26, 1993, p. 35.

50. ITAR-TASS (Russian), 1152 GMT, April 5, 1993; *FBIS,* April 16, 1993, p. 23.

51. ITAR-TASS (Russian), 1428 GMT; and Radio Rossii, 1600 GMT, April 19, 1993; both in *FBIS,* April 20, 1993, p. 14.

52. ITAR-TASS (English), 1605 GMT, April 20, 1993; *FBIS,* April 21, 1993, p. 28.

53. *Izvestiia,* May 19, 1993, p. 4; *FBISR* 069, June 4, 1993, p. 15.

54. *Trud,* April 29, 1993, p. 2; *FBISR* 060, May 14, 1993, pp. 64–65.

55. Ibid.

56. *Torgovaia Gazeta,* May 12, 1993, pp. 1, 2; *FBISR* 069, June 4, 1993, p. 32.

57. *RT,* May 7, 1993, p. 3; *FBISR* 064, May 22, 1993, p. 44.

58. Ibid., May 15, 1993, p. 1; *FBISR* 065, May 26, 1993, pp. 23–24.

59. Ibid.

60. *Trud,* May 22, 1993, p. 2; *FBISR* 069, June 4, 1993, p. 35.

61. Ibid., p. 37.

62. See ITAR-TASS (Russian), 0724 GMT, March 28, 1993; *FBIS,* March 29, 1993, pp. 82ff.

63. *Rossiiskie Vesti,* June 5, 1993, p. 2; *FBIS,* June 8, 1993, p. 32.

64. *Komsomolskaia Pravda,* May 6, 1993, p. 2; *FBIS,* May 11, 1993, pp. 28–29.

65. Ibid., June 16, 1993, p. 1; *FBIS*, June 18, 1993, p. 31.

66. ITAR-TASS (English), 0736 GMT, June 21, 1993; *FBIS*, June 21, 1993, p. 32.

67. *Nezavisimaia Gazeta* (hereafter *NG*), June 19, 1993, p. 1; *FBIS*, June 21, 1993, p. 33.

68. *Rossiiskie Vesti*, June 23, 1993, p. 1; *FBIS*, June 25, 1993, p. 26.

69. *Komsomolskaia Pravda*, June 24, 1993, pp. 1, 3; *FBIS*, June 25, 1993, p. 26.

70. *RT*, June 26, 1993, p. 1; *FBISR*, 085, July 9, 1993, p. 56.

71. *Rossiiskaia Gazeta*, July 6, 1993, p. 5; *FBIS*, July 14, 1993, p. 32.

72. *RFE/RL News Briefs* (hereafter *RLNB*), July 12–16, p. 3, citing ITAR-TASS.

73. ITAR-TASS (English), 1602 GMT, July 19, 1993; *FBIS*, July 20, 1993, p. 31; *Izvestiia*, July 22, 1993, p. 2; *FBIS*, July 22, 1993, p. 45.

74. *Rossiiskaia Gazeta*, July 20, 1993, pp. 1, 4; *FBIS*, July 21, 1993, p. 23.

75. *Izvestiia*, July 24, 1993, p. 2; *FBIS*, July 28, 1993, p. 29.

76. *RLNB*, July 26–August 6, 1993, p. 4, citing ITAR-TASS.

77. *Rossiiskaia Gazeta*, July 1, 1993, pp. 1, 2; *FBIS*, July 2, 1993, p. 43.

78. Radio Mayak, 1300 GMT, July 23, 1993; *FBIS*, July 23, p. 19.

79. *Trud*, June 17, 1993, p. 2; *FBISR* 101, August 6, 1993, pp. 43–44.

80. *Kommersant-Daily*, July 20, 1993, p. 3; *FBISR* 101, August 6, 1993, pp. 57–58.

81. *RT*, August 7, 1993, p. 1; *FBISR* 108, August 20, 1993, pp. 56–57.

82. *Trud*, August 12, 1993, p. 1; *FBISR* August 20, 1993, p. 60.

83. *Rossiiskaia Gazeta*, August 11, 1993, p. 1; August 20, 1993, pp. 57–58.

84. *Trud*, August 13, 1993, p. 1; *FBISR* 112, August 27, 1993, p. 66.

85. *Kommersant-Daily*, August 10, 1993, p. 14; *FBIS*, August 11, 1993, p. 31.

86. *Rossiiskaia Gazeta*, August 12, 1993, p. 2; *FBISR* 112, August 27, 1993, pp. 52–53.

87. The appeal appeared in *Rossiiskie Vesti*, August 20, 1993, p. 1.

88. *RT*, August 31, 1993, p. 1; *FBISR* 123, September 23, 1993, pp. 46–47.

89. *Rossiiskie Vesti*, August 20, 1993, p. 1; *FBISR* 115, September 2, 1993, pp. 76–77.

90. *Rossiiskaia Gazeta*, September 7, 1993, p. 2; *FBIS*, September 10, 1993, p. 44.

91. ITAR-TASS (English), 1457 GMT, September 10, 1993; *FBIS*, September 13, 1993, p. 35. On the Klochkov-Chernomyrdin meeting and Klochkov's characterization of the government's policy, see *Rossiiskaia Gazeta*, September 17, 1993, pp. 1, 4; *FBIS*, September 21, 1993, pp. 29–31.

92. *Rossiiskie Vesti*, August 20, 1993, p. 1; *FBISR* 115, September 2, 1993, p. 77.

93. Ibid.

94. *Trud*, September 16, 1993, pp. 1–2; *FBISR* 126, September 30, 1993, pp. 96–97.

95. *Rossiiskaia Gazeta*, August 28, 1993, p. 1; *FBISR* 126, September 30, 1993, p. 98.

96. See, on the September 17 RTK meeting, Ostankino TV, 1100 GMT, September 17, 1993; *FBIS*, September 21, 1993, p. 27.

97. *Rossiiskaia Gazeta*, September 23, 1993, p. 4; *FBIS* (supp.), September 24, 1993, pp. 38–39.

98. Ibid., p. 38.

99. *Kommersant-Daily,* September 23, 1993, p. 3; and Interfax (English), 1110 GMT, September 22, 1993; both in *FBIS* (supp.), September 23, 1993, p. 24.

100. *Kommersant-Daily,* September 24, 1993, p. 3; *FBIS,* September 28, 1993, p. 24.

101. *Segodnia,* September 28, 1993, p. 3.

102. *Kommersant-Daily,* September 29, 1993, p. 4; *FBIS,* September 30, 1993, p. 37.

103. ITAR-TASS (English), 0811 GMT, September 30, 1993; *FBIS,* September 30, 1993, p. 37.

104. *Moskovskii Komsomolets,* September 29, 1993, p. 2; *FBIS,* September 30, 1993, pp. 37–38.

105. Radio Rossii, 0900 GMT, September 27, 1993; *FBIS* (supp.), September 28, 1993, p. 31.

106. ITAR-TASS (English), 1453 GMT, September 22, 1993; *FBIS* (supp.), September 23, 1993, p. 46.

107. *Financial Times,* October 6, 1993, p. 2.

108. See accounts in *Financial Times,* October 13, 1993, p. 3, and *Kommersant-Daily,* October 9, 1993, p. 4; *FBIS,* October 12, 1993, p. 42.

109. *RT,* October 8, 1993, p. 2; *FBISR* 136, October 21, 1993, p. 68.

110. *Izvestiia,* October 9, 1993, p. 8; *FBISR* 136, October 21, 1993, p. 69.

111. Ibid.

112. *Trud,* October 14, 1993, p. 1; *FBISR,* October 28, 1993, p. 44.

113. *Trud,* October 16, 1993, pp. 1–2; *FBISR* 147, November 18, 1993, pp. 46–49.

114. *RT,* October 19, 1993, p. 2; *FBISR,* October 28, 1993, pp. 45–46.

115. *NG,* October 26, 1993, p. 2; *FBIS,* October 27, 1993, p. 29.

116. See the interview with Shmakov in *RT,* October 26, 1993, pp. 1–2; *FBISR* 142, November 9, 1993, pp. 37–38.

117. *Trud,* October 26, 1993, p. 1; *FBISR* 142, November 4, 1993, p. 39.

118. *Trud,* October 28, 1993, p. 2; *FBISR* 144, November 10, 1993, p. 67.

119. *Trud,* October 30, 1993, p. 1; *FBISR* 142, November 4, 1993, pp. 42–43.

120. An abbreviated text of the Shumeiko speech is in *RT,* November 2, 1993, pp. 1–2; *FBISR* 144, November 10, 1993, pp. 70–72.

121. Ibid.

122. *RT,* November 6, 1993, p. 1; *FBISR* 144, November 10, 1993, p. 72.

123. *Trud,* November 4, 1993, p. 2; *FBISR* 145, November 11, 1993, p. 4.

124. *Rossiiskie Vesti,* October 27, 1993, p. 2; *FBISR* 146, November 17, 1993, pp. 14–16.

125. Quoted in *Trud,* October 30, 1993, p. 1; *FBISR* 142, November 4, 1993, p. 43.

126. See *Rossiiskaia Gazeta,* November 6, 1993, p. 5; *FBISR* 147, November 18, 1993, pp. 51–53.

127. See *RT,* November 10, 1993, p. 1; *FBISR* 147, November 18, 1993, p. 15; *Kommersant-Daily,* November 10, 1993, p. 3; *FBISR* 150, November 25, 1993, p. 65.

128. *Segodnia,* November 2, 1993, p. 3; *FBISR* 147, November 18, 1993, p. 49.

129. *Trud,* November 17, 1993, p. 1; *FBISR* 150, November 25, 1993, pp. 80–81; and *RT,* November 27, 1993, p. 1; *FBISR* 153, December 4, 1993, pp. 104–105.

130. *Trud,* November 27, 1993, p. 1; *FBISR* 155, December 9, 1993, p. 23.

131. *Segodnia,* December 14, 1993, p. 2; *FBISR* 167, December 31, 1993, p. 20.

Chapter 5

1. For a discussion of the election controversies, see Vera Tolz and Julia Wishnevsky, "Election Queries Make Russians Doubt Democratic Process," *Radio Free Europe/Radio Liberty Report* (hereafter *RFE/RL R*), April 1, 1994, pp. 1–6.

2. Wendy Slater, "Russian Duma Sidelines Extremist Politicians," *RFE/RL R,* February 18, 1994, pp. 5–9.

3. See the analysis of the centrist failure in Daniel Treisman, "Russia's Disappearing 'Center': The Parliamentary Elections of December 1993," in Timothy J. Colton and Jerry F. Hough, eds., *The Russian Elections of 1993* (Washington, DC: Brookings Institution Press, forthcoming).

4. Wendy Slater, "The Diminishing Center of Russian Parliamentary Politics," *RFE/RL R,* April 29, 1994, pp. 13–18.

5. *Obshchaia Gazeta,* March 9–15, 1995, p. 8; *Foreign Broadcast Information Service–Central Eurasia* (hereafter *FBIS*), April 7, 1995, pp. 36–37.

6. *Segodnia,* May 4, 1995, p. 1; *FBIS,* May 5, 1995, pp. 21–22.

7. *Rabochaia Tribuna* (hereafter *RT*), May 5, 1995, p. 1; *FBIS,* May 9, 1995, p. 32.

8. ITAR-TASS (English), 1646 GMT, April 5, 1995; *FBIS,* April 12, 1995, p. 16.

9. *Segodnia,* April 13, 1995, p. 2; *FBIS,* April 19, 1995, pp. 39–40. See also *Nevskoe Vremia,* May 11, 1995, p. 1; *FBIS,* May 17, 1995, p. 5.

10. *Open Media Research Institute Daily Report* (hereafter *OMRIDR*), April 26, 1995, citing Interfax.

11. *OMRIDR,* May 17, 1995, citing NTV.

12. *OMRIDR,* June 5, 1995, citing Interfax.

13. Privatizing being an ongoing and complex process, any statistics are, by the date of publication, behind events. Those cited are from *New York Times,* July 5, 1994; and *Financial Times,* June 20, 1994.

14. The words are Michael McFaul's, in his "State Power, Institutional Change, and the Politics of Privatization in Russia," *World Politics* 47, 2 (January 1995), pp. 210–243.

15. See Ed A. Hewett, *Reforming the Soviet Economy: Equality vs. Efficiency* (Washington, DC: Brookings Institution Press, 1988), pp. 28–29, 358–359.

16. See McFaul's interesting analysis along these lines in "State Power."

17. An example of the latter, from a Marxist perspective, is Simon Clarke, Peter Fairbrother, Michael Burawoy, and Pavel Krotov, *What About the Workers? Workers and the Transition to Capitalism in Russia* (London: Verso, 1993).

18. See *Segodnia,* June 21, 1994, p. 3.

19. *Izvestiia,* February 8, 1992, p. 1; *Current Digest of the Post-Soviet Press* (hereafter *CDSP*), March 11, 1992, p. 26.

20. For early readings of the variants and processes of privatization, see Bozidar Djelic, "Mass Privatization in Russia: The Role of Vouchers," *Radio Free Europe/Radio Liberty Research Report* (hereafter *RFE/RL RR*), October 16, 1992, pp.40–44; Keith Bush, "Industrial Privatization in Russia: A Progress Report," *RFE/RL RR*, February 12, 1993, pp. 32–34; also, *Izvestiia*, September 28, 1992, p. 4; *CDSP*, November 4, 1992, pp. 7–8; and Roman Frydman, Andrzej Rapaczynski, John S. Earle, et al., *The Privatization Process in Russia, Ukraine and the Baltic States* (Budapest and London: Central European University Press, 1993), pp. 1–82.

21. See, for example, the thoughts of the economists Larisa Piiashcheva, Gennadi Lisichkin, and Vasili Seliunin, among others, in *Izvestiia*, February 14, 1992, p. 3; and *CDSP*, April 1, 1992, p. 5.

22. See *Izvestiia*, September 25, 1992, p. 1; *FBIS*, September 29, 1992, p. 21.

23. Moscow Radio (English), 1900 GMT, October 31, 1992; *FBIS*, October 7, 1992, p. 20.

24. ITAR-TASS (English), 1120 GMT, October 16, 1992; *FBIS*, October 20, 1992, pp. 25–26.

25. Richard Rose, "Toward a Civil Economy," *Journal of Democracy* 3, 2 (April 1992), pp. 13–26.

26. *RFE/RL News Briefs* (hereafter *RLNB*), February 14–18, 1994, p. 5, citing Interfax; *RLNB*, January 31–February 4, 1994, p. 5, citing ITAR-TASS; *RT*, January 29, 1994, p. 1; *Foreign Broadcast Information Service Report–Central Eurasia* (hereafter *FBISR*) 012, February 10, 1994, pp. 57–58; *Segodnia*, February 12, 1994, p. 2.

27. On the elections in the region, see Stephen Crowley, "Elections in Siberia's Rust Belt," in Colton and Hough, *The Russian Elections of 1993*, forthcoming.

28. *RLNB*, February 21–25, 1994, p. 6; *Nezavisimaia Gazeta* (hereafter *NG*), March 2, 1994, p. 2; *RLNB*, February 28–March 4, 1994, p. 2.

29. See *Rossiiskie Vesti*, March 15, 1994, p. 1; *FBIS*, March 16, 1994, p. 22.

30. *RLNB*, April 28–30, 1994, p. 6; *RT*, April 5, 1994, p. 1, and April 8, 1994, pp. 1, 6; *FBISR*, 038, April 15, 1994, pp. 80–82; *Segodnia*, April 1, 1994, p. 2. Also see ITAR-TASS (English), 1419 GMT, March 31, 1994; and Interfax (English), 1843 GMT, March 31, 1994; both in *FBIS*, April 1, 1994, pp. 26–27. And see ITAR-TASS (English), 1306 GMT, April 12, 1994; *FBIS*, April 13, 1994, p. 23.

31. *RLNB*, May 2–6, 1994, p. 4; *Trud*, June 7, 1994, p. 1; *FBIS*, June 8, 1994, p. 33; *Segodnia*, June 10, 1994, p. 2.

32. See *RLNB*, July 11–15, 1994, p. 3.

33. *Rossiiskie Vesti*, May 18, 1994, p. 1; *FBIS*, May 20, 1994, pp. 25–26.

34. *NG*, June 2, 1994, p. 4; *FBIS*, June 3, 1994, p. 22.

35. *Pravda*, July 15, 1994, p. 1; *FBIS*, July 18, 1994, p. 25.

36. *Rossiiskie Vesti*, September 16, 1994, p. 1; *FBIS*, September 16, 1994, pp. 23–24.

37. *Segodnia*, October 20, 1994, p. 2; *Kommersant-Daily*, October 20, 1994, p. 3; *FBIS*, October 21, 1994, pp. 17–19.

38. See *RT*, November 25, 1994, p. 4; *FBIS*, November 29, 1994, p. 25; *RT*, February 3, 1995, p. 4; *FBIS*, February 3, 1995, pp. 41–42.

39. *Izvestiia*, February 9, 1995, p. 4; *CDSP*, March 1, 1995, p. 5.

40. *Rossiiskie Vesti,* February 8, 1995, p. 1; *CDSP,* March 1, 1995, p. 4.

41. See various press services' reports on the Primorskii strike and settlement, especially *FBIS,* April 13, 1995, pp. 27–29.

42. *Izvestiia,* April 11, 1995, p. 2; *FBIS,* April 11, 1995, p. 8. The 1995 General Agreement was signed by a total of 87 people: 30 for the government, 29 on the labor side, and 28 employers. Something of the fluidity of the institutional environment was indicated by the fact that, respectively, only three, four, and five of the 1995 signatories had also signed for their sides in 1992's first agreement.

43. See *RT,* April 15, 1995, pp. 1–2; *Sovetskaia Rossiia,* April 15, 1995, p. 1; *FBIS,* April 18, 1995, pp. 25–27.

44. *RT,* January 22, 1994, p. 2; *FBIS R* 009, February 3, 1994, p. 29–30.

45. *Argumenty i Fakty,* no. 14 (April 1994), p. 5; *FBIS R* 038, April 15, 1994, p. 62.

46. *Rossiiskaia Gazeta,* April 20, 1994, pp. 1, 3; *FBIS R* 051, May 12, 1994, p. 66.

47. Ibid., p. 64.

48. *Izvestiia,* July 21, 1994, pp. 1, 4; *CDSP,* August 17, 1994, p. 9.

49. *Obshchaia Gazeta,* May 27, 1994, p. 8; *FBIS R* 066, June 21, 1994, p. 32.

50. See note 45.

51. "After all, the budget should be replenished, too," as Melikian put it to *Rossiiskaia Gazeta,* April 20, 1994, pp. 1, 3; *FBIS R* 051, May 12, 1994, p. 67.

52. *RT,* April 11, 1995, p. 1; *FBIS,* April 12, 1995, pp. 36–37.

53. *Financial Times,* September 2, 1994, p. 2.

54. *Trud,* February 8, 1994, p. 1; *FBIS,* February 8, 1994, pp. 29–30.

55. Ibid., April 30, 1994, pp. 1, 2; *FBIS,* May 4, 1994, p. 8.

56. Ibid.

57. *Rossiiskie Vesti,* March 24, 1994, p. 3; *FBIS,* March 25, 1994, p. 15.

58. Radio Rossii, 1000 GMT, April 8, 1994; *FBIS,* April 8, 1994, p. 26.

59. *RT,* April 12, 1994, pp. 1–2; *FBIS R,* April 28, 1994, p. 15.

60. Ibid.

61. *Trud,* May 26, 1994, p. 2; *FBIS,* May 31, 1994, pp. 30–31.

62. *Kommersant-Daily,* June 18, 1994, p. 3; *FBIS,* June 20, 1994, pp. 20–21.

63. Interfax (English), 1015 GMT, May 12, 1994; *FBIS,* May 13, 1994, pp. 27–28.

64. *Kommersant-Daily,* June 18, 1994, p. 3; *FBIS,* June 20, 1994, pp. 20–21; *Kommersant-Daily,* July 8, 1994, p. 3; *FBIS,* July 11, 1994, p. 21.

65. *RT,* August 20, 1994, pp. 1–2; *FBIS,* August 23, 1994, pp. 10–11.

66. *Trud,* December 9, 1994, p. 2; *FBIS,* December 12, 1994, pp. 31–32.

67. *Segodnia,* March 4, 1995, p. 2; *FBIS,* March 13, 1995, p. 22. See also *RT,* March 3, 1995, p. 2; *FBIS,* March 22, 1995, pp. 14–15.

68. *NG,* September 17, 1994, p. 3; *FBIS R* 108, October 4, 1994, pp. 26–27.

69. *Obshchaia Gazeta,* October 14, 1994, p. 8; *FBIS R* 117, October 31, 1994, pp. 39–40.

70. *Komsomolskaia Pravda,* September 27, 1994 (business supp.), p. 3; *FBIS,* September 30, 1994, pp. 33–34.

71. *Kommersant-Daily,* September 23, 1994, p. 3; *CDSP,* October 26, 1994, pp. 11–12.

72. *Kommersant-Daily,* November 17, 1994, p. 2; *FBISR* 130, December 1, 1994, pp. 40–41.

73. *OMRIDR,* May 5, 1995, citing Interfax and *Segodnia,* May 4, 1995.

74. *OMRIDR,* May 29, 1995, citing *Segodnia,* May 27, 1995.

75. *Rossiiskaia Gazeta,* April 20, 1994, pp. 1, 3; *FBISR* 051, May 12, 1994, p. 69.

76. *Obshchaia Gazeta,* June 10, 1994, p. 8; *FBISR,* June 16, 1994, p. 51.

77. *Obshchaia Gazeta,* December 3, 1993, p. 8; *FBISR,* December 23, 1993, p. 14.

78. *Rossiiskaia Gazeta,* April 20, 1994, pp. 1, 3; *FBISR* 051, May 12, 1994, p. 65.

79. *Obshchaia Gazeta,* May 27, 1994, p. 8; *FBISR* 066, June 21, 1994, p. 33.

80. Valerie Bunce and John M. Echols, "Soviet Politics in the Brezhnev Era: 'Pluralism' or 'Corporatism'?" in Donald R. Kelley, ed., *Soviet Politics in the Brezhnev Era* (New York: Praeger, 1980), pp. 1–26.

81. Ibid., p. 19.

82. Ibid.

83. See Baohui Zhang, "Corporatism, Totalitarianism, and Transitions to Democracy," *Comparative Political Studies* 27, 1 (April 1994), pp. 108–136.

84. Quotes from ibid., pp. 112–113.

85. Ibid., p. 131.

86. Quotes, and the line of argument, from ibid., pp. 131, 124–125, and 126.

87. Philippe C. Schmitter, "Interest Intermediation and Regime Governability in Contemporary Western Europe and North America," in Suzanne Berger, ed., *Organizing Interests in Western Europe* (Cambridge: Cambridge University Press, 1981), pp. 295–296.

88. Adam Przeworski, *Democracy and the Market: Political and Economic Reforms in Eastern Europe and Latin America* (Cambridge: Cambridge University Press, 1991), p. 86.

89. Randall L. Calvert, "The Rational Choice Theory of Social Institutions: Cooperation, Coordination, and Communication," p. 7, citing Douglass C. North, *Structure and Change in Economic History* (New York: Norton, 1981); and Calvert, *Institutions, Institutional Change, and Economic Performance* (Cambridge: Cambridge University Press, 1990).

90. Kenneth A. Shepsle, "Studying Institutions: Some Lessons from the Rational Choice Approach," *Journal of Theoretical Politics* 1, 2 (1989), p. 144.

91. Przeworski, *Democracy and the Market,* p. 136; Przeworski deals interestingly with a number of aspects of the political strategy of "command-to-market" reform, especially gradualism versus "shock therapy" calculations, pp. 136–187.

92. Miroslawa Marody, "The Political Attitudes of Polish Society in the Period of Systemic Transitions," in Walter D. Connor and Piotr Ploszajski, eds., *The Polish Road from Socialism* (Armonk, NY: M. E. Sharpe, 1992), p. 262. On the notion of the "common lot," Marody cites Ireneusz Bielecki, "Duch wspolnotowy," *Res Publica,* no. 4, 1990.

93. Here we quote again some of Philippe C. Schmitter's ("Still the Century of Corporatism?" *Review of Politics* 36, 1 [1974], p. 123) discussion of Manoilesco's ideas about the roots of corporatism.

94. Przeworski, *Democracy and the Market,* p. 186.

95. *Financial Times,* October 22–23, 1994, p. 2.

96. I have drawn here on a talk by Anders Aslund (Russian Research Center, Harvard University, October 19, 1994).

97. See Daniel Yergin and Thane Gustafson, *Russia 2010 and What It Means for the World* (London: Nicholas Brealey, 1994), p. 104.

98. "Survey: Poland," *Economist,* April 16, 1994, p. 3.

99. *Financial Times,* July 5, 1995, p. 2.

100. See Giuseppe DiPalma, "Legitimation from the Top to Civil Society: Politico-Cultural Change in Eastern Europe," *World Politics* 44, 1 (October 1991), p. 70, on this. DiPalma probably underestimates the similarity of material situations of workers and intelligentsia, especially in Poland and Hungary. For a different analysis from an earlier time, which may now carry some ironic implications for intelligentsia-mass relations in the present and future, see Gyorgy Konrad and Ivan Szelenyi, *The Intellectuals on the Road to Class Power* (New York: Harcourt Brace Jovanovich, 1979).

101. See various comments on this decree in *Izvestiia,* September 21, 1992, p. 1; *Segodnia,* September 21, 1994, p. 2; and *Izvestiia,* September 22, 1992, p. 2. All in *CDSP,* October 19, 1994, p. 10–12.

102. See the discussions in J. L. Cohen and Andrew Arato, *Civil Society and Political Theory* (Cambridge: MIT Press, 1992); and Giuseppe DiPalma, *To Craft Democracies* (Berkeley: University of California Press, 1990).

103. Yergin and Gustafson, *Russia 2010,* p. 48.

104. Anders Aslund, "Russia's Success Story," *Foreign Affairs* (September-October 1994), p. 64.

105. See the "instant analyses" in *Economist,* October 15, 1994, pp. 20, 63–64.

106. Alfred Stepan and Cindy Skach, "Constitutional Frameworks and Democratic Consolidation: Parliamentarianism Versus Presidentialism," *World Politics* 46, 1 October 1993), pp. 1–22.

107. Ibid., pp. 17–18.

108. Ibid., pp. 19–20, citing Guillermo O'Donnell, "Democracia Delegativa?" *Novos Estudios* (CEBRAP), no. 31, October 1991.

109. Thane Gustafson, quoted in *Financial Times,* July 8, 1994, p. 2; the term "prime movers" comes from Yergin and Gustafson, *Russia 2010.*

110. As Gustafson, ibid., did.

111. These alternatives are much along the line of what Yergin and Gustafson (*Russia 2010,* pp. 194–195) project as the two main dangers to their most optimistic scenario, the "miracle" (*chudo*), or the early achievement of a smoothly functioning market economy, albeit one that still distributes its benefits quite unevenly.

112. See, for a Gorbachev-period assessment, Gail W. Lapidus, "State and Society: Toward the Emergence of Civil Society in the Soviet Union," in Seweryn Bialer, ed., *Politics, Society, and Nationality: Inside Gorbachev's Russia* (Boulder: Westview Press, 1989), pp. 121–148.

113. Grzegorz Ekiert, "Democratization Processes in East Central Europe: A Theortical Reconsideration," *British Journal of Political Science* 21 (July 1991), p. 300.

114. Paul Kubicek, "Delegative Democracy in Russia and Ukraine," *Communist and Post-Communist Studies* 27, 4 (1994), p. 438.

115. DiPalma, "Legitimation from the Top," p. 63.

Epilogue

1. Open Media Research Institute (OMRI) Daily Report (hereafter OMRIDR), September 26, 1995.

2. OMRIDR, December 1 and December 4, 1995.

3. *Obshchaia Gazeta,* no. 38, September 21–27, 1995, p. 8; *Foreign Broadcast Information Service–Central Eurasia* (hereafter *FBIS*), September 26, 1995, pp. 75–76.

4. *Ogonek,* no. 35, August 1995, pp. 24–25; *FBIS*, September 13, 1995, pp. 57ff.

5. *Segodnia,* September 1, 1995, p. 2; *FBIS*, September 5, 1995, pp. 31–32.

6. OMRIDR, November 28, 1995, citing ITAR-TASS, November 27, 1995.

7. See OMRI Election Survey, November 28, 1995, citing ITAR-TASS, November 22, 1995.

8. OMRI Election Survey, December 8, 1995.

9. Lev Timofeyev, *Russia's Secret Rulers* (New York: Alfred A. Knopf, 1992), p. 100.

About the Book
and Author_____

IN POST-SOVIET RUSSIA'S TRANSITION to new political and economic systems, few issues are as important as labor. Although the "worker's paradise" may have been largely imaginary, the loss of job security and benefits that has accompanied marketization could well become a catalyst for yet another political upheaval. In this timely book, Walter Connor explores how the Yeltsin government attempted to avoid this pitfall of system change.

Connor examines Russia's emergent labor politics in the critical first years of the post-Soviet period, focusing on the problems Yeltsin encountered in attempting to adopt a "corporatist" solution to the conflicts of interest that have arisen between labor, employers, and the state. With many employers still heavily dependent on the state, while others are already beyond state control, the corporatist effort has been sabotaged, Connor contends, by the lack of distinct interest groups found in more mature market economies. He concludes with an analysis of what these recent developments may portend for Russian politics and government in the future.

WALTER D. CONNOR is professor of political science, sociology, and international relations at Boston University and a fellow of Harvard University's Russian Research Center. He is author, among seven previous books, of *The Accidental Proletariat: Workers, Politics, and Crisis in Gorbachev's Russia* (1991).

Index_____